GW09985835

FROM RUSHDIE TO 7/7

It is fitting, given the title of the book and its subject matter, to dedicate this work to the memory of the victims of 7/7, Muslim and non-Muslim.

FROM RUSHDIE TO 7/7:

THE RADICALISATION OF ISLAM
IN BRITAIN

Anthony McRoy

THE
SOCIAL
AFFAIRS
UNIT

British Library Cataloguing in Publication Data
A catalogue record of this book is available from the British Library

Printed and bound in the United Kingdom

ISBN 1-904863-09-4

Social Affairs Unit
314–322 Regent Street
London W1B 5SA

www.socialaffairsunit.org.uk

CONTENTS

ACKNOWLEDGEMENTS

There are a number of people whom I must thank for their help in regard to this book. I wish to thank the Director of the Social Affairs Unit Michael Mosbacher for his invitation to write this book and for giving me complete intellectual freedom to do so. This leads me on to thank Andy Bannister for suggesting to Mr Mosbacher that I would be the person to engage in this work, which again leads me on to express gratitude to Professor Peter Riddell of the London School of Theology for recommending me to Mr Bannister. Dr Riddell was my PhD supervisor and, as I have accessed parts of my doctoral research in the writing of this book, my debt to him is especially great. Dr Riddell combines rigorous scholarship with the traditional Aussie tension of cordiality and forthrightness, and I appreciated all these factors when he kindly agreed to read through the draft of this book, offering valuable suggestions.

I also wish to thank various people that I consulted during the writing of this book, including Anas Altikriti, Arzu Merali, Asghar Bukhari, Fuad Nahdi, Massoud Shadjareh and Shahed Alam among others. Special mention must also be made of the book's excellent copy-editor, Clive Liddiard, for his painstaking work. Last, but by no means least, I must thank my wife and children for their extraordinary patience as I got to work on this endeavour.

A NOTE ON WEBSITES

The existence of the Internet makes a researcher's work relatively easy on the one hand, and extremely frustrating on the other. Easy because so many groups and individuals maintain websites that often feature leaflets and booklets that they have distributed, making it possible for people everywhere to peruse them. Frustrating because, as is the nature of things, some websites – or at least some features on those sites – tend to disappear, especially when they are statements relating to topical events. This is the case with a few of the sites listed here. However, this does not affect the overall study in question.

THE AUTHOR

Dr Anthony McRoy BA BD MA (Theol) PhD is a Born-again Christian researcher and religious journalist who frequently contributes to both Evangelical Christian and Muslim periodicals, often appears on Middle Eastern/Islamic TV, and lectures in Islamics at the Evangelical Theological College of Wales. He holds dual Eire and UK citizenship and is married with three children.

GLOSSARY

'adat – principle of 'custom' in fiqh

'aql – reason

'urf – principle of customary usage in fiqh

aman – visa, guarantee of protection

Amir – leader

Ayah/Ayat – Qur'anic verse

batil – 'void'; legal principle emerged to establish a court decision

da'if – 'weak'; hadith of questionable provenance

Dar al-Ahad – 'Abode of Pact'

Dar al-Harb – 'House of War' – i.e. non-Islamic enemy territory

Dar al-Iman – 'Abode of Faith'

Dar al-Kufr – 'Abode of Disbelief'

Dar al-Sulh – 'Abode of Truce'

dawah – missionary action or call

deen – religion

dhimmi – non-Muslim living under Islamic rule

faqih – jurisprudent – expert in fiqh

fard – obligation according to Shari'ah. There are sub-categories:

> *fard 'ayn* – obligation on the *individual*, e.g. prayer
>
> *fard kifayah* – obligation on the *community*, e.g. funeral arrangements, or seeking knowledge

fassid – 'irregular'; legal principle emerged to establish a court decision

fatwa – a juridical verdict upon an issue

fiqh – Islamic jurisprudence

fuqaha – scholar of fiqh

ghairat – honour of religion

hadith – narration of the Prophet (and sometimes the Sahabah or, for Shi'ites, the Twelve Imams)

hadd – singular of hudud

hajj – pilgrimage

halal – allowed, permissible

haram – forbidden

harbi – a non-Muslim alien from the Dar al-Harb, as opposed to a dhimmi

hijab – Islamic headscarf

hijrah – migration; specifically of Muhammad and his disciples from Mecca to Medina

hudud – lit. 'limits'; usually used to define the punishments under Islamic law, e.g. stoning adulteresses, amputating the hand of a thief

ibadah – worship/ritual matters in fiqh

ijma' – consensus

ijtihad – lit. 'effort'; used in fiqh to describe the process of judgment

imam – prayer leader or head of a community or state. In Shi'ism it usually denotes the twelve infallible descendants of Muhammad prescribed to lead the Ummah

iman – belief

istisah – principle of 'preference' in fiqh

istishab – 'continuity'

istislah – principle of 'welfare' in fiqh

izzat – honour of the family or community

jahiliyyah – state of ignorance or pre-Islamic times

jama'ah – group (of people) or community

jihad – sacred struggle, often militarily, against non-Islamic believers and structures

jizyah – head tax on non-Muslims under Islamic rule

Khalifah – Caliph

khawarij – rebels; specifically the rebels against the fourth Caliph Ali Ibn Abi Talib

Khilafah – Caliphate, Islamic State

kufr – unbelief

madhab – school of fiqh

Majlis – Council, Assembly or Parliament

makruh – disapproved action according to Shari'ah. It has two further sub-divisions:

makruh tahrimi – 'that which is nearly unlawful without it being actually so'

makruh tanzihi – 'that which approaches the lawful'

maslaha – benefit, welfare

millats – autonomous confessional units in the Ottoman Caliphate

mu'amalah – legal/political matters in fiqh

mubah – permissible action in Shari'ah

mufsid – disturbing/corrupting action according to Shari'ah

mujtahid – scholar of Ijtihad

nafs – 'the self'

naskh – abrogation

niyyah – intention

nusrah – material support and aid

qisas – lawful retaliation

qiyas – measure, reference comparison, analogy or deduction by analogy

ra'y – principle of 'opinion' in fiqh

riddah – apostasy; historically used to describe the rebellion against the first Caliph, Abu Bakr

Sahabah – Companions of Muhammad

sahih – 'valid'; legal principle emerged to establish a court decision

shahid – martyr

Shari'ah – Islamic law

shi'ah – followers of Ali, the Prophet's son-in-law as his rightful successor

shura – consultation

Sirah – sacred biography of Muhammad

Sunnah – recommended according to Shari'ah. Sub-categories of this division include:
  mustahabb (prized)
  mandub (preferred)

tabligh – lit. 'to publicise' – preaching to encourage greater Islamic devotion and practice

tadarruj – gradualness

taghut – everything that is worshipped, or followed or obeyed, other than Allah (cf. Surah An-Nisa 4:60); means 'rebel' and is used of Satan himself

takfir – excommunication

taqlid – imitation, copying or blind unquestioning adoption of concepts or ideas; also means the adoption of the legal decision or opinion of a Mazhab or school of jurisprudence

taqwa – piety

tarbiya – Islamic education

tasawwuf – spirituality/character

ulema – plural of 'imam' – mullahs, religious scholars, prayer leaders

Ummah – nation, people or community

Uswah Hasanah – Muhammad as the ideal model for piety and conduct

Vilayet i-Faqih – 'Guardianship of the Jurist'; Khomeini's theory of Islamic government

wajib – duty, imperative or obligatory

zakat/zakah – purity or vindication; in Islamic Law it refers to alms-giving, alms tax or charity

INTRODUCTION

It is often said nowadays – perhaps with some exaggeration – that the world changed forever on 11 September 2001. Certainly, the event led to an increased interest in Islam and Muslims. Conflicting reports were received of Muslims across the globe praising and denouncing the action by Al-Qaida. This in itself demonstrated that the global Muslim community is not a monolith, and this is equally true of its British section. Similar divisions were noticeable in the reactions to the bombings of 7 July 2005 in London. Although the worst ever terrorist attack on mainland Britain, and despite being a 'martyrdom operation' in which the *jihadis* blew themselves up along with their victims, the event was not as traumatic for Britons as 9/11 was for Americans. Partly this was because the scale was smaller, and partly because thirty years of IRA terrorism had diluted the shock factor for the British. It was, perhaps, the revelation that the bombers were UK citizens and, with one exception, British-born that was startling. People from the UK mainland had attacked their fellow citizens. Inevitably, the question arises as to what led young Britons to kill themselves and others. This book attempts to answer that question by illustrating the historical events and theological underpinnings that have radicalised elements of the British Muslim community.

The 2001 census suggested that there were 1.6 million British Muslims: 1,524,887 in England and Wales,[1] 42,600 in Scotland,[2] and around 5,000 in Northern Ireland.[3] Statistics from the census showed both that at least 50 per cent of Muslims were born in the UK, and that the Muslim community tends to have bigger families than the non-Muslim population, with a younger age range.[4] Muslim growth occurs in three ways: natural increase, which, as we have suggested, is assisted by Muslims having bigger families; immigration, notably by many marriages being transcontinental (typically involving, for example, a woman marrying her Pakistani cousin); and conversion. This last factor distinguishes Muslims from Sikhs and Hindus. Islam, like Christianity, is a missionary religion, which actively seeks converts. No reliable figures exist for the number of white and Afro-Caribbean converts, though various Muslim sources often claim 10,000.[5] Whilst large numbers originate from the Indian subcontinent, the UK Muslim magazine *Q-News* pointed out in its 2005 pre-election issue that currently 'the majority of British Muslims are not from the sub-continent. We consist of more than 56 nationalities speaking nearly a hundred languages.'[6]

As the Muslim community has become a permanent feature of British society, it has established institutions, such as places of worship and representative bodies. The permanence of the community is best expressed in the changing character of its mosques. At first, converted homes, warehouses and churches were used, but since the 1980s we have observed a burgeoning trend towards purpose-built mosques. Much of the funding for these buildings has come from Muslim states – something that is not uncontroversial: when some Birmingham Muslims wanted to construct a purpose-built mosque, they applied to the Iraqi government for help, with the result that the imposing edifice received the nomenclature of the 'Saddam Hussein Mosque'. The Saudi and Kuwaiti governments have also funded Muslim organisations, as has the Iranian government in regard to Shi'ites.

As the Muslim community has become more established, especially with the rise of the British-born generation, the impact of global crises affecting Muslims has inevitably touched them. This has led to a general 'radicalising' of the community. This radicalism contrasts with the stance of the Union of Muslim Organisations (UMO), whose General Secretary, Syed Pasha, has stated that it seeks to project 'an image of the Muslim community as a "moderate community"'. Another example was the short-lived 'Muslim Forum', established by Zaki Badawi, Hesham El-Essawy and Akbar Ahmed to counter 'extremist' groups.[7] 'Radicalism' in this regard can be defined in different ways for the purposes of this study. One definition would be hostility to the Saudis for allowing American and other 'non-Muslim' forces to be stationed in the Kingdom since the Gulf crisis – an act many have seen as a betrayal of Islam. Other definitions of 'radicalism' would include hostility to the policies of Western governments, and specifically the British Government in the domestic sphere. Antagonism to the British Government has resulted from the Government's refusal to ban Salman Rushdie's book, *The Satanic Verses*; from its involvement in the war to remove Iraq from Kuwait; its rejection of military action to aid the Bosnian Muslims; and its commitment to President Bush's 'War on Terror', most especially the Iraq war. Another, concomitant radicalism is an Islamic identity and political agenda, especially among the youth. Many are willing to listen with approval to groups supportive of regimes that are often in conflict with the West, such as Iran and Sudan, and the former Taliban regime in Afghanistan. In some cases this has led to open support for Al-Qaida.

Some – especially the youth – support hard-line groups, such as Hizb ut-Tahrir or the Saviour Sect (now the Saved Sect). Others have given allegiance to groupings such as the Islamic Society of Britain or Islamic Forum Europe and their youth wings, and to the Muslim Association of Britain, whose ideologies originally derive from the teachings of the *Jama'at-i-Islami* and the *Ikhwan al-Muslimeen* (Muslim Brotherhood) – although, and this must be emphasised, their ideologies have been contextualised for the British situation. As it was from this milieu that the inspiration for the Muslim Council of Britain (MCB) came, supplanting UMO as the main representative federation for UK Muslims, it could be said that this form of Islamic radicalism has become mainstream. Indeed, the radical Islamist ideas this section represents have, in their contextualised form, provided another form of radicalism – a determination to be politically active and to influence British domestic and foreign policy. The most obvious example of this is the way Muslims have turned out for anti-war rallies and formed a tactical alliance with some Leftist elements in the RESPECT coalition. Again, dress is an indicator of this trend: increasingly, young Muslim girls have adopted the *hijab,* and recently, the *jilbab.* Ironically, the more 'British' the community becomes, the more 'Islamic' is its faith and practice, not least politically. The quietist attitude and often Hinduised cultural accretions of the immigrant generation are being discarded. A sign of this is the increasing popularity of *Arab*, as opposed to subcontinental sheikhs, such as Yusuf al-Qaradawi, and the fact that Palestine easily outstrips Kashmir as the definitive concern among British Muslim youth. Indeed, the shift to Islamic, rather than ethnic, identity helps to explain why the four British Muslims, none of whom was of Arab heritage, could perpetrate the bombings on 7 July 2005; their anger was directed not at India over Kashmir, but at the West over Palestine, Arabia, Iraq and Afghanistan.

The main grid by which this radicalism will be explored in this study is in relation to democracy and *jihad*, as it is these issues that most concern the wider British population. This necessitates some exposition on the Islamist theory of government, as well as the theological jurisprudence of *jihad*. Unavoidably, this section of the book involves technical explanations, but this is vital to understanding both how British Muslims responded to events, and what the aims and strategies are of the various Islamic organisations. Each of the groups that feature in Part Three will be examined in the light of their attitudes to these concepts and also their practical outworking. On the basis of their attitude to involvement with the British democratic process, I have labelled groups either *participationist* or *rejectionist*. The historical events that radicalised British Muslims will be examined in Part One.

My approach in this study is, as far as possible, to examine phenomena from a strictly objective and scholarly basis, and for this reason I have not engaged in ethical judgements with regard to statements involving, for example, violence, whatever my private views may be on the matter, because the reader is not interested in reading a sermon, but in discovering what, how and why such statements come to be made. I have been studying British Muslims for around ten years, and they were the subject of my PhD thesis. Since then I have attended numerous Muslim meetings and rallies, and read unquantifiable reams of their literature. I have met most of the individuals mentioned in this study, and some I have interviewed several times. In some ways my being a Born-again Christian is a help in this process, since I know what it means simultaneously to be part of the British nation, yet to bear a higher allegiance to God and to relate to a transnational body that is the main part of my identity – the Universal Church. Most religious communities share this dichotomy of identity. Hence, when Muslims often place their allegiance to the global *Ummah* above their UK citizenship, they are by no means unique. I mention this because avowedly secular readers might find it surprising that I see no problems with this. In a Britain that is increasingly multi-faith as well as multi-ethnic, we need to recognise the realities of plural allegiances and identities. This is vital, because we shall see that it was partly misunderstanding and insensitivity to Islamic sanctities and concerns that first led to the radicalisation of the Muslim community in Britain.

[1] Office of National Statistics, 2005;
http://www.statistics.gov.uk/census2001/profiles/64.asp.
[2] Office of the Chief Statistician, 2005;
http://www.scotland.gov.uk/stats/bulletins/00398-02.asp.

[3] Belfast Islamic Centre, 2005;
http://www.belfastislamiccentre.org.uk/visitorsguide.htm.

[4] Muslim Council of Britain, 2005;
http://www.mcb.org.uk/mcbdirect/statistics.php#2.

[5] *Ibid.*

[6] Nahdi, Fuad, 'From the Pulpit', *Q-News,* No. 362, April 2005, p. 3.

[7] Mohammed, Jahangir, *The Home Office Strategy for Islam and Muslims in Britain* (London: Muslim Parliament of Great Britain, 1996), p. 28.

PART ONE

THE IMPACT OF CRISES ON BRITISH MUSLIMS

THE CONCEPT OF THE *UMMAH* AND BRITISH MUSLIMS

How do we explain the presence of British Muslims fighting alongside Al-Qaida and Taliban *mujahidin*, and the 'Tipton Taliban', who ended up being incarcerated in Guantanamo Bay before their repatriation? Indeed, how do we explain the British Muslim bombers who caused such carnage in London on 7 July 2005? The answer is the concept of the *Ummah*. Muhammad's migration from Mecca to Medina on 20 June 622, is known as *al-Hijrah*[1] and, being the turning point in Muhammad's career, was declared to be the beginning of the Muslim era. In the *Declaration of Medina*, effectively the constitution of the Islamic city-state, Muhammad stated that the Meccan migrants and the people of Yathrib (Medina) together 'constitute one nation (*Ummah*) in distinction from the rest of the people'.

This *Ummah* is the primary community to which Muslims in Britain belong, and it can be seen from this that the strongest communal links for any Muslim – according to Islam – will be those with the *Ummah*, rather than with fellows of his race, ethnicity or nationality. As a British Muslim student declared of the American action against Afghanistan in 2001, 'I've always believed that I am Muslim first, then British.'[2] Hence the tendency for second- and third-generation Muslims to regard their Pakistani, Bangladeshi, Yemeni, etc. ethnic origins as secondary to their faith, and to identify their distinction from the rest of the British population as being essentially their membership of the *Ummah*, is not only natural, but actually 'scriptural'.

In Islam, communal solidarity is a religious obligation. In its brochure, the Muslim Parliament's Jihad Fund stated the following: 'Muslim minorities in the West have a crucial part to play in the defence of Islam. Few of us will have the opportunity to fight and die in the cause of Allah...But there is a great deal we can do, nonetheless.' The *Ummah* concept has influenced British Muslims to be actively concerned about the Gulf war and Bosnia. In a paper given at the 'International Congress on Imam Khomeini and the Revival of Religious Thought' in Tehran in 1997, Jahangir Mohammed, then Muslim Parliament of Great Britain (MPGB) Deputy Leader, argued that the 'politicisation' of the British Muslim community had been spurred by 'events like the Rushdie affair, the destruction of Iraq by US forces [;] events in Bosnia and Chechenia have played their part.'[3] The *Ummah* concept is vital for understanding British Muslim responses to the Rushdie, Gulf, Bosnian and 9/11 crises.

THE RUSHDIE CRISIS

The publication of Salman Rushdie's book *The Satanic Verses* in 1988 was the defining watershed for British Muslim identity and activism. Previously, Muslims were only seen as part of the general 'Asian' community (despite the fact that UK Muslims are racially diverse) and their activism was limited to 'race' issues. Significantly, anti-Rushdie protestors neither looked for nor were offered any 'black' solidarity; a leader of 'black' politics, Paul Boateng MP, dismissed Muslim anger as having nothing to do with 'the black discourse'.[4] During the Rushdie and subsequent crises, British Muslims found the reverse to be the case – that 'the black discourse' was irrelevant to *their* needs. *The Satanic Verses* uses the Crusader derogatory term *Mahound* for Muhammad, as well as reversal of faith in the employment of *Jahiliya* for the holy city of Mecca, and the names of the wives of the Prophet for the prostitutes in the city. The Islamic Foundation stated that 'it is...*Shatm al-Rasul* [blasphemy against the Prophet] to which Rushdie remains accountable'.[5] We shall see that *fiqh* regards blasphemy as a capital crime. Once British Muslims became aware of the nature of the book in October 1988, one of their first moves was to contact the Muslim states, and that month Faiyazuddin Ahmad, Public Relations and Administration Director of the Islamic Foundation, who had been planning a visit to Saudi Arabia, met the Secretary-General of the Organisation of the Islamic Conference (OIC).[6] On 5 November 1988, the OIC condemned the book as a 'malicious slander against the holy prophet', stated that Rushdie had committed blasphemy, and further resolved that those committing such acts 'are definitely apostates'.[7] Let this be understood: the OIC, by declaring him to be an apostate, usually considered a capital offence in Islamic law (except by some modern scholars, such as Sheikh Yusuf al-Qaradawi), effectively stated that Rushdie should be executed. That, however, was as far as it went: 'the Saudis adopted an unduly soft approach, failing even to protest strongly to the British government'.[8] Lewis comments in similar vein: 'One aspect of the Rushdie affair, often invisible to non-Muslims, was a growing impatience with the seeming lack of zeal exhibited by Saudi Arabia in using its influence to bring pressure to bear on the British government.'[9]

An umbrella lobby group, the United Kingdom Action Committee on Islamic Affairs (UKACIA), was formed in October 1988, following a circular sent to Muslim groups by the Islamic Foundation.[10]

The circular urged recipients 'to take a united stand on this issue and demand the authorities/publisher to withdraw this novel immediately and make a public apology for the offence caused to Islam and Muslims'.[11] The role of the Islamic Foundation in UKACIA demonstrates an underlying sub-agendum in the crisis – the struggle for power in the Muslim community. Whilst the Union of Muslim Organisations (UMO) had called for the book's proscription on 20 October 1988, one feature of the crisis was the effective marginalisation of the group, which does not figure prominently in any account of the affair.[12] UMO started lobbying the Government by urging the Prime Minister to prosecute the author and publishers under the Race Relations and Public Order Acts, describing the book as 'a ferocious and savage attack on our Holy Prophet', which had left the Muslim community 'seething with indignation'.[13] Prime Minister Margaret Thatcher replied on 11 November that there were 'no grounds in which the Government would consider banning'.[14] UMO's failure to make any real impact opened the way for British allies of the *Jama'at-i-Islami* to seize community leadership. Ruthven writes:

> Not the least of the ironies flowing from the anti-Rushdie agitation has been the consolidation of right-wing control, including that of the Jamaatis, over mosques and other Islamic institutions that had previously been open to more liberal elements. *The Satanic Verses* provided the Mawdudists and other hard-liners the opportunity to increase their influence, vindicating their thesis that no compromise was possible between the absolute truths of Islam and the falsehoods of the infidel, *jahili* West.[15]

Ruthven further alleges that the primary concern for the 'Mawdudists' (followers of the Pakistani Islamist scholar Abul A'la Mawdudi, founder of the *Jama'at-i-Islami*) was 'escalation' of the agitation 'to bring it under fundamentalist' control.[16] Kepel notes that the Islamic Foundation organises training schemes for Muslim youth, the aim being to overcome sectarian differences and subcontinent 'tribal superstitions', replacing these things with 'true' Islam.[17] The overall goal, however, relates directly to the internal British Muslim power struggle:

These training courses also constitute a vital element in the movement's strategy aimed at achieving hegemony within the Islamic field: by 'targeting' English-speaking Muslim youth on one hand, and state employees on the other, the Foundation has prepared the way for transition from a fragmented, locally based communalism towards community activism on a national scale.

Thus, by launching the campaign against *The Satanic Verses,* the Foundation hoped to mobilize around its own set of demands the mass of Muslims whom it had not yet succeeded in purging of their popular 'superstitions'.[18]

Hence, given that the Islamic Foundation was responsible in the first place for contacting Saudi Arabia and the OIC to enlist their support, it is not presumptuous to infer that the formation of UKACIA was an attempt not only to unite British Muslims on a specific issue of concern, but also to unite them *behind* the pro-*Jama'at* element. Kepel argues that this was the case; by being the first to launch the campaign, 'the Mawdudiites had a real chance of taking over the leadership of a movement which promised to mobilize large numbers and thus considerably extend their influence over British Islam'.[19] Significantly, as far back as 1980 Murad had called for the formation of a federation of all Muslims residing in any Western state.[20] This call was echoed in 1995 by Iqbal Sacranie, UKACIA Convenor and later Muslim Council of Britain (MCB) Secretary General, who stated that he would like 'all Muslim organisations to interact and co-ordinate their activities so as to represent a united Muslim voice'.[21] In the light of this, it would seem that UKACIA and subsequently the MCB are the result of longstanding plans by pro-*Jama'at* forces to take over the leadership of British Muslims. The Rushdie crisis enabled them to effect this plan.

Kepel credits pro-*Jama'at* forces with having 'initiated' the Rushdie affair with street demonstrations.[22] Again, this suggests that, whilst Muslim leaders may have been genuinely concerned about *The Satanic Verses,* Bosnia, Islamophobia, etc., they also had an interest in *intensifying* and perpetuating such concerns so as to win community support for their distinctive agenda. The pro-*Jama'at* element was more capable of performing that task precisely because of its commitment to English, its interaction with non-Muslims, especially in the public sector, and because of its special orientation to Muslim youth. These were advantages that set them apart from some other elements that were subcontinent-oriented, uneasy with English, and inexperienced in dealing with state institutions.

By the start of 1990, passions were reaching boiling point, fanned by the Government's negative attitude, the unsympathetic indifference of the race constituency, hostility from the media and liberal Establishment, and the ineffectiveness of the world Muslim bodies and their campaign, all of which led to intense frustration.[23] As Webster affirms, the famous book-burning occurred

> ...only when all means of democratic protest had been exhausted, when Muslim leaders had knocked on the doors of the High Court and found that they were barred against them, when their impassioned letters had been ignored by the author, and treated with disdain by the publishers.[24]

On 14 January, the Bradford Council of Mosques, at a thousand-strong protest, publicly burnt the book, one aim being to assuage the feelings of frustration of the Muslim community, the other to impress upon public opinion the intensity of Muslim outrage at the novel.[25] Another motive may be inferred – the desire to escalate the campaign; however, the media ignored them. For that reason an amateur video of the event was sent to TV stations, to be aired with the aim of attracting public attention. In this the organisers were successful, but the resultant attention was almost entirely negative, with Muslims being compared to the Nazis or the Inquisition.[26] Indifference was superseded by hostility, and still the campaign had been unsuccessful. What changed everything was the intervention of Iranian leader Ayatollah Khomeini, who, on 14 February, issued his famous *fatwa* sentencing Rushdie and those associated with the book to death.[27] Throughout the Muslim world and Europe itself, Muslims demonstrated in support of the *fatwa*.[28] Anti-British and anti-American feeling was strong, but so was something else:

> Arab governments, particularly the Saudis, were condemned for their silence over the Anglo-Rushdie scandal; they were passionately accused of being co-conspirators with the West in a plot to destroy Islam. Khomeini, by contrast, emerged as the isolated but celebrated hero who had saved Islam in the hour of trial. Muslims the world over were deeply impressed by the courageous stance of the Iranians.[29]

Despite UKACIA's campaign, the Government still refused to act. Home Secretary Douglas Hurd was perceived as less than sensitive in the manner he addressed the Birmingham Central Mosque in February 1989.[30] Hurd urged that Muslims should join 'the mainstream', and essentially integrate.[31] The *Guardian*, commenting on his speech, noted that in one tabloid headline this came out as 'Behave like British, or don't live here.'[32] This fuelled the underlying psychological anxieties of Muslims about their children becoming 'brown Sahibs' that helped to generate the crisis. The great fear of many British Muslims was that their children would be contaminated by 'infidel' ideas, resulting in the younger generation becoming morally loose, even practically apostate. Rushdie was seen as a paradigm of this. Sardar writes about this phenomenon:

> Rushdie is an instantly recognizable historical type, the 'brown sahib' who is at once an insider and a total, alien, outsider...The brown sahib has an acute inferiority complex about his original identity: he hates his Indian/Muslim self. Yet, on the other hand, he knows he can never be accepted as a *pukkah* sahib...Rushdie wrote *The Satanic Verses* in the full knowledge...that the secularist establishment will rush to protect and defend him.[33]

Indeed, Hurd's junior, John Patten, caused outrage by, in their view, effectively inviting Muslims to become 'brown Sahibs'. On 4 July 1989 he wrote to Muslim leaders, stating that the crisis had caused everyone 'to think deeply' about 'what it means to be British, and particularly what it means to be a British Muslim'.[34] Patten stressed the need for younger Muslims to know about the democratic process, which, in the context of Thatcher's reason for doing nothing about Rushdie's book, could only be seen as an invitation to Muslims to uphold Rushdie's right to 'blaspheme'. He repeated the Government's refusal to act against *The Satanic Verses,* a position reiterated in his reply to UKACIA's response on 19 July.[35] A point that should be considered with regard to Patten's letter is the effect of Khomeini's *fatwa*. At the time of its pronouncement, Britain had only recently restored relations with Iran, and was looking forward to new contracts to aid the reconstruction of Iran after its recent long war with Iraq. The *fatwa* undermined this, leading to a breach in diplomatic relations, and hence the loss of potential contracts. Moreover, the Iranian action naturally upped the stakes in the Islamic world, putting pressure on other Muslim states to be more forthright against the book. This escalation potentially imperilled British contracts in other parts of the Muslim world. In this context, it is not cynical to see Patten's letter to British Muslims, the main instigators of the anti-Rushdie protest, as a call to abandon their campaign, not simply because it was pointless or divisive as his letter implied, but because it threatened British interests abroad, and because the Government wished to prevent anything similar occurring in the future.

Unlike all the protests, Khomeini's *fatwa* was effective: Rushdie was forced into hiding – virtual imprisonment. The effect on British Muslims was startling. Ruthven notes how antagonistic many became to the Saudis, even calling them 'heretics', whilst 'almost all the Muslims' he met in Bradford agreed with the *fatwa* in principle.[36] Jahangir Mohammed observes that 'Muslims also began to identify with the Islamic State in Iran and Khomeini. At demonstrations, Sunni Muslims proudly carried placards bearing the Imam's photograph.'[37] This success allowed Khomeini's supporters, principally Kalim Siddiqui, to bathe in his reflected glory. Siddiqui was later to form the Muslim Parliament, but because of Sunni–Shia rivalry, too close an identification between Iran and his own person, and the hostility of other Muslim groups, the venture failed, essentially collapsing soon after his death. A continuing legacy was the radicalisation of the community – hostility towards the Saudis and the UK Establishment, a concern over the desecration of Islamic sanctities, an assertion of Islamic identity, and the need to address the problem of powerlessness in Britain, which the Government's peremptory dismissal of calls to ban the book had demonstrated.

THE GULF CRISIS

British Muslims scarcely had time to catch their breath before another crisis intervened. The Iraqi invasion of Kuwait captured the imagination of Muslims across the globe as an anti-imperialist action, reversing the artificial colonial borders imposed after the First World War by Britain and France. British Muslims reacted similarly, and for many of the same reasons. Foreign Office Minister Douglas Hogg was subjected to 'continuous heckling' at the UMO February conference for supporting the war against Iraq whilst rejecting similar action to end the Israeli occupation of Arab lands.[38] At a Muslim conference in Manchester at the time of the Gulf crisis one speaker '…condemned the sham and hypocrisy of Western claims to be following "international law". Like others at the meeting, he evoked the problems of Kashmir and Palestine.'[39]

The doctrine of the *Ummah* ensured that Islamic solidarity – at least among the masses – would go to the one Muslim ruler who stood up to the infidel West. Saddam was praised 'because he dared to challenge the West directly'.[40] We can understand why such sentiments could be easily transferred to bin Laden for some UK Muslims. When the Saudis allowed American troops to enter their territory, Muslims throughout the world were outraged by what they saw as the desecration of the Islamic Holy Land, which many viewed as violating the *hadith* (narration of the Prophet) banning non-Muslims from Arabia.[41] This should be remembered when we consider why bin Laden enjoys support from some British Muslims today; the US presence was seen as a defilement, just like the purported desecration of the *Qur'an* at Guantanamo Bay, revealed in 2005, or like the abuse of prisoners in Abu Ghraib. As such, it had to be ended and avenged. Thus, for some, the destruction of the World Trade Center would be seen as *qisas* – retaliation, a feature of Islamic law.[42] The Americans were anyway hated because of their perceived pro-Israeli bias, and the Iraq/Kuwait issue was compounded by the fact that the Americans were allowed to 'attack' Iraq from the Muslim Holy Land. Lewis observes of British Muslim reaction: 'Anti-Saudi sentiment amongst Muslims…was much more public during the Gulf crisis. Many Muslims…were aghast that the Saudis could invite American and European forces onto Saudi territory.'[43] As Werbner observes, a popular Mancunian Muslim reaction to protests that Saddam was a tyrant was the rhetorical question 'Which is the greater evil, America or Saddam Hussein?'[44] At this point we should understand that 'the lesser of two evils' is a feature of Islamic law.[45] In the eyes of Muslims, the answer was obvious. At a national Muslim meeting in Bradford on 20 January 1991, a few days after the start of the Gulf war:

> …the resolutions insisted that 'the USA led aggression against Iraq' must stop and these forces withdraw from Muslim territories; the Saudi ruling family was condemned for allowing non-Muslim forces access to the Islamic heartlands and declared

unfit to be the custodian of Mecca and Medina; therefore it was every Muslim's duty to 'restore the Khilafat [Caliphate]'.[46]

We see here emphases that we will meet when studying the various radical Islamic groups in Britain: hostility to US policy; antagonism to the 'puppet rulers'; opposition to UK policy; the need for the *Khilafah*. A national Muslim meeting of thirty-five British Muslim organisations on 12 August 1990 condemned 'the presence of non-Muslim foreign troops in the Gulf and demanded their withdrawal'.[47] The anti-Western emphasis of the conference was clear, and so was the intensifying anger at the Saudi 'transgression' of the ban on non-Muslims in the Arabian Peninsula:

> We cannot tolerate the intervention of non-Muslim powers in this essentially internal Muslim affair...The build up of non-Muslims [*sic*] military forces in the vicinity of Islam's most holy shrines (Makkah, Madinah and Jerusalem) is not acceptable...any government in Muslim lands co-operating with the non-Muslim armies cannot demand the support of Muslims world wide.[48]

The Saudis had always enforced the *hadith* against church services in the country, and especially forbade non-Muslims from entering the holy cities. Yet now the Saudi regime had 'violated' this command, allowing the superpower usually hated by Muslims for its support of the Israelis to establish a military presence in their Holy Land, not to fight atheistic Communism – something the Saudis had never allowed even at the height of the Cold War – but to combat another Muslim state.

As the overwhelming Western technological and military supremacy made its presence felt with the bombing of Iraq, so overt support for Saddam became more intense, to the level that anything approximating to a dispassionate approach to the crisis by British Muslims disappeared. The issue was now 'simple': Muslims were being killed by the Great Satan. At a Bradford conference, Sher Azam's attempts at a balanced call for simultaneous withdrawal of Iraqi and Western forces were loudly rejected.[49] Instead, the resolutions demanded only a Western withdrawal, accusing the Western powers of 'aggression' against Iraq.[50] Also denounced was the Saudi royal family for allowing the non-Muslim military presence, which rendered it 'unfit to be the custodian of Mecca and Medina'.[51] The fact that this was a national conference of Muslims, and not simply a gathering of militants, demonstrates how pervasive anti-Saudi feeling had become among the community, and also how far British Muslims were prepared to go in confronting their own Government in times of war. A more extreme case occurred after the Baghdad air-raid shelter episode, when an Allied missile caused a large number of civilian deaths through incineration, leading to outrage across the Muslim world. British Muslim opinion was likewise angered, with the Bradford Council of Mosques issuing a heated statement entitled 'Baghdad Massacre', accusing the British Government of responsibility for the incident. This was strong enough in itself, but the statement went on to demand an avenging *jihad* against the Allies and Muslim 'puppets':

> ...these deaths must...be avenged in accordance with Islamic law...The House of Islam is at war with all those who attack its interest including those so called Muslims who are...fellow conspirators with the forces of western imperialism.[52]

The Bradford Council of Mosques' reaction, informed by the concept of *qisas*, is interesting because it represents the view of a leading and broad representative body of British Muslims on the nature of the war. That being the case, it provides an insight into the community's opinion in general about the nature of the conflict and British Muslim response to it. The perception was that Muslims were under attack by the West, aided by puppet Muslim regimes. The Rushdie crisis had seen them attacked intellectually; now they were being attacked militarily. The Saudis had 'betrayed' the honour of Islam by their soft approach in the Rushdie affair; now they betrayed its very holy texts by allowing non-Muslims to 'defile' the Islamic Holy Land and attack and 'massacre' fellow Muslims. In neither case did the Saudis rush to the aid of British Muslims. As with the Rushdie affair, during the Gulf crisis British Muslims were denounced, insulted, threatened and physically attacked. The Runnymede Report notes the increase in attacks during this period:

> At the time of the Gulf War...the West Yorkshire Police noted a 100 per cent increase in racist attacks in Bradford and a 58 per cent increase in West Yorkshire as a whole. A senior police officer was quoted as saying that 'dark-skinned people were attacked

because they were considered to be supporters of Saddam Hussein.'[53]

Vertovec sees the Gulf war as a stimulus to violent incidents against British Muslims and to Islamophobic opinion among the wider British population: 'there has been an evident rise in anti-Muslim sentiments (especially during and following the Gulf War)'.[54] The media's 'vilification' of Muslims during the Gulf crisis, the hostility of the general public, the very fact that holy buildings were defiled and Muslims were physically assaulted, all in a sense brought the 'attacks' on Muslims in Iraq home to Muslims in Britain. Albeit on a much lesser scale, they produced a microcosm of events in the Gulf, with 'Western infidels' defiling the holy sites of Islam by their very presence, and indeed engaging in physical attacks on Muslims. Hence sympathy moved to empathy, and to the perception that Muslims worldwide were under attack from the West – that Western people hated them and their religion, were determined to keep them weak and powerless, and even to humiliate them. Ultimately, this perception was to lead to the terrible events of 7/7.

The crisis situation for British Muslims was not helped by the deafness of the Government to their concerns. There was little reason for the Government to pay them attention. The Rushdie crisis had demonstrated how powerless they were, and had left them virtually friendless. With Iran neutral and Saudi Arabia actually a main coalition ally, there was not even minimal pressure from the Muslim states to change policy. British Muslims were totally isolated in their support for Saddam's '*jihad*'.

At the Manchester conference, one speaker first attacked the 'misrepresentation' of British Muslims in the media. This he blamed on a mixture of Crusader attitudes in the 'Christian psyche' and 'Jewish and Zionist' control of the media, which prevented Muslims from getting 'a fair hearing'. He also bemoaned the Muslim community's lack of 'proper political organization and mobilization'.[55] Werbner refers to the 'sense of frustration' at the 'basic political inactivity of Muslims in Britain', to the call for 'more activism', not just about the Gulf crisis, but over domestic concerns such as immigration rules and 'discrimination' against Muslim schools, and to the warning that in order 'to preserve our rights, to preserve our identity, to preserve our integrity we need to fight, and fight hard'.[56]

It should be noted, however, that no British Muslim group objected to Britain and America bombing Serbia during the Kosova crisis in 1999 without UN authorisation; *Muslim News* supported this action, describing it as 'a welcome move'.[57] British Muslims opposed the Gulf war not for any quasi-pacifist reasons, but rather out of solidarity with the *Ummah* – which explains why they opposed US–British air strikes against Iraq, and supported them against Serbia. With regard to the former, the Western action was perceived as being against the *Ummah* and its interests; in the latter, the action by the same states was viewed as a positive move with respect to the situation of the *Ummah*. The first was a crusade against Allah, the second was a military action sanctioned by God – or at least His believers in the Balkans and Britain. Hence, as far as British Muslims were concerned, there was no contradiction or hypocrisy in their position. In fact, their stance was consistent throughout all the crises that the *Ummah* – including its British section – encountered in the last decade of the twentieth century: solidarity with their Muslim brethren. This led them into conflict with the position of their Government over Iraq, and an enthusiasm bordering on zeal with regard to the policy of their Government over Kosova. It is likely that any Western action against a Muslim state will be met with hostility, whereas if America and Britain were to use military action to liberate the Palestinians, British Muslims would be their cheerleaders.

THE PSYCHOLOGICAL EFFECT OF BOSNIA

To understand contemporary British Muslim radicalism, we must understand the *psychological* impact of the crises Muslims faced after 1988, in terms of both the temporal sequence and the distinctive, but related, natures of the affairs themselves. In temporal terms, everything seemed to hit the community at once. The Rushdie affair began in 1988 and continued into 1990. In 1990–91, the Gulf crisis occurred. Soon after began the disintegration of Yugoslavia, and the resultant Bosnian conflict. The Rushdie affair had seen Muslims accused of possessing values hostile to the cultural norms of modern Britain. During the Gulf crisis, there had been accusations that they were disloyal to Britain in a war situation. The insinuation was that Muslims were not really 'British' and therefore not part of 'Western' or 'European' civilisation. The implication of these sentiments, added to the abuse and sometimes violence that British Muslims experienced at street level during these crises, was that Muslims were unwelcome in Britain because of their religion, or more specifically, because of their *assertiveness* about it. As British Muslims understood the words of Home Office ministers, they could only fully function, or even reside, in Britain if they became 'integrated', passive about their religious identity.

The Bosnian crisis shocked the community, partly because Bosnian Muslims held the very identity that government ministers were understood to be suggesting for British Muslims, yet this did not prevent their being slaughtered. This discredited government statements at the time of the Rushdie crisis yet further in the eyes of Muslims. Their perception was that Muslims were unwanted in Europe, and that this prejudice had led to the massacre of their brethren elsewhere on the continent. Given Bosnia's 'proximity' to Britain, Muslim voices expressed concern that they could be the next victims of European Islamophobia. There are indications of widespread fear in the community resulting from the crisis. The depth of this anxiety can be measured by the fact that when Jacobson engaged in field research amongst the Muslim youth of East London, one interviewee stated 'that some young men of his acquaintance did not wish to be interviewed by me because, in the wake of events in Bosnia, they felt that Muslims in Britain should be wary of researchers gathering information about them'.[58] Jacobson found that Bosnia was the regular international issue raised by interviewees.[59] She quoted one of them as an example of the 'vulnerability' Muslims felt 'even in Britain':

> 'In Yugoslavia, Muslims are being slaughtered by the Serbs...And [my mum is going] I told you it can happen – look it's happening there.' This sense of vulnerability in the face of the Bosnian war was made apparent to me in another context. A teacher at a local sixth-form college arranged for me to conduct interviews with some of his students, but told me that a few of them had not wanted to take part in my research. One had said to him, 'What about Bosnia?', and then explained that research could be used against Muslims in this country – in the same way that in Germany statistics had been used in the efforts to round up and kill the Jews.[60]

That young men could feel threatened by a lone writer engaged in innocent research indicates the degree both of the psychological trauma inflicted by the Bosnian crisis on the community, and of the sense of conspiracy involving the British Government. Ataullah Siddiqui, observing the effect of various crises on young British Muslims, noted how this led them to see 'non-Muslims as potential enemies of Islam, conspiring and colluding against the wider Muslim community', and to view *The Satanic Verses* as a 'conspiracy' against Muslims, supporting evidence for which was found in events such as 'the massacre of Muslims in Bosnia'.[61] The Runnymede Trust's *Islamophobia* report noted:

> Many Muslims believe Islamophobia has played a major part in Western attitudes to events in Bosnia, and has prevented so far a just and lasting settlement. One of our correspondents (not himself a Muslim) wrote as follows:
>
> *'During the Bosnian war I had many encounters with politicians, including a senior cabinet minister. It was clear to me that irrespective of their political loyalties their reluctance to sanction military intervention in Bosnia was rooted in a large degree in their reluctance to support the creation of a new Muslim polity in Europe. "Muslims have a tendency to radicalism," the cabinet minister told me, when I asked why the government was refusing to lift the arms embargo against the Bosnian government.'* [62]

It is important to recognise the existence of such fears in the community, before examining how Muslim organisations responded. It is essential to remember that since the Rushdie crisis, a struggle for power in the community had been waged between UMO, Kalim Siddiqui and the Mawdudists. Therefore, whilst the genuineness of their outrage at the carnage in Bosnia need not be doubted, neither should it be dismissed that those elements vying for influence had an interest in *promoting* those fears to compete against each other and to undermine tendencies towards more secularised approaches, such as those suggested by government ministers. The very fact that Bosnian Muslims were often nominal Muslims assisted this campaign, since the more religious elements were able to argue that such an identity provided no defence against Islamophobia.

Prior to the outbreak of the Balkan conflict, most British Muslims were unaware of even the *existence* of the Bosnian Muslims: 'A few months ago few Muslims in this country had even heard of Bosnia or knew that there was such a large and important community of indigenous European Muslims.'[63] This in itself contributed to the shock experienced when the crisis began. The community suddenly discovered a nation of co-religionists native to Europe. But they received this revelation through TV pictures depicting weeping women complaining of rape; forced deportations; burning houses; and corpses, including dead children. The message they imbibed – and that Islamic activists promoted – was that Muslims in Europe were endangered. The suddenness of the recognition of Bosnian existence reinforced arguments that British Muslims were just as likely to suffer for their religion as for their race.

FULFILMENT OF PROPHECY?

In the British context, there was a link between the Rushdie and Bosnian crises. Writing in 1992, Shabbir Akhtar reminded readers of his comment in the *Guardian* on 27 February 1989 – that 'next time there are gas chambers in Europe, there is no doubt concerning who'll be inside them'.[64] Akhtar argued that Bosnia demonstrated that his words were 'terrible prescience'. Over the years, British Muslim organisations and media have recalled both these words and the perceived 'fulfilment of prophecy' in Bosnia, and have related both to the situation of their community. The relation of the Bosnian tragedy to the condition of British Muslims is crucial to understanding developments in the community. There is a distinct nuance with regard to what occurred in Bosnia on the one hand, and what happened during the Gulf crisis on the other. When many British Muslims opposed the war against Iraq, the prevailing sentiment was ideological solidarity with the *Ummah*. With Bosnia, whilst solidarity was certainly a constituent in their reaction, the response was also motivated by *psychological* considerations: anxiety about their own situation. The demographic character and religious attitudes of the Bosnian Muslims must be considered when we try to understand the British Muslim response to the crisis. LeBor notes that 'Bosnian Muslims were largely secular and those that were religious emphasised that they were "European Muslims", something quite different to the Ayatollahs of Iran and the Islamic clergy of Saudi Arabia.'[65] They were committed to multi-ethnicity and a multi-faith constitution, yet years of stressing 'multi-ethnicity' did not prevent their tragedy.[66] They were native Europeans rather than immigrants, indistinguishable in culture and language from their neighbours. Moreover, Bosnian Muslims were *white*. This enabled

British Islamic activists to play the *race*, as well as the religious card – if genocide could happen to native white European Muslims, how much more at risk were British Muslims, who were comparatively more religiously observant, largely of migrant origins, and, frankly, for the most part brown – and thus more visible and easily identifiable than their Bosnian brethren. Akhtar noted the secularisation of the Bosnian Muslims, and observed that neither this fact, nor 'the European appearance – their blue eyes, their blond hair...availed them anything'.[67] The comments by government ministers about 'integration' were undermined for British Muslims by the Bosnian crisis: integration and state policies on 'multi-ethnicity' had not saved the Bosnians. A more relaxed attitude towards their religion had not helped either.

Every Muslim attempt at lobbying the British Government to suggest a Kuwait-style UN military intervention to aid the Bosnians was met with a firm refusal. Suspicions arose in the community, encouraged by figures like Siddiqui, that the Government was unwilling to help Bosnia because the victims in that conflict were Muslims. This impression was intensified by the response of the Bosnian Government, represented by the words of Dr Ejup Ganic, Vice-President of Bosnia-Herzegovina, prominently displayed in text form on the video of the MPGB Bosnia conference in 1993: 'You all know that the West would do something for Bosnia if the Bosnians were not Muslims.'[68] *Trends* reproduced a letter sent by the Foreign and Commonwealth Office in response to a letter sent by a British Muslim to the Prime Minister:

> Many voices, including a large number from the Muslim community in the UK, have argued for international military intervention to force an end to the fighting. No government is contemplating this and we do not believe that this is viable...We do not believe that lifting the arms embargo would improve the situation. Indeed, the likely effect would be to increase the suffering and the killing...The only way to achieve a lasting peace is through a negotiated settlement.[69]

Hurd was criticised for his justification for retaining the arms embargo on the grounds that it would produce a 'level killing field'. The *Muslim News* editorial condemned him for this remark, arguing that 'He only prefers one-sided "killing fields", that is, killing fields full of Muslim bodies.'[70] The problem of government 'deafness', manifested during the Rushdie and Gulf crises, arose again. In 1995, the Prime

Minister refused to see a UKACIA delegation about Bosnia.[71] Iqbal Sacranie, its Joint Convenor, not normally someone given to hard-line statements, accused the Government of playing a 'negative role' by 'discouraging any decisive action and giving the Serbs clear signals to attack and ethnically cleanse the rest of the so-called safe areas'.[72] Psychologically, the effect was serious. If their Government was indeed an accomplice to what they saw as Europe's Muslim Holocaust, what might befall *British* Muslims one day? By the time of the Bosnian conflict, the Government's unwillingness even to permit the Bosnian Government access to self-defence made such fears plausible.

ISLAMOPHOBIA

Whilst all these crises were continuing, a new phenomenon was receiving attention in the community: Islamophobia. Seen by Muslims as essentially the equivalent of anti-Semitism, it first manifested itself during the Rushdie crisis. The generally negative reaction to the anti-Rushdie campaign shocked Muslims, especially since this response was not confined to traditionally working-class racist elements that objected to Muslims as coloured immigrants, but included those previously seen as sympathetic and supportive – liberals and leftists. The focus of the antagonism displayed by the latter, as opposed to the 'Alf Garnett' types, was not a biological (and to some extent cultural) difference, but an *ideological* distinction. Essentially, there occurred a clash of values. The media and general public viewed British Muslims as intolerant Nazi bigots, as was implied by the press reaction to the Bradford book-burning.[73] Akhtar comments on public reaction to the burning of Rushdie's book: 'it was fair to speculate that the resentment really centred around the fact that these foreigners – blacks, Muhammadans, immigrants – were taking liberties in someone else's country'.[74] The Rushdie affair affected even those normally sympathetic to Muslims as a minority – especially liberal/left elements. A particularly ironic response came from Roy Jenkins, former Labour Home Secretary and architect of the 1976 Race Relations Act. In the *Independent* of 4 March 1989, he lamented that 'we might have been more cautious about allowing the creation in the 1950s of a substantial Muslim community here'.[75] This quote, and the fact that Jenkins was responsible for introducing the 1976 Act, was noticed by Muslims, and helped to undermine confidence in traditional race structures and policy.[76]

The emphasis on Islamophobia, and the pressure for legislation against religious discrimination that has been exerted with special vigour since the 1990s by Muslim representatives, are directly traceable to the shock of the widespread and largely uncontested anti-Muslim animosity experienced during the Rushdie crisis. Since backing down on the issue was not an option, Muslims began to believe that, unless they redressed their socio-political marginalisation, Akhtar's 'prophecy' might be fulfilled. This point was made by Islamic Human Rights Commission (IHRC) Chairman Massoud Shadjareh at the launch of the report entitled *Anti-Muslim Discrimination and Hostility in the United Kingdom, 2000*: 'The report's findings indicated that unless something is done urgently at governmental level, Muslims in Britain and Europe are likely to face the same fate this century as Jews in Europe in the last.'[77] The remarks by Akhtar and others all point to the sense of embattlement that began to characterise British Muslims during and after the Rushdie crisis, as they witnessed what they saw as the prevailing Islamophobia in British and Western society. Islamophobia was to intensify their assertion of the priority of Muslim identity and the political radicalism that accompanied it. The Muslim campaign received a major fillip in 1997 when the Runnymede Trust published its report *Islamophobia – A Challenge for Us All*. Since then, the phrase has entered public discourse and has received increasing recognition.

One area where Muslims felt that they were victims of active Islamophobia was in education. The Government persistently found reasons to reject state funding applications by Muslim schools. UKACIA asserted that the attitude of the authorities, which it denounced as 'double standards', could only 'deepen the disillusionment with government'.[78] This disillusionment appeared to stretch beyond the assertions of Muslim interest groups. La'Porte refers to a TV broadcast where young Muslims cited the denial of state funding for Muslim schools, in contrast to that for Catholic, Anglican and Jewish schools, as evidence of 'a conspiracy against Muslims'.[79] Another area where British Muslims persistently complain of Islamophobia is in the media. The IHRC report *Anti-Muslim Discrimination* devoted a section plus an appendix to the issue of 'The media and incitement to hostility against Muslims'.[80] It observed the negative effect of media Islamophobia on the community, and its relation to the anti-Muslim discrimination in other sectors, suggesting that British Muslims face pervasive animosity and discrimination:

Regular and usually incorrect portrayals of Muslims as violent threats to social stability are, in and of themselves, likely to stir up hatred against Muslims...A headline from the *Today* newspaper of April 1995 showing a burned baby in the arms of an Oklahoma fire officer, carried the banner headline, 'In the Name of Islam.' As events transpired, the bombers were white supremacists...The impact of such reporting cannot be underestimated. The persistent analogising of Muslims with all that is despised in society reinforces the prejudice that is exemplified throughout this report. In this context a Headteacher of a Primary school justifies her violent attack on a 9 year old child, and the NUS justifies ignoring the victimisation of Muslims on campus, and its own targeting of Muslims as a problem on campus.[81]

Apart from portrayals of Muslims as violent and 'extremist', the other area in which Muslims feel that they have been demonised by the media is purported Islamic attitudes to women. The Runnymede Report referred to a *Daily Mail* article that claimed '...Moslem men can continue to treat women as second-class citizens in Britain without a murmur from the equal opportunities brigade'.[82] A particularly important observation was made that 'Another stock story or image is of the *hijab*, seen by the western media as a symbol of male oppression.'[83]

Just as the Government during the Rushdie crisis refused to extend the Blasphemy Law to protect Islam, both Conservative and Labour Governments likewise declined to extend the laws against religious discrimination and incitement from Ulster to the mainland, where most Muslims live – that is, until two phenomena intervened. Firstly, the British National Party (BNP) started winning council seats – sometimes from Labour – often employing Islamophobic language, which heightened Muslim concerns that anti-Muslim sentiment was now entering the electoral sphere. Secondly, Muslims started deserting Labour as a result of the Iraq war. It is not implausible to conclude that Labour's policy change in introducing a Bill against religious hatred was at least partly motivated by a concern to retrieve votes lost on both counts by making things harder for the BNP and undoing the electoral damage among Muslims caused by Iraq.

2001 – THE YEAR OF LIVING DANGEROUSLY

The year 2001 was a watershed for British Muslims. The first crisis in the year occurred when riots by Muslim youths erupted in Oldham, Burnley and Bradford. In consequence, the Government commissioned reports on these disturbances. These reports approached the riots from the sociological twin poles of ethnicity and socio-economic issues. This methodology virtually ensured that their conclusions would effectively reflect their presuppositions. Little serious attention was given by the reports to the *religious* context of these riots.

Significantly, Marsha Singh, Labour MP for Bradford West, declared after the Bradford riot: 'We have to put the events into some sort of perspective. It was nothing to with deprivation [*sic*], this was sheer criminality.'[84] A police report stated that 'The majority of violent racist incidents are perpetrated by Asians on whites, which is an ongoing trend involving primarily Pakistani and Bangladeshi teenagers.'[85] Some Muslim community leaders questioned the figures on the grounds that Asian Muslims in the area frequently do not report attacks where they are the victims.[86] However, even if some crimes on 'Asians' went unreported, there clearly *was* a problem of anti-white violence, and Oldham Christian sources stated that attacks on *whites* were often underreported.[87] The police report into 'racial' attacks reveals that 'the issue of racist attacks on whites dates back to 1992...'[88] This fact is important, since apparently the British National Party did not exist in Oldham until about 1999.[89] Thus, the attacks could not have been a response to the BNP presence in the town.

The old 'sociological' explanations for the Northern riots crucially ignore the fact that the riots did not involve blacks, Hindus or Sikhs. Indeed, reports from Oldham recorded Muslim youth attacks on Hindus and blacks.[90] Another important fact ignored by the reports was that Hindus and Sikhs thereafter pronounced the 'Asian' tag to be dead. 'The word "Asian" has outlived its usefulness. Raj Ruia, an Indian businessman in Manchester, said: "The word lumps us all together."'[91] Significantly, the reason given for this new policy was the riots: 'A growing number of Indians in Manchester say they no longer want to be described as "Asians" because it places them in the same category as rioting Muslim youths of Bangladeshi and Pakistani origin in nearby Oldham.'[92] Crucially, this reaction from other minorities undermines traditional sociological analysis based on race and social deprivation. Clearly, Hindus and Sikhs identified the riots as Muslim-based, and the lack of 'Asian' or 'ethnic minority' solidarity perhaps indicates that these communities held local Muslims to blame for the riots, not least because Indian non-Muslims had also been victims of sectarian attacks prior to the disturbances. Media articles and subsequent government reports were flawed by their emphasis on *ethnicity* above *religion*. Community relations 'experts' seemed reluctant to take the religious factor seriously, probably because of secular-humanist presuppositions. The Home Office *Community Cohesion* report (hereafter called the Cantle Report) notes 'This was a question which consultees preferred to steer clear of.'[93]

The failure to take religion seriously naturally led the reports to address the disturbances from the standpoint of *race* and thus, subliminally and in effect, to view them in terms of previous riots involving people of Afro-Caribbean heritage, such as the riots in Toxteth and Brixton. This led the reports to largely ignore the impact of both domestic and international issues on British Muslim youth, as well as the influence of certain *ulema* preaching *jihad* and a negative attitude towards non-Muslims. The Cantle Report rarely mentions religion, merely observing that 'Islamaphobia [*sic*] was also identified as a problem...'[94] It can be argued that these secular-humanist presuppositions prejudiced an objective analysis of the causes and nature of the riots. Arguably, this attitude is an *English* problem; outside Merseyside, with its Orange–Green divide, sectarian divisions have not been a problem in England for many generations, and possibly Scots or Ulster-dominated committees would have found it easier to understand the character of the problem, since sectarian issues have been traditional problems in these two parts of the UK. The riots and the emergence of BNP electoral Islamophobia demonstrate that sectarianism is now also an English issue.

ISLAMIC RADICALISM/SECTARIANISM

Certainly, considering the character of BNP electoral propaganda, which specifically called for a boycott of *Muslim* – as opposed to other minority – businesses, it is clear that, as the Cantle Report suggests, anti-Muslim sectarianism was a feature of the events surrounding the riots.[95] No reference, however, was made in the Oldham Independent Review to claims from local Hindus and Christians that local mullahs were to blame for sectarian incitement.[96] It is hard to understand – and certainly to justify – why no mention was made of non-Muslim 'Asians' dissociating themselves from the Muslim community in the wake of the riots, and specifically rejecting a catch-all *ethnic* designation. For example, a letter from a Pakistani Christian in the *Guardian* during May asserted:

> During the past three years, a mini ethnic cleansing, largely encouraged by mullahs from mosques, has been taking place in Oldham. Young Muslims have been encouraged to attack Hindu homes and shops. The mainstream media have ignored this terrorism, but the ethnic press has reported it. The most terrifying incident was in 1999 when the Diwali celebration lights in a Hindu enclave were torn down and destroyed by Muslim thugs. Any extremism is wrong; but to lay the blame wholly on the BNP and NF [National Front] is not only one-sided, it also frees Muslim extremist groups from any involvement and responsibility.[97]

Oldham appeared to be a stronghold of Taliban supporters.[98] A Kashmiri guerrilla group (albeit one on ceasefire) openly held a meeting in the local Pakistani community centre soon after the riots.[99] The town had already been linked with Kashmiri Muslim radicalism by the Government's attempt to deport a young Oldham imam, Shafiq ur-Rehman, on the charge that he had recruited British Muslims to fight in the *jihad* for Kashmir.[100] It may be argued that the *jihad* message against non-Muslims preached by the supporters of the Taliban and Kashmiri rebels had been 'transferred' by some Oldham youths to local residents. The fact that Oldham's Hindu Diwali festival was attacked by Muslim youths underlines that the problem was sectarian, rather than racial, yet the reports ignore this. Thus, since other minorities have been regularly targeted, the 'sociological' explanation of the riots – that they were the venting of outrage against a white racist society – is deficient in terms of objective analysis.

The Oldham Review admits that 'there have been many examples of attacks by Asians on whites', but in complete contradiction it denounces the 'assertion, without any substantiation, that "Muslims" were guilty of...for example terrorising white people'.[101] The report asserts that 'the claims of no-go areas are not borne out by experience...'[102] This was despite contrary claims by locals. For example, a Muslim youth in the Glodwick estate, where the majority of residents are Muslim, told Radio 4's *Today* programme (19 April 2001): 'There are signs all around saying whites enter at your risk. It's a matter of revenge. It's about giving as good as you can take.'[103] This implies that the Report, rather than being objectively empirical, was an exercise in politically correct propaganda, with a predetermined conclusion. Significantly, Gerry Sutcliffe, Labour MP for Bradford South, recognised the reality of this problem: '...there is a core of people who...want to create no-go areas'.[104]

In Burnley, Muslim youth violence was particularly vicious and openly sectarian. Churches were vandalised.[105] In 2000, Muslims purchased some land behind the Living Hope Christian Fellowship's chapel, and unsuccessfully approached the church to sell its property to allow construction of a mosque. In March, cars outside the chapel were vandalised, and leaflets were attached to windscreens warning 'Allah is the one true God. Leave now.' In April, the chapel doors were daubed with the word 'ALLAH', and once again the same leaflets were found. Two weeks later, whilst the congregation were at Bible study, the chapel was petrol-bombed. Fortunately, the distressed congregation was able to escape unscathed, if petrified. Summer saw the church's evangelistic caravan overturned and vandalised by 'Asian' youths. In October, the car belonging to Dave Bullock, church pastor, was petrol-bombed whilst parked outside his house, and a leaflet was attached: 'Allah is the one true God. You must leave – it could be you next.'[106] Bullock did not claim that those *specific* Muslims seeking the property were behind the violence. However, the wording of the leaflets suggests that *some* Muslims were definitely the culprits.

Incredibly, the Burnley Task Force Report makes no reference to these incidents. Had it done so, it would have brought the issue of *sectarianism* to the fore, rather than the *ethnic* emphasis that characterised it. The omission is particularly surprising in the light of the 1999 Channel Four *Despatches* programme that played a tape purportedly showing Supporters of Sharee'ah (SOS) leader Abu Hamza preaching in a Burnley mosque and advising Muslims to learn martial arts, to disguise themselves, and to 'rip the intestines' out of local infidels![107] Abu Hamza denied he was the speaker involved, but certainly *someone* incited sectarian violence. Yet the Burnley Report ignored this, only focusing on white racist groups when it considered preaching 'hatred and prejudice'.[108]

This immediately raises the question of why the report chose to ignore these facts? At best, one can accuse the report writers of incompetence in failing to examine this incident, when two mosques invited someone who not simply preached inflammatory sermons, but actually incited the murder of innocent local non-Muslims in Burnley itself. The issue here is not the person in question, but the fact that two Burnley mosques saw fit to allow their premises to be employed in this way. Had the committee examined this at length, it might have altered its conclusion that the riots were largely gang-related hooliganism. The timeline at least suggests the influence of Islamic sectarianism. Considering the attacks on Christian places of worship in the area, this conclusion seems irresistible.

A feature highlighted by the reports was the 'self-segregation' practised by all communities in these towns, and the need for 'planned' (enforced?) housing and educational integration. The Ouseley Report on Bradford observes 'Self-segregation is driven by fear of others...and the belief that it is the only way to promote, retain and protect faith and cultural identity and affiliation.'[109] The report observed not only 'white flight', but also that 'Sikhs and Hindus' were leaving, and that the inner city was seen as 'Muslim dominant'.[110] The fact that Sikhs and Hindus were quitting the area, and that they were uninvolved in the riots, again challenges the emphasis the reports on the disturbances place on 'race'. Perhaps a major reason for 'non-Muslim' flight was that non-Muslim homes were being attacked by 'Asian' (i.e. Muslim) youths: 'Stone-throwing yobs as young as ten have turned a Bradford street into a "war zone", residents claimed today. Many householders in the Girlington street fear leaving their homes at night as out-of-control youngsters hurl bricks through windows, set fire to fences and clamber across the roofs of bungalows.'[111] A related point, unmentioned by the reports, but broadcast by BBC Radio 4 (18 November 2001) was that Bradford churches had been vandalised, pastors and church officials physically attacked.[112]

Rev. Paul Bilton of St Columba's and St Wilfrid's, Horton Grange, stated that he had received physical threats from Muslim youths, and had also had his church threatened with arson. Sexual threats were made against his wife. In his area, Muslim youths had also intimidated other whites and Hindus. Similarly, Rev. Paul Hackwood of St Margaret's, Thornberry, faced intimidation from Muslim youths. The word 'HAMAS' was spray-painted on his church. Threats were made against his family. St Phillip's Church, Girlington, was attacked by about 50 Muslim youths, who dumped rubbish into the church and set

THE IMPACT OF CRISES ON BRITISH MUSLIMS

it on fire in November.[113] They also smashed a stained-glass window dating back to 1860. Furniture was destroyed. Its minister, Rev. Tony Tooby, was chased with cries of 'Get the white bastard!', and had the back windscreen of his car smashed as he attempted to escape the gang.

This was the latest in a stream of assaults on the building; the front door had been vandalised a number of times and had even suffered an attack with a battering ram! At Easter, Lucy-Jane Marshall, the leader of the Brownies, a young girls' group based at the church, was chased by a Muslim mob shouting 'Christian bitch' (significantly, a *sectarian*, rather than *racist* taunt).[114] Ms Marshall rejected claims from the community that this was simple thuggery or, as Ayub Laher, Vice-President of the Bradford Council of Mosques, suggested, Muslim youths' idea of 'fun'. She was adamant that it was definitely 'racist'.[115] Thereafter, Muslim youth mobs threw eggs and stones at Brownies and their parents.[116] This caused the Brownies to quit the church after twenty years.

The BBC programme reported the priest at St Cuthbert's RC church as stating that Muslims from the neighbouring mosque had urged him to close the building, and when he refused, Muslim youths began to threaten him, warning 'we'll get it [the church] one day!' This intimidation climaxed with the hanging of the caretaker's dog. Another church, St Clement's, was the victim of arson, which caused tens of thousands of pounds' worth of damage – first in October, and again in November. This followed an unsuccessful approach by the neighbouring mosque to purchase the building.

It would be easy to dismiss this as youth vandalism or as mirror-image racism, except for two factors. A black majority Pentecostal church, Victor Road Church of God of Prophecy, was also intimidated, again over a period of several years.[117] A spokesman reported that virtually all the building's top windows had been stoned, and the protective mesh cut. At various times Muslim youths had stormed in and overturned the chairs, shouting that the Christians should get out and sell the church to be turned into a mosque. Just before Bonfire night, some Muslims threw fireworks into the church and then smashed the pastor's car window. Muslims – including even children – often abused worshippers outside the building. An Asian family who joined the church was the object of particular harassment, and Muslims would often storm in, demanding to speak to them.

33

It may be argued, then, that whilst Asian against black racism (and vice versa) is a reality, the assaults on this black church demonstrate that the attacks were not a response to increasing white votes for the BNP. The clincher is that, according to the BBC programme, Leeds Road Ahmadiyya Mosque (which is frequented by a sect deemed heretical by orthodox Muslims) had also been attacked by Muslim youths and had its windows smashed in. This proves that the motivation for the attacks is neither simple yob violence, nor racism, but rather sectarianism. Philip Lewis has stated that, traditionally, Muslims enhanced their power by consolidating their territory.[118] Police reports of 'no-go' areas and 'ethnic cleansing' in Oldham seem to tie in with this.[119] The fact that this information was open to the committees investigating the riots raises crucial questions as to why it was ignored, and thus raises further questions about the integrity and accuracy of their analysis and recommendations. Perhaps referring to the attacks on the black church and Ahmadiyya mosque would have undermined the emphasis in the reports on ethnicity and deprivation. At the time of the Oldham riots, the *Guardian* leader said:

> The term 'Asian' is too broad to be useful: there are so many different communities grouped under that umbrella. In Oldham, the 'Asians' are mainly Pakistanis and Bangladeshis and they are mainly Muslim. Few dispute that Muslims are finding it harder to find their place in British society than, say, Sikhs or Hindus. There is greater misunderstanding and prejudice against their faith, and perhaps greater exclusion, too.[120]

The failure of successive governments to address this problem, added to the foreign policy of those same governments on the Bosnian and Middle East crises, has alienated British Muslims, especially their youth. The Cantle Report noted: 'most of the disturbances have involved youths of Pakistani origin and this seems to point to a growing disaffection...Islamaphobia [*sic*] was also identified as a problem in the areas we visited and for some young people was part of their daily experience. They felt that there [*sic*] were being socially excluded because of their faith and that this was not being recognised or dealt with.'[121] British Muslims often perceive an Islamophobic bias in British society, and fear that one day they might share the fate of their Bosnian brethren. Hence, government policy – especially in the international sphere – has impacted on Muslim youth in northern towns, causing both fear and an assertive reaction.

The reports observed disaffection with the police, and an MCB release indicates why this is so: 'The Police are perceived by the Asian Muslim community – by youth, parents and community leaders alike – to be indifferent to their complaints and racist. The Police are not trusted by an important section of the Asian Muslim community.'[122] The *Yorkshire Post* produced an excellent analysis of the underlying causes of the Bradford riot, which applies equally to the disturbances in Oldham and Burnley:

> Taught to think of themselves as an oppressed and victimised minority, hounded by a police force which even a noted Law Lord labelled as institutionally racist, the modern Muslim young male despises the seeming docility of his father's generation, rejects the disciplines and values of his religion but turns Islam instead into a militant, violently rebellious credo, along the lines of Hamas and the intifada (Saturday night's running battle with police bore a striking resemblance to the confrontations on the Gaza strip). Add drugs and crime into the mix, and Bradford becomes a simmering, poisonous stew of racial resentment.[123]

It is significant that youths in these places identified with groups such as HAMAS, the Taliban, and Al-Qaida, calling themselves *mujahidin*. During the Bradford riot, Muslim youths left 'tributes to the Hamas Islamic militant movement sprayed on Bradford shops', implying that their resistance to a National Front rally was analogous to the *jihad* of HAMAS.[124] There were reports of some youths wearing T-shirts in support of bin Laden.[125] Others stated that their model was the Taliban, with one informing the *Independent*: 'Some of the older boys are forming a mujaheddin group.'[126] Some Burnley Muslims wore bandannas with Arabic inscriptions, terming themselves 'Mujahids'. Hundreds of young Muslims in Bradford and Oldham reportedly formed a vigilante group 'Combat 786' (the numerical value of 'Allah') to fight the white racist group 'Combat 18'.[127] There were confirmed reports of young Muslims from places like Bradford and Leeds going to fight for the Taliban against British and US forces.[128] After 9/11, local police began stopping Muslim youths wearing pro-Taliban T-shirts.[129] There were also major incidents of Muslim youth violence in support of Usama bin Laden:

There was a string of incidents across West Yorkshire on Monday night with reports that people on their way to a family bonfire and fireworks display in Roundhay Park, Leeds, were approached by youths chanting 'Get out of Afghanistan' and demanding drivers say 'Osama bin Laden rules'. When they refused, the terrified drivers and passengers tried to escape as their cars were pelted with bricks and stones thrown through their windows.[130]

As a *Guardian* editorial immediately after the Oldham riots observed about Muslim youth, 'Many have turned to communal vigilantism to protect themselves.'[131] The message was: 'we are ready to fight'. It is noteworthy that the 7/7 bombers originated from West Yorkshire, scene of some of the events under consideration in this section. Significantly, as we observed earlier, police reports from Oldham suggest that Muslim youth attacks on non-Muslims became a problem around 1992 – i.e. around the time of the Gulf and Bosnian crises. Similarly, the attacks on churches in Bradford go back to about the same time.[132] This may indicate that a more positive government policy towards Muslims – especially in terms of *foreign* policy – may assist in the reconciliation of communities in these places.

In many ways, the attempt to form Muslim self-imposed ghettos should be seen not so much as a natural social and cultural development, but rather as an act of defensive *jihad*, by consolidating Muslim settlement and power, removing non-Muslims from the area, and establishing places that are more easily protected from an Islamophobic society. As the Cantle Report observed:

> Of course, some minorities choose to live within their own communities. For example, some would choose to live in a distinct area dominated by one culture and to ensure that there is a sufficient critical mass to support facilities such as shops and places of worship – and to try to ensure safety of community members.[133]

The Bradford riot was an overreaction to a planned, but later proscribed, National Front march. As previously noted, the Muslim youths clearly saw themselves as *mujahidin,* identifying with HAMAS, defending their areas from a racist invasion. The immediate cause of the riot in Burnley was an inter-racial altercation, possibly between two criminal groups.[134] The Oldham riot was the consequence of police action, and a desire on the part of Muslim young men to defend their community.[135] The speed with which the riots developed, and the large numbers of young people involved, suggest that the recommendations of some Muslims in the 1990s on the need for British Muslims to organise almost on a paramilitary basis had been heeded. Ultimately, to a large extent, the riots were the result of perceived government insensitivity to Islamophobia since the Rushdie crisis, as well as of British foreign policy in the Middle East and especially its perceived negative role during the Bosnian conflict. The riots showed that 'skinhead'-type yob behaviour is not the prerogative of white youth; ironically, it shows that the more 'British' Muslims become, the more certain elements will mimic modern British dysfunctional misconduct. Such violence is also a reaction to Akhtar's prophecy; the British-born generation of Muslims have no intention of meekly marching to the gas chambers – they will resist. Perhaps 7/7 should be seen as the most extreme illustration of this tendency.

9/11 AND IRAQ

The next crisis to hit the British Muslim community in 2001 was 9/11. The massacre led to attacks on Muslims and mosques across the UK, including in Glasgow, Edinburgh and Belfast. All major UK Muslim groups condemned the 9/11 attacks. The MCB stated:

> British Muslims, along with everyone else, are watching events in America with shock and horror. Whoever is responsible for these dreadful, wanton attacks, we condemn them utterly. These are senseless and evil acts that appal all people of conscience. The MCB stands shoulder to shoulder with remarks made by our Prime Minister Tony Blair. Our thoughts and prayers are with all the innocent victims, their families and communities. We convey our deepest sympathies to President Bush and the people of America. No cause can justify this carnage. We hope those responsible will swiftly be brought to justice for their unconscionable deeds.
>
> As the British Muslims come to the full realisation of these most awful events, which they condemn wholeheartedly, they too are beginning to feel a huge sense of fear. **Terror makes**

victims of us all, it is beyond reason. Terror on this scale must not be compounded by knee-jerk reactions that would make victims of other innocent peoples of the world. This would only **add** to the devastation caused.[136]

However, SOS actually blamed the Israelis for the attack:

ZIONISTS ARE THE ONLY BENEFICIARIES FROM THIS PLOT!...The towers owned by a Jew [*sic*]. It is reported that 4000 Jews did not go to work at the World Trade Center on that day, 11 September 2001. Reported Stern-Intel...Aeronautical Experts suggest that the plane was not even hijacked, the tranponder [*sic*] was not even on, it was infact [*sic*] programmed to hit its target. Civil engineering experts suggest that, it was a pure demolition, no steel framed towers fell like the way WTC's fall.[137]

A poll by *Muslim News* displayed the following attitudes among British Muslims to 9/11:

According to a 'temperature-gauging poll' conducted by *The Muslim News* on line, the single most difficult issue for British Muslims to reconcile was the Government role in international affairs. A massive 86 per cent believed the UN and the West had double standards in dealing with the injustice in the world. More than two out of five agreed that if the West had been more tough and exacting against Israel, with regard to the Kashmiri conflict and on Bosnia, they would have been more supportive of action against Usama bin Ladin...

Regarding the events of September 11, just over half of the respondents said they reacted to news of the attacks with a combination of 'sadness and understanding;' 36 per cent said it was a 'moral outrage;' only 8.5 per cent agreed that it was a 'good strike.' But an overwhelming 79 per cent of Muslims disagreed that it was right to bomb Afghanistan, 73 per cent said they would have preferred a criminal investigation and extradition process. More than two-thirds believed it was wrong by the US and West to describe September 11 as an act of war.[138]

This was not the first time British Muslims had been forced to cope with the effects of bin Laden's *jihad*. In 1998 bombs had exploded in Kenya and Tanzania outside the US embassies, killing and maiming a number of people. Al-Qaida were blamed by America for this action, and in retaliation US forces had bombed Sudan and Afghanistan, because of their purported links with the dissident leader. British Muslim organisations unanimously condemned this action. The MCB charged that 'The American action is a clear violation of international law and takes us back to the days of gunboat diplomacy when might was right, and the law of the jungle prevailed.' It accused Clinton of trying to divert attention from the Monica Lewinsky crisis (where the President was accused of sexual misconduct and perjury).[139] The IHRC similarly attacked the bombings as abuses of international law, echoing the link with the Lewinsky crisis; it also saw a parallel with the Gulf war.[140] It further noted US Secretary of State Madeleine Albright's comment that the death of half a million Iraqi children as a result of sanctions was justified.

These reactions demonstrate how widespread and deep-rooted overt opposition to US policy had become in the British Muslim community. It should be noted, however, that this is not analogous to the way migrant minorities often sympathise with their home governments in confrontation with the host country. Pakistan, Bangladesh and Yemen, for example, are US allies. The support for Sudan and Taliban-Afghanistan was not based upon a sentiment of ethnic nostalgia – few British Muslims are of Sudanese or Afghan heritage. Rather, it is *ideological* – a support for religious comrades. The reaction of British Muslims cannot be characterised as South Asian or Arab, but rather is only comprehensible as a *religious* response – demonstrating the priority of their identity with, political allegiance to, and sympathy for two radical Islamist states.

Prior to 9/11, Usama bin Laden emerged as the hero of some young British Muslims, with his writings and tapes enjoying increasing circulation, as was observed by Fuad Nahdi on the BBC1 programme *The Koran and the Kalashnikov*.[141] *Q-News*, reviewing the programme, noted that it ended with how British Muslims are responding: 'The increasing frustrations of seeing their fellow Muslims as the enemy is provoking many young men to seek combat training and voice their anger against Western power in more controversial ways.'[142] This is an important observation: it is not only 'solidarity with the *Ummah*' that is provoking this response from British Muslim youth, but their feeling of alienation towards the governments in the West for their 'complicity' in the oppression of Muslims in the Middle East, the Caucasus and the Balkans. The article also noted the comments of white convert Muhammed Yusuf, 'If the police and the Government won't protect us then we have to protect ourselves', which the article saw as 'a chilling reminder' to the 'powers that be' that Muslims must have 'greater input' into government decision-making – and specifically (and this is what is so pertinent for our theme) 'in the area of foreign policy'. This demonstrates how the legacy of the Gulf and Bosnian crises persists, and that British Muslims are concerned to influence Western policy towards the Muslim world. A *Sunday Times* article, 'Britain's Islamic Army', noted that 'According to Muslim sources, in Britain, about 2,000 young Muslims travel abroad each year for training.'[143] The *Guardian* ran an article about this trend after a 24-year-old Birmingham Muslim, Bilal Ahmed, was killed in an alleged suicide bombing in Kashmir, in which his actions also killed six Indian soldiers.[144] He was purportedly fighting for an Islamist group called *Jaish-e-Mohammed*. Apparently, another Birmingham Muslim, this time a convert, was killed when America bombed the Al-Qaida base.[145] The article quoted Omar Bakri Muhammad of Al-Muhajiroun as claiming that 1,800 young British Muslims go abroad annually to fight in places like Kashmir, Palestine and Chechenya.

It appears that many of these volunteers are students, recruited on campuses, motivated by a desire to 'defend fellow Muslims anywhere in the world'.[146] This in itself tends to undermine traditional sociological explanations that people are motivated to undertake such violence by poverty or ignorance. For example, the first British Muslim to be convicted in the UK of terrorism at a 2005 trial, Saajid Badat, was notably intelligent. Moreover, whilst involvement in Kashmir or even Afghanistan could, perhaps, given the Pakistani heritage of many British Muslims, be understood as partly ethnically oriented, this is not the case with other incidents. The British 'martyr' *mujahidin* Omar Khan Sharif and Asif Mohammed Hanif, who sacrificed their lives in Tel Aviv in 2003, killing three people, were not of Arab heritage; their motivation was based on solidarity with the *Ummah*. This is even more pronounced in the case of the 'shoe bomber', Richard Reid, who tried to blow up an American plane in 2001; he was of mixed Afro-Caribbean and white heritage. This shows how overt Islamic radicalism among British Muslims has spread in response to the various crises since Rushdie, and how this has impacted on the issue of identity.

Arguably the greatest event to undermine the yob violence that characterised the 2001 riots and the call for *jihad* occurred in response to the US–UK coalition that attacked Afghanistan in the wake of 9/11 – the anti-war movement. The Stop the War Coalition, formed shortly after 9/11 to protest against the Afghanistan war, was a broad alliance of leftists, pacifists and Muslims, notably the Muslim Association of Britain (MAB). Undoubtedly, most Muslims were opposed to the conflict; the MCB had issued a statement to this effect, urging 'British Muslims to voice their protest in peaceful ways through demonstrations and vigils'.[147] Thousands of people took part in the initial rallies, and the sight of non-Muslims aiding Muslims in their darkest hour (with widespread physical attacks on Muslims after 9/11) undoubtedly prevented a retreat into Bosnia-type anxieties. What made even more impact, however, was the growth of the movement in the wake of US–UK plans to attack Iraq. There was widespread – indeed majority – public scepticism about this war. Muslims were therefore not part of a minority on this issue; most Britons were with them. This was expressed in a very practical way on 15 February 2003, when up to two million people congregated in Hyde Park to protest about the war plans. The fact that this number represented a cross-section of 'Middle Britain' reinforced Muslim buoyancy. The rally organisers went further than opposing war on Iraq: they demanded 'Freedom for Palestine', which further convinced Muslims of the goodwill of most Britons about their central concern. Even a hard-line rejectionist group like SOS was moved to observe: 'The Worldwide anti-war demonstrations by non-Muslims is [*sic*] appreciated and noted.'[148] It is noticeable that MCB releases on Iraq were uncompromising and forthright, unlike the somewhat apologetic tone of those on Afghanistan, undoubtedly reflecting the fact that Muslims were far from isolated on the issue. Examples are their 20 March 2003 release 'A Black Day in Our History', which accused the war of being 'part of a plan to redraw the map of the Middle East in accordance with the agenda of Zionists and American neo-Conservatives', or their subsequent release on 11 April 'UK Muslims Reject Neo-Conservative/Zionist Plans For Iraq':

> The imminent US announcement that pro-Israeli Retired General Jay Garner is to head an interim Iraqi administration, coupled with the crass threats against Syria and Iran from the most senior US officials only serve to confirm the worst fears of those

41

who assert that the real objective of the war against Iraq was to promote US/Israeli geo-political interests in the Middle East.

The anti-war rallies, and the prominent role taken by the MAB therein, were a victory for the participationist wing of Islamic radicalism in Britain, signalling to British Muslims that they were not a totally isolated body in the UK, and that therefore a second Bosnia was less likely. The 2003 Hyde Park rally, the biggest in British history, probably did more for community relations and to prevent a recurrence of the 2001 riots than any government initiative. The fact that many non-Muslim Britons then joined with Muslims to desert Labour at subsequent elections has accentuated this.

POWERLESSNESS AND THE MUSLIM VOTE

The simple reason why the Muslim community had been ignored by the Government on issues such as Rushdie, Iraq, Bosnia, Muslim schools, etc., was that it *could* be ignored, because it lacked serious political influence. As Akhtar observed, 'British Muslims are a powerless minority...[F]or most practical purposes, Muslims in Britain remain poor, isolated and weak. In the Rushdie affair, their protest is a proof of their powerlessness; powerful groups do not need to demonstrate on the streets.'[149] It was in the wake of the Rushdie campaign that investigations and suggestions to remedy the community's powerlessness emerged. The purported economic and political influence of the British Jewish community was seen as a model of what a minority could do if properly organised. *New Statesman and Society* editor Stuart Weir noted that:

> There are signs that some Muslim leaders at least want more tangible results for their ability to 'deliver' their vote and are seeking to emulate the influence of American Zionists over government policy. And they have observed that British Jews have been able to block the production of a historical play [Jim Allen's *Perdition*] which offends them.[150]

Ruthven, interviewing Shabbir Akhtar, noted the latter's comment that if Muslims 'had been a powerful, well-organised lobby like the Jews, Rushdie's outrages would never have got into print'.[151] Similarly, Raza writes:

The Muslim community has not yet learnt how to approach the British political system. It lacks the political experience which is practised by other communities like the Jews. The implicit trust placed on the state and its political elites by the Muslim community has not paid off. Working in the anti-Islamic context the Muslims have to adopt various sophisticated ways of political participation. [152]

This refrain has continued to the present, notably among groups like the Muslim Public Affairs Committee (MPAC). It has been increasingly suggested that the potential electoral power of the Muslim community should be properly utilised. *Muslim News* saw tactical voting as the answer to the Government's refusal to proscribe religious discrimination in mainland Britain, and did so by making the points about the Jewish experience and the number of Muslim electors. Referring to a speech by then Home Secretary Michael Howard at the 24th winter conference of UMO that rejected any such legislation, the editorial stated 'Muslim voters mean business this time, Mr Howard…Muslims might not be as influential as the Jewish community, but they have the voting power and this time they should not be taken lightly.'[153]

To be effective, the call to tactical voting must be delivered and practised on a *national* basis. Attempts to found UK-wide institutions, equipped to formulate and effect such a policy (such as UKACIA, the MPGB or the MCB), reflect the need for a co-ordinated national response. UKACIA's July 1989 Bulletin recognised that the Rushdie affair had revealed the community's need for an empowerment strategy:

> Compared to other communities it has as yet no effective clout in the seats of power, in the media or in economic circles…Muslims as a result of this campaign are beginning to learn more about the political…and legal processes of the country.[154]

If a single major reason for the failure of the 1988–90 British Muslim campaign against Rushdie may be identified, it is the community's inexperience and even incompetence in the political field. This picture is no longer as valid at the beginning of the twenty-first century as it was then. The formation of the MCB has given Muslims more unity than they previously enjoyed. In 1997 UKACIA urged a mass turnout of Muslim voters for the general election.[155] The community was urged 'to exert its numerical strength by extracting promises from candidates in constituencies where Muslims can alter the balance of power'.[156] UKACIA Convenor Sacranie argued that it was 'crucial that we maximise our potential to get a return from those candidates who will not be able to make it to the Commons without our votes'.[157] UKACIA reckoned that, in around twenty seats, the number of Muslim voters exceeded the majority held by the sitting MP.[158] A *Muslim News* editorial noted how better organisation encouraged tactical voting:

> The General Election results showed that the Muslim community used tactical voting...as we predicted...Both the Labour and Conservative parties need to take note. The Muslim community is better organised now and with better leadership and information about issues and will use their vote tactically. The days of the parties taking support for granted are over.[159]

The evidence for this was the voting strategy in constituencies like Bradford West, where Muslims turned to vote Tory, and in Bethnal Green and Bow, which saw a 5.9 per cent swing to the Muslim Tory candidate. In Batley, the Tory lost, which the paper attributed to his breach of a 1992 promise of support for the Muslim Zakaria School. More vital at local level, the radicalised Muslim youth of 1988 were, at the dawning of the new millennium, often around the age of thirty. Many enjoyed a superior education to that experienced by their migrant forebears, and, having been born or raised in Britain, they were more *au fait* with its political and legal structures, not least because of the Rushdie crisis. They held the potential for a more effective, independent and objective leadership at both local and national levels.

Among indications of the potential for *bloc* tactical voting is the phenomenon of Birmingham's Justice For Kashmir party, devoted to Kashmiri self-determination, which began 'as a protest against the continuing imprisonment in Britain of two Kashmiri separatists jailed for the killing of an Indian diplomat'.[160] However, the party grew into 'a protest against Labour which is accused of heel-dragging on Kashmir and neglecting the Muslim community'.[161] Labour, they claimed, took 'the Muslim vote for granted'.[162] The party's election triumphs were not only related to Kashmir, but also reflected 'years of frustration with the Labour Party at a local level...'[163] The party initially won two seats in

1998, was then joined by a Labour defector, and the May 2000 elections saw it emerge with five councillors.[164] *The Economist* observed 'The JFK is already Britain's most successful ethnically based party, outside Northern Ireland.'[165]

This demonstrates that, in certain council wards, tactical voting by Muslims can be effective. However, unless a small number of councillors hold the balance of power, such results are unlikely to lead to major changes in government policy, or even party policy at a national level. In Birmingham, though, such a situation did lead to some changes – 'Labour has already taken note. Last month, the city council passed a resolution supporting the self-determination of Kashmir.'[166] This shows that, since the three major crises they have faced since 1988, Muslims have shown themselves prepared, in some cases, to be more assertive in electoral terms. Daniele Joly, director of the Centre for Research into Ethnic Relations at the University of Warwick, observed: 'although the Asian communities have traditionally had a strong allegiance to the Labour Party, "it has not met their aspirations." The party has for too long taken their support for granted, but "the new generation expects a lot more."'[167] Another indication of this trend was demonstrated in the 1999 European elections. *Q-News* examined the prospects for Muslims resulting from the use of proportional representation, and the possibility of *bloc* voting: 'According to research carried out by a prospective candidate Muslims could return as many as four British MEPs without the help of any established party if they voted strategically and en bloc in the June elections.'[168] *Q-News* was pessimistic about the chances of such a breakthrough, but in the event, one Muslim Conservative candidate – Bashir Khanbhai – was actually elected as MEP for the Eastern region.[169]

The 2001 election saw the first major steps in the direction of tactical voting, when the MCB produced the document *Electing to Listen*. The issues of political marginalisation, religious discrimination and Islamophobia (especially in the media), the priority of faith identity, and international concerns such as Iraq, Kashmir and Palestine were highlighted.[170] A major indication of the move to tactical *bloc* voting was the 'Votesmart' campaign for the 2001 election, informally linked to the MCB. 'Votesmart' urged 'British Muslims: Don't just vote, vote smart.'[171] The campaign included an 'Activist's Toolkit', and information on marginal seats where Muslim votes could be crucial. It sought 'to empower Muslims' by informing them how individual MPs voted or spoke on issues such as Palestine, Kashmir, Iraq, Section 28, etc., with advice on whether the MP should receive Muslim votes. These records were sent to mosques to educate Muslim electors. This displays a necessary move from previous Muslim electoral interventions – organisation at both local and national levels, identification of 'unsympathetic' MPs, and a campaign to remove them. Significantly, the 'Votesmart' campaign was a consequence of British Muslim concern for the Palestinians, illustrating how, since the Gulf and Bosnian crises, the *Ummah* concept and external issues have impacted on community activism.[172] *Muslim News* observed:

> The Palestinian intifadah has provided a wake-up call for Muslims to become more involved in politics. But there are also many other issues. Some are detailed on vote card drawn up by the Muslim Council of Britain. But they will only become topical if they are raised and put on the political agenda by sustained lobbying. This needs for Muslims to be involved in the democratic process, whatever the shortcomings, and not only in the run-up to a General Election every four or five years.[173]

To aid the campaign, the MCB distributed a broadsheet entitled *Election Supplement 2001*. It included a cut-out 'Muslim VoteCard', asking prospective candidates to literally sign up to the MCB agenda involving legislation against religious discrimination, opposition to the Terrorism Bill, and support for 'suffering Muslims in Palestine, Kashmir, Chechnya and Iraq'.[174] Muslim communal voting 'provides politicians with...incentives and disincentives'.[175] The broadsheet, noting that the community faced big challenges, realistically observed that, irrespective of the strength of arguments, 'sometimes it boils down to numbers'.[176] Numbers being their only real strength, British Muslims were finally facing up to the use of that weapon to realise their aspirations, through the call to tactical *bloc* voting. In close elections, such a lobby might be a principal factor in deciding the outcome. The 'Votesmart' campaign represents the community's response to the powerlessness so evident during their three main crises of recent history.

It was actions by foreign Muslims and a US President that, ironically, made the Muslim vote a major factor of British political life. The 9/11 attacks by Al-Qaida led to President Bush declaring the 'War on Terror', first against Afghanistan for sheltering them, and then against Iraq. In both cases the British Government, under Blair, backed

Bush. The Iraq war was, arguably, the most unpopular war in modern British history and, like most Britons, Muslims were unconvinced of any links between Iraq and Al-Qaida. The significant point was that Labour, the major beneficiary of Muslim votes, was intent on this war, and ignored even the biggest demonstration in UK history in 2003. Suddenly, the voices urging tactical voting fell on welcome ears. The local elections produced the 'Baghdad Backlash'. Birmingham saw Labour lose eleven seats to the Liberal Democrats, mainly in wards with large Muslim concentrations. In Leicester, home to another substantial Muslim community, Labour lost eight seats and the Liberal Democrats emerged as the single largest party on the city council. Muslim disillusionment in Luton cost Labour thirteen seats, eleven of them to the Liberal Democrats, and elsewhere, such as in Preston, Labour lost ground because of Muslim tactical voting. In the Scottish parliamentary elections, Muslims voted for the Scottish Socialist Party, the Greens and the SNP rather than for Labour. Muslim groups campaigned for a tactical vote to punish Labour for its Iraq policy and to empower the Muslim community. A Scots MAB leaflet stated: 'Despite our large numbers, our own inaction has left us impotent and ignored by the political parties. Politicians have not felt the need to ensure that Muslims are on their side, knowing that they can obtain power anyway. That is because Scottish Muslims have either not voted or not voted smart.' It is difficult to judge how far the Muslim vote was spontaneous, and how much it was the result of organised lobbying. However, especially in Scotland, the high level of local media publicity generated awareness of the Muslim 'Use Your Vote' campaign, which employed a dedicated website that advised on the suitability of candidates, and vigorous leafleting on the issue.

The anger over Iraq continued into the 2004 Greater London Authority (GLA), European and council elections. Nationally, the Liberal Democrats ate into the Labour vote. Overwhelmingly, this was because of Iraq. The Muslim *bloc* tactical vote was a major factor in this, but it must also be emphasised that the Lib Dems benefited from anti-war sentiment among the wider British community, too. It follows that the effect of Muslim tactical voting is intensified when the wider community shares the same concerns. In terms of actual electoral analysis, it seems that, despite Ken Livingstone's return to Labour, many London Muslims voted for him because of his high-profile anti-war and pro-Muslim stance. What was particularly interesting were the results for George Galloway's new party, RESPECT, which polled well in some Muslim-intensive areas, notably the East End. RESPECT polled 91,175 votes (or 4.8 per cent) in the European elections in London, and 87,533 votes (4.57 per cent) for the GLA. Their candidate, Lindsey German, came fifth in the mayoral ballot. In Newham, RESPECT obtained 11,784 votes (21.41 per cent), and in Tower Hamlets 10,611 (20.36 per cent). In the City and East constituency, Oliur Rahman won 19,675 votes. More significantly, a few weeks later the same candidate was successful in the St Dunstan's and Stepney Green ward by-election for Tower Hamlets Council. The two boroughs of Newham and Tower Hamlets have a high Muslim concentration, which until recently was solidly Labour. It is clear that the Muslim vote was also responsible for the reasonably good result for RESPECT candidate Yvonne Ridley (herself a Muslim convert), who polled 12.66 per cent in the Leicester South by-election and contributed to the Lib Dem victory, which was partly the result of electoral education by the Friends of Al-Aqsa, a Muslim pro-Palestinian group. Equally, in Birmingham Hodge Hill, RESPECT's John Rees won 6.27 per cent in the by-election and, had he not stood, the anti-war Lib Dems would have taken the seat.

The 2005 election may not have been 'the khaki election', but it was certainly 'the Iraqi election'. In many ways the community became electoral kingmakers. The day after the election the *Daily Telegraph* observed: 'The Muslim community appears to have vented its fury over Tony Blair's support for the war in Iraq by turning its back on Labour. Constituencies with high Muslim populations demonstrated an average nine per cent swing away from the party they have traditionally voted for. Although many live in areas with seemingly unassailable Labour majorities, their impact was felt by the significant erosion in those Labour majorities.'[177] It was not only a case of reduced majorities: the paper further noted that 'Labour's Barbara Roche lost her Hornsey and Wood Green seat in north London to the Liberal Democrat Lynne Featherstone after a huge 14.6 per cent swing. The Muslim vote – they make up 7.2 per cent of the population – undoubtedly contributed to her demise.'[178]

It was not only in Hornsey that the Muslim vote was effective. Rochdale Labour MP Lorna Fitzsimmons – opposed for her pro-Israeli views – lost out to the Lib Dems. The most spectacular result was in the previously safe Labour seat of Bethnal Green and Bow, where voters elected the outspoken opponent of the Iraq war George Galloway. The result was interesting because, despite claims by some commentators, race and gender played little or no role in the result. Ms King was regarded by the local community as an excellent constituency MP and was outspoken in her pro-Palestinian views, but she made what was, in the view of the locals, the catastrophic error of voting for the war against Iraq. Galloway, by contrast, is a hero to many Muslims worldwide because of his uncompromising stance on Iraq and Palestine. In many ways, it was not so much King as it was Blair who lost. The MAB welcomed 'the role of the Muslim vote in numerous constituencies which affected clearly either the outcome of the vote or the share thereof. It was absolutely clear that the Muslim community decided to utilise their numbers in several dozen constituencies to bring about a recognition of the issues of concern to them, particularly the anti-terror laws and the war in Iraq.'[179] The Muslim electoral defection from Labour that began in 2003 was clearly no hiccup. A definitive shift in allegiance appeared to have occurred, with large numbers of Muslims giving their votes to the Liberal Democrats rather than Labour. Overwhelmingly, the reason was Iraq.

There were several factors in this result. Firstly, it appears that, as with the wider British electorate, the Muslim community was no longer bound by the tribal allegiance to parties that once characterised British politics. 'Public' outrage was the second factor. It was not only Muslims who were aggrieved; it is clear from the results across the UK that the wider British public were also galvanised by Iraq. Hence, Muslims were simply the vanguard of a crest of national disillusion with both Tories and Labour over the war. Thus, Muslims can influence results when the wider public are in sympathy with them. The final major factor in the results was the impact of lobbying and guidance. The Muslim Council of Britain issued a pamphlet *Electing to Deliver*, which offered ten issues on which to confront candidates. The MAB was bolder, giving specific advice as to which particular candidates in certain constituencies should receive the Muslim vote. A further step was undertaken by MPAC, which established teams on the ground to confront certain MPs. The election displayed an increasing sophistication by Muslim voters. The fact that Muslims have exercised tactical *bloc* voting over a space of three years demonstrates that the political radicalisation of the community envisaged since the Rushdie crisis has come about; henceforth politicians have to consider the reality of 'the Muslim vote', especially when it comes to foreign policy.

49

Moreover, this shows that British racial and religious diversity has now affected the electoral system. As in America, ethnic and faith community caucuses are now a significant factor in how elections turn out. The 2005 election may well prove to have been a watershed in UK politics in more ways than one.

7/7 – AL-QAIDA HITS HOME

Another watershed in 2005 was the attack against London on 7 July. Bombings occurred on the underground in Aldgate, Edgware Road and Russell Square, and on a bus in Tavistock Road. Britain had faced terrorist outrages before, notably by the IRA, but there were two essential differences: three of the four bombers were from mainland Britain, and the attacks were all 'martyrdom operations'. Mohammad Siddique Khan, a 30-year-old from Leeds who had worked in schools as a teaching assistant, was the Edgware Road bomber, and may have been the unit's leader; Shehzad Tanweer, 22, blew up the underground train at Aldgate; Hasib Hussain, 18, was the bus bomber; and it was a West Indian convert, Lyndsey Germail or Jamal, originally from Jamaica and married to a white convert, who attacked Russell Square. Over fifty people were killed in the attacks.

The bombings provoked a wave of Islamophobic attacks across the country, including attacks on mosques, assaults on Muslims, anti-Muslim graffiti and, in one case, the murder of a Muslim man in Nottingham. On 12 July, the Muslim Safety Forum (MSF), a coalition of Muslim groups,[180] issued two press releases, the first listing Islamophobic attacks.[181] A later release announced examples of the backlash: 'Arson, Bomb hoaxes, Criminal Damage/Graffiti, Assault, Abuse/Threats…The day after the attack, there was a large increase in Faith Hate and Race Hate Crimes. This rate decreased the few days after and slightly increased after the announcement of the suspects.'[182] The *Guardian* reported:

> The number of faith hate crimes has risen fivefold in the fortnight since the London bombings…The Metropolitan Police has recorded 800 race and faith hate crimes since the July 7 attacks.
>
> The number of faith hate crimes, predominantly directed at British Muslims, has passed the 200 mark. In the same

fortnight last year, 30 faith hate incidents were reported by the Met.

Nationally, the figure for hate incidents directed at Muslims has passed 1,200 as a backlash continues.[183]

Response from Muslim organisations to the bombings was swift. The MCB stated that it 'utterly condemns today's indiscriminate acts of terror in London'.[184] The IHRC were equally forthright: 'The Islamic Human Rights Commission condemns in no uncertain terms the attacks perpetrated in London this morning.'[185] The Muslim Public Affairs Committee (MPAC) conveyed similar sentiments, but then went on to attack UK foreign policy as the cause of the attacks – a refrain to be heard from Muslim groups soon after – and furthermore urged Muslims to be proactive in countering Islamophobia:

> London's Muslims are shocked as our city has been the victim of what appears to be a co-ordinated terrorist attack.
>
> The perpetrators of this horrific crime need to be caught and brought to justice, but no matter who is responsible for this attack British Muslims and MPACUK do not have any sympathy for those who continue to use violent methods to raise very important issues...
>
> Mosque media teams around the country need to start brainstorming ideas to counter a rise in Islamophobia, and Mosque leaders should start condemning the attacks and calling for a rethink in the root cause of these horrific incidents that affect our country.
>
> The British government and present politicians seriously need to consider how the effects of their dangerous foreign policy are putting at risk lives of innocent Britons at home. British citizens have been at the forefront of raising these issues with the current government and we hope the government keeps these in mind as we all go through what will be a very difficult time for our country.[186]

On 12 July, the MSF issued this statement:

'Whoever kills a person unjustly it is as if they have killed the whole of humanity.' *(The Holy Quran, Chapter 5: verse 32).*

Last Thursdays [*sic*] attack was a crime against all of London's 2000 different communities. The UK's Muslim Community is united in condemning the attacks.

Unfortunately, there have already been over three hundred faith and hate crimes against the Muslim community since last Thursday, also Nottinghamshire witnessed an Islamophobic murder.

It is unacceptable for anyone who seeks to take advantage of this tragedy and use it to spread hate and violence amongst the communities in Britain.

This is the time for **all of us** to show resilience, tolerance and mutual support.

We must maintain and preserve our unity, anything less is a capitulation to those who seek to divide us.[187]

Hizb ut-Tahrir (HT) were more equivocal, waiting for evidence before issuing any condemnation, but nonetheless observing that such acts contradicted Islamic law:

At a time when fingers will be pointed at us from the wider community we need to come together as a community with one voice. Yes, the rules of Islam do not allow the harming of innocent civilians, but at the same time the rules of Islam do not allow us to condemn Muslims with little evidence in order to remove the pressure from ourselves. Condemnation with scant information will only aid the leaders of the West who want to use fear as a tool to change our Ummah and our Deen as well as allow them to arrest more Muslims unjustly under draconian terror laws.[188]

The MAB was uncompromising in its condemnation of the attacks, and was concerned to address the need 'for more emphasis to be placed on tackling the causes of terrorism', a theme that came to the fore as responses to the crisis developed:

What happened in London completely and utterly repulses us. The finger of suspicion has been pointed on Muslims as being responsible for the atrocity. It goes without saying that if this is the case, these people are acting outside the framework of Islamic teachings. Nothing justifies the killing of innocents.

As British Muslims, there is a great responsibility on us. We are uniquely placed in this global faultline between Islam and the West, to help bridge this gap. We fully understand the psychology and background both of this country and the Muslim world.

With this in mind, we have to state once again that until the grievances of the Muslim world are addressed, the open wound from which blood trickled onto London will continue to exist. That wound is the injustices felt in Palestine, in Iraq and other parts of the Muslim world. It is the installing and propping up of dictators and stems from hundreds of years of colonialism. In the West, we have forgotten most of this – the Muslim world with its past hasn't.

Once this is addressed, global security will prevail. Re-evaluating our foreign policy is not as [sic] easy task but must be done. We can throw as many counter-terrorism measures at the problem, lock up people indefinitely, stop and search people indiscriminately, make them carry ID cards, but we are not even sticking elastoplasts on the gaping wound this way.

To borrow and adapt one of the Prime Minister's own phrases, we need to be tough on terrorism, and tough on the causes of terrorism.[189]

The followers of Omar Bakri Muhammad were late in responding to the crisis. His own response was to blame both the British Government and British people for creating the circumstances that led to the bombings:

> The British people did not make enough effort to stop its own government committing its own atrocities in Iraq and Afghanistan. They showed Tony Blair full support when they elected him prime minister again even after he waged the latest war in Iraq.[190]

He went on to say that the bombings were a surprise, and that if he saw anybody he 'would stop them'.[191] A website influenced by his teachings issued a release echoing and expanding upon his points, and it is worth examining these in detail, because of the difference in view from other Muslim statements:

In truth there is a joint responsibility for the London bombings which rests on the necks of not just those who carried them out but also on the necks of the following:

- The British government
- The general public in Britain and
- Secular and moderate so-called 'muslims' such as the Muslim Council of Britain (MCB), the Muslim Association of Britain (MAB), the Muslim Public Affairs Committee (MPAC) etc.

The British government has responsibility due to the following:

- Their crusader war against Islam and Muslims manifest in their wholesale murder of Muslims in Afghanistan, the occupation and murder of Muslims in Iraq and their support of the fascist state of Israel.
- Their colonial views expressed in the claim of Tony Blair that British values and civilization are universal and superior to Islamic values and civilization and his loathing for the Shari'ah (Islamic law).
- Their policy of 'divide and rule', wishing to divide the Muslims into 'moderates' and 'extremists' in order to isolate practicing Muslims from the apologists.
- Their terrorizing the Muslim community in the 'war on terror', which has given them the excuse to violate the sanctity of the house of Allah and the sanctity of Muslim homes and honour.

The general public in Britain are responsible due to the following:

- Their disregard for the cease-fire offered to them by Sheikh Usama Bin Laden in 2004. This is an indication of people who are irresponsible and who do not pay attention to or give proper priority for their own security.
- Their silence towards the brutal foreign policy of the Blair government against the Muslims all around the world since they publicly re-elected him despite the atrocities he has committed in Afghanistan and in Iraq.

The secular and moderate so-called 'Muslims' in the UK are responsible due to the following:

- Their neglect for the concerns of the Muslim Ummah abroad, their pre-occupation with unimportant issues and their propagation of corrupted ideas such as competing for government positions.
- Their labelling [*sic*] and underestimation of Sheikh Usama Bin Laden.
- Their oppression against Muslims who support their brothers abroad and their labeling [*sic*] them as extremists in addition to spying on them and handing them over to the British authorities.[192]

As a result of the bombings, there was much concern that London had become a centre for foreign militant mullahs – 'Londonistan' – although no evidence was presented to suggest that any such individual was actually responsible for 'inciting' or influencing the bombers. There were also comments on the need to counter 'extremist' teaching, although 'extremism' was not actually fully defined. For example, some commentators defined Sheikh Yusuf al-Qaradawi as an extremist for his support of martyrdom operations by the resistance movements in Palestine and Iraq, whilst virtually all Muslims regarded him as a moderate, who condemned Al-Qaida actions in America and Britain. Prime Minister Blair met with twenty-five Muslim leaders on 19 July to tackle extremism: 'They agreed to set up a task force that would explore the extent of disaffection among the Muslim population.'[193] However, the composition of the group (hand-picked by the Prime Minister) that met with Blair was questioned. One of them was Sir Gulam Noon, whose only qualification seemed to be that he was a millionaire donor to the Labour Party; other obscure figures included Azhar Ali from the Labour National Policy Forum, as well as controversial Labour parliamentarians Khalid Mahmood and Lord Patel, who have upset younger Muslims with their comments on certain issues, such as the Iraq war. In fact, there was a dearth of younger Muslims in the delegation, save for *Emel* editor Sarah Joseph OBE. The *Guardian* observed that the delegation were 'mostly established figures in their 40s and older'.[194] Considering that the bombers were from the younger generation, this was a questionable response to the events of 7/7, as the article reported:

> Among groups not invited to the meeting was the Muslim Association of Britain, which was active in organising opposition

to the Iraq war, and the Islamic Human Rights Commission (HRC) which has been critical of the police.

Massoud Shadjareh, of the Islamic HRC, said: 'The overwhelming majority of youth and others in the Muslim community are alienated not just from British institutions, but from Muslim institutions as well. Mr Blair met too narrow a group of Muslims. He invited those who he knew would agree with him.'[195]

A similar reaction was reported by Muslim youth in Luton:

Ali dismissed Tony Blair's meeting at Downing Street with the country's 20 most prominent members of the Muslim community as a 'PR exercise', and said he believed these 'elders' were out of touch with disenchanted Muslim youth.

Many others acknowledged anger at not being heard or represented and admitted to feeling less pride in being British than Muslim, with a strong emotional bond to the concept of Ummah, or the Muslim community, that extends across geographic and nationalistic boundaries.

A shop assistant at a Muslim bookshop said: 'The injustices that Britain is inflicting through their foreign policy is unacceptable. There are angry men who sympathise with the people who are oppressed.'

Abu Zulfiqer, 24, a Bangladeshi-British Muslim, said while he disagreed with killing innocent people, some felt it was legitimate to defend the 'brotherhood'.[196]

As part of their response to the bombings, on 15 July the MCB gathered over forty leading Islamic scholars to issue a *fatwa* (ruling in Islamic law) condemning the bombers:

Along with all Londoners and the people of Britain, we are deeply shocked and saddened by the bombing attacks of 7 July...We regard these acts as utterly criminal, totally reprehensible, and absolutely un-Islamic...There can never be any excuse for taking an innocent life. The Qur'an clearly declares that killing an innocent person was tantamount to killing all mankind and likewise saving a single life was as if one had saved the life of all mankind. (The Qur'an, Al-Maidah 5:32) This is both a principle and a command.

We are firmly of the view that these killings had absolutely no sanction in Islam, nor is there any justification whatsoever in our noble religion for such evil actions. It is our understanding that those who carried out the bombings in London should in no sense be regarded as martyrs.[197]

Two points should be noted in relation to this declaration. Firstly, it is not cynical to view this as mainly a PR exercise to set the record straight before the general public. That is, the main intended audience would not have been Muslims, but rather wider British society, to clarify that the bombings were not sanctioned by Islam. Had any of these scholars been asked before 7/7 whether such an attack was *halal*, he would, of course, have replied in the negative. The *fatwa* did not suddenly make the action *haram*; it was so already. Secondly, a *fatwa* is only effective in influencing people who freely choose to follow the Islamic scholars in question. Islam is not like the Catholic Church, with a hierarchical structure that can determine dogma, for example when the Pope gives an *ex cathedra* declaration, such as the 1950 Papal ruling on the Assumption of the Virgin Mary into Heaven. The bombers, following Al-Qaida, will have regarded these scholars as apostates, and the *fatwa* will be ineffective in preventing future attacks. This is illustrated by those who openly support bin Laden, such as the Al-Ghurabaa website, which denounced the *fatwa*:

> As for the recent Fatwa signed by 500 'imams', it is clear blasphemy against Islam. To begin with, a Fatwa is not issued by two, three or 500 people, rather it is issued by one person. Moreover a Fatwa must be based on the Qur'an and Sunnah (sayings and actions of the Messenger Muhammad (saw)) and not on pressure from the government or the wider community.[198]

It should be noted that there are indications that the *fatwa* should not be read as a blanket condemnation of the use of martyrdom operations as a tactic in *jihad* in all spheres. As we shall see in the next section, Muslims – including those in Britain – differentiate between the *jihad* of HAMAS and Hezbollah and that of Al-Qaida. They will usually accept such operations against Israelis and occupation soldiers in Iraq, whilst condemning them in Britain. This is neither hypocrisy nor special pleading, but is based on Islamic jurisprudence. Essentially, the issue revolves around two factors: whether the operation's principle is *halal,* and the identity of the victim. Suicide is a sin in Islam, but the definition of suicide concerns one's intention (*niyyah*). If self-destruction is motivated by despair of one's life, that is suicide, and thus is sinful.[199] If it is to please God by fighting the enemies of Islam, necessitating self-sacrifice in the process, that is not suicide, but martyrdom. The main issue concerns the objects of the action. If they are combatants, such as people who serve in an occupation army and ancillary services (such as an occupation administration) and/or have taken homes belonging to Muslims and covenanted Christians,[200] they are viewed as legitimate targets, and thus most Muslims see Israelis, Serbs who have taken Muslim homes in Bosnia, and occupation troops and administrators in Iraq as legitimate targets, but reject such attacks against US, Spanish and British civilians in their own countries. Thus condemning the London bombings provided no ethical dilemmas for mainstream Muslims. That this qualification was probably in the minds of the London *fatwa* authors is illustrated by the following comment:

> However, after the statement, Sayed Mohammed Musawi, the head of the World Islamic League in London, later called for a 'clear distinction' between suicide bombings.
>
> 'There should be a clear distinction between the suicide bombing of those who are trying to defend themselves from occupiers, which is something different from those who kill civilians, which is a big crime,' he said.
>
> 'The media in the West are mixing the difference between these two, and the result is that some of our Muslim youth are becoming more frustrated and they think that both are the same, even though Muslim law forbids killing any innocent lives.'[201]

Indeed, the *fatwa* itself raised the topic of global issues concerning Muslims, itself an indication of the main intended audience: 'We also call on the international community to work towards just and lasting peace settlements in the world's areas of conflict and help eliminate the grievances that seem to nurture a spiral of violence.'[202] The Al-Ghurabaa website's release was explicit on this issue, even to the point of warning of a recurrence of the bombings unless international issues such as Iraq were addressed:

> As for Jack Straw claiming that the bombings have nothing to do with Iraq and his reference to the bombings in Kenya,

Tanzania and Yemen (and others) as examples of bombings in countries which did not support the war in Iraq, he wishes to distort the facts that all these bombings were clearly against American embassies and US warships.

...[We] believe that they [the London bombings] are not the first and that they will not be the last; that is because these bombings were an effect stemming from a particular cause that has remained present and uncanged [*sic*].

As for the British people, we would like to state that it is never too late to review your stance towards the cease fire with Sheikh Usama Bin Laden and to thereby secure your safety like the people of Spain, otherwise you have nobody to blame but yourself for what has and will most probably happen again. [203]

Considering the failed London tube and bus bombings that occurred two weeks later (21 July), this seemed almost prophetic. After those attacks, Bakri '...called on Tony Blair to resign', saying 'the British people did not deserve to be the victims of American and UK foreign policy'.[204] This was an unusual step for Sheikh Omar, who normally regards internal UK politics as irrelevant. He continued: 'Tony Blair must resign. He has brought this on everyone with his position with American policy...I condemn the killing of any innocent people, whether it be in London or anywhere...The British public does not deserve it, and muslims do not serve it.'[205] The MAB was one of the contributing groups to the London *fatwa*, and its statement about the attacks, its causes, global Muslim issues and the position of Sheikh al-Qaradawi is worth observing in detail, since it illustrates the pulse of the British Muslim community on all these factors, and how mainstream Muslims differentiate martyrdom operations in Britain from those in Iraq and Palestine:

A section of the media, who are providing platform for the extreme right and the pro-Israel lobby in the country, have been adamant to confuse the London atrocities with what goes on in Palestine. Whereas the Palestinian scene witnesses a conflict between illegal Israeli occupation and its Palestinian victims, who have been struggling for freedom and liberation, the London bombings, and those that took place in other places where innocent people have been targeted such as in New York,

Madrid, Rabat, Bali, Riyadh and Istanbul, are unjustifiable and should be unconditionally denounced.

To seek to understand what prompted four young Muslims born and brought up in this country to turn into suicide bombers against their own country and their own people is not to justify the act but to find ways of preventing the atrocity from ever recurring in the future. Many people in this country and around the world believe the war on Iraq was a major contributing factor to the state in which we find ourselves today. Many also point to the plight of the Palestinian people.

A number of prominent Muslim figures, from within the Muslim community here in the UK as well as from abroad, have been pointed fingers at [*sic*] in a malicious attempt to undermine them and tarnish their reputation despite their unequivocal condemnation of the attacks on London and similar atrocities world-wide. Sheikh Yusuf Al-Qaradawi, a highly respected and world-renowned scholar of Islam, is once again put under the spotlight despite having been among the first to denounce all these atrocities. His crime, it would seem, is that he supports the right of the Palestinian people to resist the oppression to which they have been subjected for more than sixty years.

Those who insist on attacking leading Muslim figures such as Al-Qaradawi…only play into the hands of the terrorists whose recruiting powers are enhanced by the discrediting of mainstream authoritative scholars and thinkers. During his visit to the UK last summer, Sheikh Al-Qaradawi told the Muslim youth in this country that they had only one option and that is to integrate into society, engage in the political process and be law-abiding citizens…[206]

A MAB spokesman, Osama Saeed, rejected the idea that mosques and community organisations have tolerated 'extremism' in their midst: 'The position of Muslim organisations and mosques has been consistent for years. Killing civilians is murder, and a crime in Islam. We have consistently said that Muslims must help the police to track down those responsible.'[207] Saeed went on to link the bombings with UK foreign policy, and to place responsibility on the Government:

By putting the onus on Muslims to defeat terror, the prime minister absolves himself of responsibility. Muslims are not in denial of our duties, but who are we meant to be combating? The security services had no idea about all that has gone on in London, so how are we as ordinary citizens to do better?

It is not Muslims but Mr Blair who is in denial. He was advised that the war in Iraq would put us in more danger, not less. Silvio Berlusconi has admitted Italy is in danger because of his alliance with Bush; Mr Blair should do the same.

Jack Straw has just apologised for Britain's role in the Srebrenica massacre. This is a welcome development, but these apologies need to be extended to Britain's explicit roles in creating the injustices in the Muslim world – from the mess that colonial masters left in Kashmir to the promising of one people's land to another in Palestine. We need to recognise our past mistakes and make a commitment not to repeat them. Western leaders are outraged about London but show no similar anger for other atrocities across the world. What happens abroad matters to British Muslims as much as what happens here.[208]

The generation gap in British Muslim society that we have observed in the reactions to 7/7 was best expressed in the response of MPAC. Like the Government, MPAC wanted mosques to educate their youth, but rather than emphasising the need to educate them against undefined 'extremism', it demanded that mosques educate their youth in the British political process as a way of addressing issues of concern:

Every single British organisation has been attempting to do its up most [sic] to ensure that the chance of an attack in Britain was minimized, yet two thousand institutions that represent the very community the attackers were most likely to come from did not lift a finger.

This gross negligence directly resulted in the attacks in London by British born Muslims on their own countrymen.

Since 7/7 MPACUK has carried out a survey of over a hundred Mosques to check if Mosque Leaders had in fact taken any serious steps to stop this happening again by educating the youth and channeling their anger into a more constructive route.

Every single mosque we called had not taken any steps to change their syllabus or reach out to young Muslims to ensure they were...educated about how they could practically make a difference. Despite the deaths of 54 Brits and the further bombing of London today. Muslim Leaders do not seem to be taking the threat seriously…We urge the Media not to focus on the Muslim public but the Leaders who fail in their responsibility.[209]

As the investigation into the bombings proceeded, it emerged that, whilst the Edgware Road bomber Siddique Khan did have some tenuous links with militants, the four were 'cleanskins' – men with no established ties to extremist or terrorist groups. This is a vital point to note: it cannot be assumed that it is membership of a 'radical' organisation or exposure to 'radical preachers' that radicalises British Muslims. At any rate, the role of mosques in producing the kind of radicalised Al-Qaida types who carried out 7/7 is questionable. Most mosques usually prohibit groups like SOS and Al-Muhajiroun from meeting on their premises, and even a 2004 Cabinet report on 'Young Muslims and Extremism' observed one pattern of recruitment:

> …a significant number of young radicalised British Muslims have been recruited through a single contact, often by chance, outside either of these environments. Such individuals are encouraged to maintain a low profile for operational purposes and do not develop the network of associates or political doctrines common to many other extremist Islamists.[210]

Rather, it was the impact of events, notably abroad, that most probably radicalised them. Even among the most moderate Muslims there is exasperation about US and UK foreign policy. From what they see as pro-Israeli bias, to the Gulf war, the stationing of US forces in the Islamic holy land of Arabia, the invasion of Afghanistan and finally, the straw that broke the camel's back, the occupation of Iraq, which engendered immense anger among Muslims, Muslims have come increasingly to see themselves as victims of a modern-day crusade. After all, that was how President Bush first described the 'War on Terror'. MPAC encapsulated the younger generation's response to 7/7 and the failed bombings a fortnight later, claiming that the Government:

> …sowed the seeds in this disaster and Londoners paid the price. They needed a scapegoat and they got it, it was an evil version of Islam. Muslims did this because they simply want all women to wear the headscarf and hate everything British. In short it was

an evil religious group and nothing to do with political blunders...

Blair took us to war...despite the British public's overwhelming desire not to send our troops abroad...

No one is saying what happened was not wrong; it was a disaster and a human tragedy. What Muslims are saying however is stop lying to the public about why this happened, because unless we can get to the bottom of what drives these people, it will happen again, and again and again!

This happened because of foreign policy, a policy that creates extremists. This isn't an Islam issue; this is a cause and effect issue...

This attack is due to foreign policy; the men who did it were driven because they felt it was unjust. Both the perpetrators of this crime and the Government who created the environment for them to breed must be held accountable.[211]

Islamic ethics, unlike Christianity, eschew turning the other cheek. Rather the *Qur'an* tells Muslims: 'Fight in the cause of God those who fight you' (Surah 2:190). Young, educated British Muslims do not need 'extremist' preachers and groups to tell them how to respond to the suffering of their brethren abroad: they need only read the *Qur'an* and *hadith* where these sources refer to military *jihad*. Because of the *Ummah* concept, Muslims in Britain view themselves as part of the oppressed – when Muslims in Palestine or Iraq suffer, British Muslims see it as though they themselves are suffering. Since the British Government was a close ally of America, it follows that the British Government is at war with God, so it is clear where the loyalties of resident members of the *Ummah* in Britain should lie, at least in the views of the bombers. Al-Qaida have argued, against the tradition of Islamic jurisprudence, that anyone in a country that is occupying Muslim lands, who pays taxes and votes for the Government engaged in 'aggression' shares its guilt, and is a legitimate target. If any Muslims are killed, they are simply collateral damage. Hence, killing their compatriots – and even their co-religionists – presented no ethical problems for the bombers.

Another casualty of the bombings was politically correct sociological explanations for the attacks. One bomber worked as a community worker and teaching assistant, another was a student –

scarcely the 'wretched of the earth' to borrow from Frantz Fanon. Moreover, neither Sikhs nor Hindus carried out the bombing, so one cannot blame anti-*Asian* racism. Further, it cannot be asserted that domestic Islamophobia was the progenitor; the Government was pledged to introduce a law against religious hatred. The bombers were 'cleanskins', people with no previous history of terrorist or extremist involvement, so one cannot blame 'extremist preachers'. The anti-Muslim backlash ironically supplied the answer; it is unlikely that any of the violent incidents following 7/7, including the murder of a Muslim man, resulted from Far Right incitement. Rather, it was the massacre itself that 'incited' that violent backlash. To observe this is not to excuse, but rather to analyse the causes of the backlash.

Equally, it was the foreign policy of the US and UK that 'incited' the bombers. This point was observed by London Mayor Ken Livingstone:

'I think you've just had 80 years of western intervention into predominantly Arab lands because of the western need for oil.

'We've propped up unsavoury governments, we've overthrown ones we didn't consider sympathetic.

'...If at the end of the First World War we had done what we promised the Arabs, which was to let them be free and have their own governments, and kept out of Arab affairs, and just bought their oil, rather than feeling we had to control the flow of oil, I suspect this wouldn't have arisen.'

He attacked double standards by Western nations, such as the initial welcome given when Saddam Hussein came to power in Iraq.

There was also the 'running sore' of the Palestinian/Israeli conflict.

'A lot of young people see the double standards, they see what happens in Guantanamo Bay, and they just think that there isn't a just foreign policy,' said Mr Livingstone.[212]

Livingstone's words were given a ringing endorsement by MPAC, demonstrating how his analysis – which was certainly no apologist defence of the bombers – reflected the pulse of the British Muslim community.[213] The Mayor of London's analysis of the causes of 7/7 was borne out by a video of the bomber Mohammed Siddique Khan aired by Al-Jazeera television on 1 September 2005. Khan explained his motivation for his martyrdom and the attack he was later to perpetrate:

> ...our words have no impact upon you, therefore I'm going to talk to you in a language that you understand.
>
> Our words are dead until we give them life with our blood...
>
> Our driving motivation doesn't come from tangible commodities that this world has to offer.
>
> Our religion is Islam – obedience to the one true God, Allah, and following the footsteps of the final prophet and messenger Muhammad...This is how our ethical stances are dictated.
>
> Your democratically elected governments continuously perpetuate atrocities against my people all over the world.
>
> And your support of them makes you directly responsible, just as I am directly responsible for protecting and avenging my Muslim brothers and sisters.
>
> Until we feel security, you will be our targets. And until you stop the bombing, gassing, imprisonment and torture of my people we will not stop this fight.
>
> We are at war and I am a soldier. Now you too will taste the reality of this situation...
>
> I ask you to make dua to Allah almighty to accept the work from me and my brothers and enter us into gardens of paradise.[214]

Analysing his words demonstrates the futility of trying to persuade Al-Qaida supporters of the immorality of their actions, because, as Khan indicates, their source of ethics is not based on secular humanism, but rather on what they see the *Qur'an* and *hadith* as enjoining. They cannot be enticed by improved social conditions – there is no reference to 'social exclusion' as a motive, and Khan rejected worldly commodities in favour of the eschatological promise of paradise as the reward of martyrdom. Khan clearly identified with Al-Qaida, referring to 'today's heroes like our beloved Sheikh Osama Bin Laden, Dr Ayman al-Zawahri and Abu Musab al-Zarqawi'. Echoes of bin Laden could be heard in his claim that the support of 'hostile' governments by their electorates makes the voters culpable in government actions, and his warning that Westerners would not enjoy security until Muslims do, as can be seen from bin Laden's comments:

> [T]he American people… are not exonerated from responsibility, because they chose this government and voted for it despite their knowledge of its crimes in Palestine, Lebanon, Iraq and in other places…[215]

> We swore that America wouldn't live in security until we live it truly in Palestine.[216]

Above all, what Khan saw as the provocation of the attack is government foreign policy. There is no sense that Khan was motivated, as the Government claimed, by 'an evil ideology' that sought to conquer Britain for Islam, but rather he and his brothers were responding to what they saw as attacks on Muslims worldwide, as seen by his reference to 'atrocities against my people all over the world'. The language of the *Ummah* and *defensive* jihad could be seen in his words: 'I am directly responsible for protecting and avenging my Muslim brothers and sisters…[U]ntil you stop the bombing, gassing, imprisonment and torture of my people we will not stop this fight.' If 7/7 had been an act of *offensive* jihad, as the Government implied, Khan would have demanded submission to Islamic law and government as the price of peace. Instead, he urged the ending of military actions against Muslims. The emphasis on the *Ummah* concept is demonstrated by his reference to 'my people'. Clearly, the UK and US governments are not 'bombing' *British* Muslims; he is clearly referring to overseas contexts, such as Iraq. Khan gave his life – and took the lives of others – for the sake of the *Ummah*.

The second part of the video carried a message from bin Laden's right-hand man Ayman al-Zawahri, where he clearly linked 7/7 to Iraq, and indeed, Palestine and Afghanistan:

> We have warned over and over again and we repeat the warning that we shall respond to anyone who participates in the aggression against Iraq, Afghanistan and Palestine in kind.

> And that as they made rivers of blood flow in our countries, so shall we, with the help of Allah, make volcanoes of anger erupt in their countries.

The lands and interests of the countries which took part in the aggression against Palestine, Iraq and Afghanistan, are targets for us all…

Blair not only disregards the millions of people in Iraq and Afghanistan but he does not care about you as he sends you to the inferno in Iraq and exposes you to death in your land because of his crusader war against Islam…

I talk to you today about the blessed London battle which came as a slap to the face of the tyrannical crusader British arrogance.

It's a sip from the glass that the Muslims have been drinking from.[217]

In the light of both these statements, it is reasonable to infer that 7/7 was the blowback from the Iraq war, even as it indicates the alienation of some British Muslims as the consequence of UK foreign policy and what they see as the suffering of the *Ummah*. The Government refused to listen to the 2003 protest which rallied against the war – the biggest demonstration in British history. It also refused to listen to the electors – especially Muslims – who deserted Labour for the anti-war parties. Rallies failed, elections failed – leaving only one option in the eyes of some Muslims. Muslims are influenced by the concept of family and communal honour (*izzat*) and defence of the honour of Islam (*ghairat*). Al-Qaida echoes the feelings of most Muslims about how 'humiliated' they feel by the occupation of Arabia, Iraq and Palestine, and honour can only be satisfied by blood. The bombings were a message to America and Britain to listen and change course – to stop 'shaming' Muslims, by quitting the Muslim world. Until that happens, it is likely that we should expect more outrages like 7/7.

[1] Muslims object to the translation 'flight'.

[2] 'Ready for jihad: Young, Muslim and angry', *Q-News*, No. 337, October 2001, p. 15.

[3] Mohammed, Jahangir, *The Muslim Parliament of Great Britain: A Unique Experiment in the Political Mobilisation of Muslim Minorities in Europe* (London & Manchester: Muslim Parliament of Great Britain, 1997), p. 12.

[4] Modood, Tariq, 'Political Blackness and British Asians', *Sociology,* Vol. 28:4, 1994, p. 869; quoting Kramer, J., 'Letter from Europe', *New Yorker,* 14 January 1991, p. 75.

[5] Ahsan, M. M. and Kidwai, A.R. (eds), *Sacrilege versus Civility: Muslim Perspectives on the Satanic Verses Affair* (Leicester: Islamic Foundation, 1991, second edition, 1993), p. 57. This book is also a compendium of articles, letters and statements by various individuals and bodies issued during the crisis.

[6] Personal communication from Ahmad, 9 October 2001.

[7] Ahsan and Kidwai, *Sacrilege versus Civility*, p. 351.

[8] *Ibid.*, p. 83.

[9] Lewis, Philip, *Islamic Britain* (London: I. B. Tauris, 1994), pp. 164–165.

[10] Kepel, Gilles, *Allah in the West* (Cambridge: Polity Press, 1997), p.133.

[11] Islamic Foundation, 'Letter sent to "Muslim Organizations, Mosques, and Prominent Muslim Leaders in Britain, 3 October 1998"' in Ahsan and Kidwai, *Sacrilege versus Civility*, p. 336.

[12] Centre for the Study of Islam and Christianity, *The 'Rushdie Affair': A Documentation* Research Papers, No. 42 (Birmingham: CSIC, 1989), p. 2.

[13] Appignanesi, Lisa and Maitland, Sara, *The Rushdie File* (London: Fourth Estate, 1989), p. 57.

[14] *Ibid.*

[15] Ruthven, Malise, *A Satanic Affair: Salman Rushdie and the Rage of Islam* (London: Chatto & Windus, 1990), p. 68.

[16] *Ibid.*, p. 107.

[17] Kepel, *Allah in the West*, p. 133.

[18] *Ibid.*

[19] *Ibid.*, p. 131.

[20] Murad, Khurram, *Islamic Movement in the West: Reflections on Some Issues* (London: Islamic Foundation, 1981), pp. 21, 23.

[21] Islamic Society of Britain, *Islam – a Vision for Britain* convention brochure (Leicester: Islamic Society of Britain, 1995), p. 41.

[22] Kepel, Gilles, 'Foreword: Between society and community: Muslims in Britain and France today' in Joly, Danièle, *Britannia's Crescent: Making a Place for Muslims in British Society* (Aldershot: Avebury, 1995), p. xiii.

[23] Webster, Richard, *A Brief History of Blasphemy* (Southwold: Orwell Press, 1990), p. 128.

[24] *Ibid.*, p. 127.

[25] Akhtar, Shabbir, *Be Careful with Muhammad!: The Salman Rushdie Affair* (London: Bellew Publishing, 1989), p. 43.

[26] Kepel, *Allah in the West*, p. 138.

[27] Lewis, *Islamic Britain*, p. 88.

[28] *Ibid.*, p. 69.

[29] *Ibid.*

[30] Faruqi, M. H., 'Muslims and Britain', *Impact International*, 10–23 March 1989, p. 198.

[31] *Guardian*, 25 February 1989, quoted in Appignanesi and Maitland, *The Rushdie File* p. 134.

[32] *Ibid.*

[33] Sardar, Ziauddin, 'The Rushdie Malaise: A critique of some writings on the Rushdie Affair' in Ahsan and Kidwai, *Sacrilege versus Civility*, pp. 281–282.

[34] United Kingdom Action Committee on Islamic Affairs, 'Letter from the Rt Hon John Patten, MP, Minister of State at the Home Office' in *Muslims and the Law in Multi-Faith Britain: The Need for Reform* (London: UKACIA, 1993), p. 28.

[35] 'Mr Patten's Reply' in *ibid.*, pp. 34–35.

[36] Ruthven, *A Satanic Affair*, p. 121.

[37] Mohammed, *The Muslim Parliament*, p. 9.

[38] 'Hogg barracked over Gulf policy', *Muslim News*, No. 24, February 1991, p. 1.

[39] Werbner, Pnina, 'Islamic radicalism and the Gulf War: Preachers and political dissent among British Pakistanis' in Lewis, B. and Schnapper, D. (eds), *Muslims in Europe* (London: Pinter, 1994), p. 105.

[40] *Ibid.*, p. 105.

[41] Ibn Shihab

Al-Muwatta 45.5.18

The Messenger of Allah (peace be upon him), said, 'Two deens [religions] shall not coexist in the Arabian Peninsula.'

[42] 7501 Al-Risala (Maliki Manual)

37.07 Talion (Qisas)

In respect of wounds deliberately inflicted retaliation is prescribed except when it is feared that death may result from such an action…or when the retaliation involves the thigh, the testicles and the backbone and some similar vital organs. For each of those a full blood-wit is prescribed.

[43] Lewis, *Islamic Britain*, p. 165.

[44] Werbner, 'Islamic radicalism', p. 100.

[45] 1260 Al-Majalla (The Ottoman Courts Manual (Hanafi))

28. In the presence of two evils, the greater is avoided by the commission of the lesser;

1261 Al-Majalla (The Ottoman Courts Manual (Hanafi))

29. The lesser of the two evils is preferred;

610 Fiqh-us-Sunnah

Fiqh 3:65 3:66

Zakat recipients: Eligible (General Categories): (5/9) Those whose hearts are to be reconciled: (2/2) Non-Muslim:

...the principle of inclining to the lesser of two evils and to the best benefit of the society...

[46] Lewis, *Islamic Britain,* p. 167.

[47] 'Withdraw non-Muslim forces', *Muslim News,* No. 18, August 1990, p. 1.

[48] *Ibid.*

[49] Lewis, *Islamic Britain,* pp. 167–168.

[50] *Ibid.,* p. 167.

[51] *Ibid.*

[52] *Ibid.,* p. 168.

[53] Runnymede Trust, *Islamophobia: A Challenge for Us All.* Report of the Runnymede Trust Commission on British Muslims and Islamophobia (London: Runnymede Trust, 1997), p. 10.

[54] Vertovec, Steven, 'Muslims, the state, and the public sphere in Britain' in Nonneman, Gerd, Niblock, Tim, and Szajkowski, Bogdan (eds), *Muslim Communities in the New Europe* (Reading: Ithaca Press, 1996), p. 183.

[55] Werbner, 'Islamic radicalism', pp. 108–109.

[56] *Ibid.,* p. 109.

[57] 'Nato forced into war with Serbia' (editorial), *Muslim News,* No. 120, April 1999; http://www.muslimnews.co.uk/120/120-2-1.html.

[58] Jacobson, Jessica, *Islam in Transition: Religion and Identity Among British Pakistani Youth* (London and New York: LSE/Routledge, 1998), pp. 55–56.

[59] *Ibid.,* p. 149.

[60] *Ibid.,* pp. 150–151.

[61] Siddiqui, Ataullah, 'Muslims in Britain: Past and present', *The Bulletin* (Hyderabad: Henry Martyn Institute, July–December 1996), p. 48.

[62] Runnymede Trust, *Islamophobia,* p. 12 (emphasis in original).

[63] Muslim Parliament of Great Britain, *The Work of the Human Rights Committee Bosnia Group* (London: MPGB, 1993), p. 3.

[64] Akhtar, Shabbir, 'Palestine within Europe?', *Muslim News,* No. 42, August 1992, p. 5.

[65] LeBor, Adam, *A Heart Turned East: Among the Muslims of Europe and America* (London: Little, Brown and Company, 1997), p. 20.

[66] Duran, Khalid, 'Bosnia: The other Andalusia' in Abedin, Syed Z., and Sardar, Ziauddin (ed.), *Muslim Minorities in the West* (London: Grey Seal, for the Institute of Muslim Minority Affairs, 1995), p. 33.

[67] Akhtar, Shabbir, 'Bosnia: The end of the long night?', *Muslim News,* No. 54, August 1993, p. 5.

[68] Video of MPGB World Conference on Bosnia, 1993 (London and Manchester: MPGB, 1993).

[69] 'FCO letter from Gerard Healy to Mr Ali', *Trends,* Vol. 5:4, 15 October 1993, p. 14.

[70] 'West delays sanctions as slaughter continues' (editorial), *Muslim News*, No. 50, May 1993, p. 2.

[71] 'PM rebuffs Muslims on Bosnia', *Muslim News,* No. 75, July 1995, p. 1.

[72] *Ibid*.

[73] Lewis, *Islamic Britain,* p. 158, refers to the *Yorkshire Post* (18 January 1989), which made the analogy with the Nazis.

[74] Akhtar, *Be Careful!,* p. 44.

[75] Parekh, Bhiku, 'The tale of instant experts on Islam' in Ahsan and Kidwai, *Sacrilege versus Civility,* p. 117.

[76] Mohammed, Jahangir, *Discussion Paper on Race Relations and Muslims in Great Britain* (London: Muslim Parliament of Great Britain, 1992), p. 14.

[77] 'Anti-Muslim abuse at dangerous high', *Paigaam,* No. 84, March 2000, p. 1.

[78] UKACIA, *Elections 1997 and British Muslims: For a Fair and Caring Society* (London: UKACIA, 1997), p. 6.

[79] La'Porte, Victoria, *An Attempt to Understand the Muslim Reaction to the Satanic Verses* (Lampeter: Edwin Mellen Press, 1999), pp. 140–141. The programme was 'Muslims and Britain', *Open Space,* BBC2 (no date, but La'Porte described it as 'recent').

[80] Islamic Human Rights Commission, *Anti-Muslim Discrimination and Hostility in the United Kingdom, 2000* (London: IHRC, 2000), pp. 5, 24–26.

[81] *Ibid.,* p. 5.

[82] Runnymede Trust, *Islamophobia,* p. 28 (quoting Richard Littlejohn, 'Moslem lambasted', *Daily Mail,* 12 May 1995).

[83] *Ibid.*

[84] Clayton, Emma, 'Sheer criminality is the root cause', *Bradford Telegraph & Argus*;
http://www.thisisbradford.co.uk/bradford__district/bradford/riot/BRAD_NEWS 11.html.

[85] Manchester Online;
http://www.manchesteronline.co.uk/news/content.cfm?story=106714.

[86] Vasagar, Jeevan, Ward, David, Etim, Abigail, and Keating, Matt, '"No go for whites" in race hotspot', *Guardian,* 20 April 2001;
http://www.guardian.co.uk/Archive/Article/0,4273,4172796,00.html.

[87] McRoy, Anthony, 'BNP's anti-Muslim crusade', *Q-News,* July 2001, p. 19.

[88] Manchester Online;
http://www.manchesteronline.co.uk/news/content.cfm?story=106714.

[89] Vasagar, Jeevan, 'Far right aims to gain foothold in Oldham', *Guardian,* 30 May 2001;
http://www.guardian.co.uk/Archive/Article/0,4273,4194701,00.html.

[90] McRoy, 'BNP's anti-Muslim crusade', pp. 18–19.

[91] Roy, Amit, 'Indians try to escape catch-all "Asian" tag', *Daily Telegraph,* 19 June 2001;
http://www.telegraph.co.uk/news/main.jhtml?xml=%2Fnews%2F2001%2F06 %2F19%2Fncric319.xml 2002; McRoy, Anthony, 'Bradford, "Saint James" and the white knights', *Q-News,* August 2001, pp. 14–15.

[92] Roy, 'Indians try to escape catch-all "Asian" tag'.

[93] Home Office, *Community Cohesion: a Report of the Independent Review Team* (London: Home Office, 2001), p. 63; http://image.guardian.co.uk/sys-files/Guardian/documents/2001/12/11/communitycohesionreport.pdf

[94] *Ibid.,* p. 41.

[95] British National Party, 'Boycott Asian businesses';
http://www.oldhamharmony.org/old27.pdf.

[96] McRoy, Anthony, 'Racism cuts both ways', *Third Way,* Vol. 24, No. 5, July 2001, p. 4.

[97] *Guardian,* 31 May 2001, letter from Yakoob Masih;
http://www.oldhamharmony.org/articles.htm.

[98] Muslim leaders admitted to Christian leaders at a meeting held after the riots that they had given the Taliban access to their mosques.

[99] This was the Jammu-Kashmir Liberation Front.

[100] Gregoriadis, Linus and Wilson, Jamie, 'Cleric accused of terrorist links can stay', *Guardian*, 11 September 1999, p. 7.

[101] Oldham Independent Review, 11 December 2001; http://image.guardian.co.uk/sys-files/Guardian/documents/2001/12/11/Oldhamindependentreview.pdf, p. 24.

[102] *Ibid*., p. 34.

[103] Vasagar, Jeevan *et al.*, '"No go for whites" in race hotspot'.

[104] Clayton, 'Sheer criminality is the root cause'.

[105] Sturdy, Gareth and McRoy, Anthony, 'Reasons for the riots', *Christianity & Renewal*, September 2001, p. 4.

[106] Author's interview with Dave Bullock.

[107] McRoy, Anthony, 'The anti-Muslim backlash: a godsend to the BNP', *Q-News*, No. 336, October 2001, p. 28.

[108] Burnley Task Force Report, 2001; http://image.guardian.co.uk/sys-files/Guardian/documents/2001/12/11/Burnleytaskforce.pdf, p. 24.

[109] *Community Pride, Not Prejudice*. The Ouseley Report; www.bradford2020.com/pride, p. 10.

[110] *Ibid*., pp. 9–10.

[111] Harley, Nick, 'Stoned by yobs aged 10', *Bradford Telegraph & Argus*, 20 November 2001; http://www.thisisbradford.co.uk/bradford__district/archive/2001/11/20/brad_news01.int.html.

[112] McRoy, Anthony, 'No more cheeks to turn: Bradford's Christian minority', *Q-News*, No. 338, December 2001, p. 11.

[113] Walsh, Sarah, 'Race-hate mob tries to burn church', *Bradford Telegraph & Argus*, 6 November 2001; http://www.thisisbradford.co.uk/bradford__district/archive/2001/11/06/brad_news01.int.html.

[114] Stokes, Paul, 'Brownies forced to quit church after "race attacks"', *Daily Telegraph*, 14 November 2001; http://www.telegraph.co.uk/news/main.jhtml?xml=%2Fnews%2F2001%2F11%2F14%2Fbrad14.xml.

[115] *Ibid*.

[116] Cope, Sally, 'Thugs force out Brownies', *Yorkshire Post*, 12 November 2001; http://www.ypn.co.uk/scripts/editorial2.cgi?cid=4&aid=419379.

117 Alibhai-Brown, Yasmin, 'When Muslims behave badly', *Independent*, 28 January 2002; http://www.independent.co.uk/story.jsp?story=116691.

118 Lewis, Philip, 'Belief in an ethnic constituency', *Third Way*, Vol. 24, No. 5, July 2001, p. 17.

119 'BNP denies stirring racial tension', *Guardian*, 29 May 2001; http://www.guardian.co.uk/Archive/Article/0,4273,4194240,00.html.

120 'When frustration erupts' (editorial), *Guardian*, 28 May 2001; http://www.guardian.co.uk/Archive/Article/0,4273,4193676,00.html.

121 Home Office, *Community Cohesion*, pp. 40–41.

122 MCB press release, 'The Bradford disturbances 7–9 July 2001', 16 July 2001.

123 'Bradford's troubles', *Yorkshire Post*, 11 July 2001; http://www.ypn.co.uk/scripts/editorial2.cgi?cid=45&aid=392486.

124 Wainwright, Martin, 'Riot-torn city voices dismay at "lawless idiots"', *Guardian*, 10 July 2001; http://www.guardian.co.uk/Archive/Article/0,4273,4218872,00.html.

125 McRoy, 'The anti-Muslim backlash', p. 28.

126 Whitaker, Raymond, 'Oldham is not alone. Other communities are retreating into a form of apartheid', *Independent*, 17 June 2001; http://www.independent.co.uk/story.jsp?story=78613.

127 Harris, Paul, 'Far Right plot to provoke race riots', *Observer*, 3 June 2001; http://www.guardian.co.uk/racism/Story/0,2763,500768,00.html.

128 Baig, Anila, 'Bradford Taliban fighter "should be tried as a traitor"', *Bradford Telegraph & Argus*, 17 December 2001; http://www.thisisbradford.co.uk/bradford__district/archive/2001/12/17/brad_news01.int.html. See also *Bradford Telegraph & Argus*, '"Some Bradford Muslims joining Taliban," says aid worker', 2 November 2001; http://www.thisisbradford.co.uk/bradford__district/archive/2001/11/02/brad_news02.int.html.

129 Herbert, Ian, 'Masked Asian youths stone vicar in attempt to burn down his church', *Independent*, 7 November 2001; http://www.independent.co.uk/story.jsp?story=103549.

130 Sutcliffe, Robert, 'Muslims in show of solidarity with attacked vicar', *Yorkshire Post*, 11 November 2001; http://www.ypn.co.uk/scripts/editorial/frontpage/419149/,2,page.html.

131 'When frustration erupts', *Guardian*.

132 McRoy, 'No more cheeks to turn: Bradford's Christian minority', p. 11.

133 Home Office, *Community Cohesion*, p. 29.

[134] Burnley Task Force Report, p. 36.

[135] Oldham Independent Review, pp. 8, 42.

[136] Muslim Council of Britain press release, 'MCB expresses total condemnation of terrorist attacks', 11 September 2001.

[137] Supporters of Sharee'ah, 'Who is behind WTC bombings...THINK???'; http://www.angelfire.com/sk3/ok5/teror1.html.

[138] Press release, *Muslim News,* 17 December 2001; http://www.muslimnews.co.uk/index/press.php?pr=139.

[139] MCB press release, 'American airstrikes against Afghanistan and Sudan', 21 August 1998.

[140] IHRC press release, 'Judge, jury and executioner', 21 August 1998.

[141] BBC1, *The Koran and the Kalashnikov* (broadcast 23 January 2000).

[142] Chaudhry, Humayun, 'Islam on our side', *Q-News,* No. 316, February 2000, p. 30.

[143] Colvin, Marie and Gadher, Dipesh, 'Britain's Islamic Army', *Sunday Times,* 17 January 1999, p. 15.

[144] Vasagar, Jeevan and Dodd, Vikram, 'British Muslims take the path to jihad', *Guardian,* 29 December 2000, p. 3.

[145] *Ibid.*

[146] Taher, Abul, 'Call to arms', *Guardian*, 16 May 2000, pp. 12–13.

[147] MCB press release, 'MCB opposes war on Afghans – insists on justice', 9 October 2001.

[148] SOS press release, 'On the war with Iraq'; http://www.shareeah.org/news/release3.html.

[149] Akhtar, *Be Careful with Muhammad!*, p. 111.

[150] Sardar, Ziauddin and Davies, Merryl Wyn, *Distorted Imagination* (London: Grey Seal, 1990), p. 218.

[151] Ruthven, *A Satanic Affair,* p. 128.

[152] Raza, Mohammad S., *Islam in Britain* (Leicester: Volcano Press, 1991), p. 44.

[153] 'Muslim voters mean business this time, Mr Howard' (editorial), *Muslim News,* No. 95, March 1997, p. 2.

[154] Quoted in Lewis, *Islamic Britain,* p. 161.

[155] UKACIA, *Elections 1997,* p. 3.

[156] Sacranie, Iqbal, 'Why you should exercise your vote', *Q-News*, No. 255–259, March 1997, p. 26.

[157] *Ibid.*

[158] 'Parties play the numbers game', *Q-News*, Nos. 255–259, March 1997, p. 16.

[159] 'Muslims wake up to tactical voting' (editorial), *Muslim News*, No. 97, May 1997, p. 2.

[160] 'JFK will stand in elections', *Q-News*, No. 319, May 2000, p. 7.

[161] *Ibid*.

[162] *Ibid*.

[163] 'Kashmir comes to Birmingham', *Economist*, 22 April 2000, p. 26.

[164] Birmingham City Council; http://birmingham.gov.uk/epislive/legal.nsf/437194deb01c293b802564d600476 24b/379c366ca914bb3e802568c7002cce71?OpenDocument.

[165] 'Kashmir comes to Birmingham', *Economist*, p. 26.

[166] *Ibid*.

[167] Quoted in 'Kashmir comes to Birmingham', *Economist*, p. 26.

[168] Bodi, Faisal, 'Muslims threaten to organise for Euro elections', *Q-News*, No. 305, May 1999, p. 8.

[169] 'Europe gets first Muslim MP', *Q-News*, No. 309, July 1999, p. 10.

[170] Muslim Council of Britain, *Electing to Listen: Promoting policies for British Muslims* (London: MCB, 2000). p. 2.

[171] Votesmart; http://www.votesmart.org.uk.

[172] 'The art of lobbying'(editorial), *Muslim News*, No. 143, March 2001; http://www.muslimnews.co.uk/paper/index.php?article=143-13-02.

[173] *Ibid*.

[174] Muslim Council of Britain, *Election Supplement 2001* (London: MCB/Muslim News, 2001), p. 1.

[175] *Ibid*.

[176] *Ibid*.

[177] Davies, Caroline, 'Muslims use vote to vent fury over war', *Daily Telegraph*, 6 May 2005; http://www.telegraph.co.uk/news/main.jhtml?xml=/news/2005/05/06/nelecmus. xml&sSheet=/news/2005/05/06/ixnewstop.html.

[178] *Ibid*.

[179] MAB press release, 'Election results indicate strong influence of Muslim vote and issue of war', 6 May 2005.

[180] Muslim Directory, MAB, IFE, MCB London Affairs Committee, YMO UK, Muslim College, FAIR, Amal Trust, The London Central Mosque, London Muslim Centre, Muslim Parliament, FOSIS, ISB, Muslimaat UK, Avenues

School, Somali Muslim Community, UKIM, MPAC, Stop Political Terror, Ershad Centre, BanglaMedia, Iqra Trust, Association of Muslim Police, Al-Khoei Foundation, UMO, Muslim Welfare House, Women's Relief.

[181] Mosque fire bombed. – Berkinhead [*sic*], Liverpool; Mosque criminal damage nineteen windows damaged – Stepney Green; Islamophobic graffiti, Stepney Green School; Criminal damage – Mosque NW London; Bomb hoax, Mosque North London; Youth assaulted – Barking & Dagenham; Bomb hoax – Harrow; Bomb hoax – Newham; Criminal damage – Battersea; Threats to cause criminal damage – Haringey; Attempted arson – Sikh Temple (Kent); Large number of Islamophobic e-mails / texts sent to various organisations; Bomb hoax – Kensington.

[182] Muslim Safety Forum press release, 15 July 2005.

[183] Dodd, Vikram, 'Religious hate crimes rise fivefold', *Guardian,* 23 July 2005; http://www.guardian.co.uk/attackonlondon/story/0,16132,1534518,00.html.

[184] MCB press release, 'British Muslims utterly condemn acts of terror', 7 July 2005.

[185] IHRC press release, 'IHRC urges caution in wake of London attacks', 7 July 2005.

[186] MPAC press release, 'Muslims shocked by attack', 7 July 2005.

[187] MSF press release, 12 July 2005 (emphasis in original).

[188] Hizb ut-Tahrir press release, 7 July 2005.

[189] MAB press release, 12 July 2005.

[190] Mendick, Robert, 'Bombings are all <u>your</u> fault', *Evening Standard,* 19 July 2005, p. 1.

[191] *Ibid*., p. 4.

[192] Al-Ghurabaa press release, 'The British policy of divide and rule: *Falsely classifying Muslims as extremist and moderate*', 18 July 2005; http://www.al-ghurabaa.co.uk/pr/divideandrule.htm.

[193] Morris, Nigel and Bennetto, Jason, 'Muslim leaders pledge to root out the extremists in their community', *Independent,* 20 July 2005; http://news.independent.co.uk/uk/crime/article300345.ece.

[194] Dodd, Vikram and White, Michael, 'Muslims agree network to fight extremists', *Guardian,* 20 July 2005; http://www.guardian.co.uk/guardianpolitics/story/0,,1532088,00.html.

[195] *Ibid*.

[196] Akbar, Arifa and Duff, Oliver, 'In Luton, summit is treated with contempt', 20 July 2005; http://www.ezilon.com/information/article_6873.shtml.

[197] MCB Ulama statement, 15 July 2005;

http://www.mcb.org.uk/Signed_Ulama_statement.pdf.

[198] Al-Ghurabaa press release, 'The British policy of divide and rule'.

[199] Narrated by AbuHurayrah

Sahih Al-Bukhari 8.603

We witnessed with Allah's Messenger…the *Khaybar* (campaign). Allah's
Messenger…told his companions about a man who claimed to be a Muslim,
'This man is from the people of the Fire.' When the battle started, the man
fought very bravely, received a great number of wounds and was crippled.

On that a man from among the companions of the Prophet came and said,
'O Allah's Messenger! Do you know what the man whom you described as one
of the people of the Fire has done? He has fought very bravely for Allah's cause
and he has received many wounds.' The Prophet said, 'But he is indeed one of
the people of the Fire.' Some of the Muslims were about to have some doubt
about that statement. However, while the man was in that state, the pain caused
by the wounds troubled him so much that he put his hand into his quiver, took
out an arrow and committed suicide with it. Off went some men from among
the Muslims to Allah's Messenger and said, 'O Allah's Messenger! Allah has
made your statement come true. So-and-So has committed suicide.'

Allah's Messenger said, 'O Bilal! stand up and announce in public: None
will enter Paradise but a believer, and Allah may support this religion (Islam)
with a wicked man.'

[200] Covenanted Christians are the Christian descendants of the indigenous
inhabitants of the areas of the first Muslim conquests, who were given a
Covenant of Protection at the time.

[201] Barnwell, Matt, 'Bombers "should not be regarded as martyrs"', 16 July
2005;

http://www.telegraph.co.uk/news/main.jhtml?xml=/news/2005/07/16/ncleric516
.xml.

[202] MCB Ulama statement, 15 July 2005.

[203] Al-Ghurabaa press release, 'The British policy of divide and rule'.

[204] 'Bakri calls on Blair to resign', *Life Style Extra*, 21 July 2005;

http://www.lse.co.uk/ShowStory.asp?story=CZ2115600U&news_headline=
bakri_calls_on_blair_to_resign.

[205] *Ibid.*

[206] MAB, 'Attacking Al-Qaradawi only plays into the hands of the terrorists';
http://www.mabonline.info/english/modules.php?name=News&file=article&sid
=451.

[207] Saeed, Osama, 'Back to you, Mr Blair', *Guardian*, 23 July 2005; http://www.guardian.co.uk/attackonlondon/story/0,16132,1534715,00.html.

[208] *Ibid.*

[209] MPAC, '100 MOSQUES CALLED – None Combat Terror', 21 July 2005; http://www.mpacuk.org/content/view/4/835/103/.

[210] Foreign and Commonwealth Office/Home Office, 'Young Muslims and extremism', 2004.

[211] MPAC, 'MPACUK accuses the government of cover up over bombing', 10 July 2005; http://www.mpacuk.org/content/view/4/791/103/.

[212] BBC News Online, 'Mayor blames Middle East policy'; http://news.bbc.co.uk/1/hi/uk_politics/4698963.stm.

[213] MPAC, 'Livingstone under attack! Defend the pro-Muslim Mayor NOW!'; http://www.mpacuk.org/content/view/828/102/.

[214] BBC, 'London bomber: text in full', 1 September 2005; http://news.bbc.co.uk/1/hi/uk/4206800.stm.

[215] Transcript of CNN interview with bin Laden by Peter Arnett; http://www.robert-fisk.com/usama_interview_cnn.htm.

[216] Al-Jazeera interview with Tayseer Alouni, October 2001; http://www.jihadunspun.net/BinLadensNetwork/interviews/aljazeera10-21-2001-1.cfm.

[217] BBC, 'Extracts from al-Zawahri message'; http://news.bbc.co.uk/1/hi/uk/4207158.stm.

PART TWO

ISLAM AND ISLAMISM IN RELATION TO DEMOCRACY AND *JIHAD*

THE *QUR'AN*

To understand Muslim radicalism, it is essential to have some acquaintance with Islamic beliefs. Muhammad is held to have stated the following:

> Narrated by Abdullah ibn Umar
> Sahih Al-Bukhari 1.7
> The Prophet (peace be upon him) said: Islam is based on (the following) five (principles):
> 1. To testify that none has the right to be worshipped but Allah and that Muhammad is Allah's Apostle. 2. To offer the (compulsory congregational) prayers dutifully and perfectly. 3. To pay Zakat (i.e. obligatory charity). 4. To perform Hajj (i.e. Pilgrimage to Makkah). 5. To observe fast during the month of Ramadan.

Fundamental Islamic doctrines involve monotheism, belief in angels (who play an even more important role in Islam than they do in the Bible, notably in being the agents of God's revelation to humanity), revelatory scriptures – normally listed as the 'Pages of Abraham', the *Tawrah* (Torah), *Zabur* (Psalms of David), *Injil* (Gospel of Jesus) and climaxing in the *Qur'an* – which are delivered by Messengers who are prophets, and finally, a developed eschatology (Doctrine of Future Events):[1]

> Narrated by AbuHurayrah
> Sahih Al-Bukhari 6.300
> One day while Allah's Messenger (peace be upon him) was sitting with the people, a man walked up to him and said, 'O Allah's Messenger! What is Belief?'
> The Prophet (peace be upon him) said, 'Belief is to believe in Allah, His Angels, His Books, His Messengers, and the meeting with Him, and to believe in the Resurrection.'

The foundation of Islamic belief and practice is the *Qur'an*, which Sunni Muslims believe to be the uncreated divine speech, whereas the Shia believe it to be created. It is not quite accurate to compare the *Qur'an* to the Bible: the traditional Christian position is that the Bible reveals Jesus, who is held to be the eternal, uncreated Word of God, whereas in Islam it is *Muhammad* who reveals the eternal, uncreated

Word of God – i.e. the *Qur'an*. Thus, the Bible corresponds to Muhammad, and Jesus to the *Qur'an*. This is essential if we are to understand the progress of Islamic radicalism. One offence caused to Muslims by Salman Rushdie's book *The Satanic Verses* was its seeming denigration of the *Qur'an*: it was the equivalent, for Christians, of blaspheming Jesus. Equally, the riots in Muslim countries and the angry protests outside the US embassy in London about the desecration of the *Qur'an* by US military in Guantanamo Bay in 2005 can be traced back to this belief. The *Qur'an* is considered to be the literal speech of God, free of any human involvement. When a Muslim quotes the *Qur'an*, he will often declare 'Allah says...' The source of this belief is found in the *Qur'an* itself, in the concept that there eternally exists in Paradise (and is therefore free from human influence) the Preserved Tablet (*Lawh-i-Mahfuz*), the eternal Word of God, from which revelation descends to humanity.[2] It is termed 'The Mother of the Book' (*Umm-al-Kitab*).[3] The Pakistani Islamist scholar Abul A'la Mawdudi, whose influence on the ideology of important British Muslim groups has been considerable, stated:

> 'Umm al-Kitab': the 'Original Book': the Book from which all the Books sent down to the prophets have been derived...[described] in Surah al-Buruj: 22 as Lauh-i Mahfuz (the preserved Tablet), that is, the Tablet whose writing cannot be effaced, which is secure from every kind of interference...[4]

The *Qur'an* is divided into chapters called *surahs,* meaning 'fences'. They are arranged in order of *length* rather than chronology. The themes within each *surah* are not entirely sequential, but rather, according to Sunnis, purportedly reflect the order established by Muhammad. Shi'ite Muslims assert that the *Qur'an* should be in chronological order. The verses are called *ayahs*, meaning 'signs'. The *Qur'an* is held to have been gradually revealed over twenty-three years, reflecting the prophetic career of Muhammad. Sometimes the reader encounters contradictory injunctions or comments in the text, and this reflects the changing circumstances of Muhammad. Muslim scholars believe in a concept called *naskh*, 'abrogation', and the *Qur'an* itself refers to the process.[5] Basically, the later verses abrogate the earlier – specifically, certain verses that materialised when Muhammad was a powerless preacher in Mecca are replaced by those emerging when he was a ruler in Medina following the *hijrah* (migration). This becomes very relevant when we consider *jihad*: for example, Surah 43:89 enjoins that pagans be ignored, but Surah Baqarah 2:190–191 orders that they be resisted and slain.[6] The latter verse abrogates the former.

THE *HADITH*

The second source of authority for Muslims is the *Sunnah*, or the 'path, way, manner of life'. This concept is held to be taught by the *Qur'an*: Surah Ahzab 33:21 'Ye have indeed in the Apostle of Allah a beautiful pattern of (conduct) [*Uswah Hasanah*] for anyone whose hope is in Allah...' Hence, Muhammad's acts, judgments, policies, strategies, words and silences collectively constitute the norm of conduct and ethics for all Muslims:

> Narrated by Malik ibn Anas
> Al-Muwatta 46.1.3
> The Messenger of Allah, may Allah bless him and grant him peace, said, 'I have left two matters with you. As long as you hold to them, you will not go the wrong way. They are the Book of Allah and the Sunnah of His Prophet.'

Essentially, the difference between the two aspects of revelation is that with the *Qur'an*, Muhammad is said to have brought the direct speech of God, precise and incorruptible, whereas the *Sunnah* is human speech and action, unprotected and subject to fallibility. In practice, however, Muslims do not markedly differentiate the two in their everyday lives. The *Sunnah* is transmitted through the *hadith*, a word meaning 'news' or 'narration', i.e. records of the life of the Prophet. This becomes relevant to the British situation in several ways. For example, on the question of how to interact with wider British society, such as whether to participate in elections, sides both for and against will look to the prophetic model for guidance. It is often argued by those supporting such activity that in Medina Muhammad established a multi-faith society with a constitution. Moreover, the Prophet Joseph was effectively Prime Minister in pagan Egypt, and therefore involvement in non-Muslim structures is allowed; opponents of voting, however, claim there is no record of Muhammad acting in this way.

Another example is community relations. Islam is a strongly eschatological faith; indeed, Muslims are defined as those who believe in Allah and the Last Day, in contrast to the pagan Arabs who purportedly denied the reality of the Hereafter.[7] One *hadith*, which probably reflects the strained relationships Muhammad eventually had with some Jewish tribes in Medina, is the following:

> Narrated by AbuHurayrah
> Sahih Muslim 6985
> Allah's Apostle (peace be upon him) said: The Last Hour would not come unless the Muslims will fight against the Jews and the Muslims would kill them; until the Jews would hide themselves behind a stone or a tree and a stone or a tree would say: Muslim, or the servant of Allah, there is a Jew behind me; come and kill him; but the tree Gharqad would not say, for it is the tree of the Jews.

After the Second Palestinian Intifada broke out, many in the British Jewish community were concerned when Al-Muhajiroun distributed posters stating 'The Hour will not come until the Muslims fight the Jews'; we can infer that the group was quoting this *hadith*. It can be seen that knowledge of the *hadith* and Islamic eschatology is essential for mapping the course of Islamic radicalism in the UK.

A major division between Sunnis and Shia is in their *hadith* collections. Sunni Muslims regard six of these collections as authoritative: Sahih Bukhari (d. 870); Sahih Muslim (d. 875); Abu Dawud (d. 888); Al-Tirmidhi (d. 892); An-Nasai (d. 915); Ibn Madja (d. 886). Also of note is the *Mishkat al-Masabih* collection. Shia Muslims adhere to their own collections and regard many of the Sunni *ahadith* as forged. The most important Shia collections are the two collations of Mohammad Ibne Yaqoob Abu Jafar Kulaini (d. 939), *Usool al Kafi* and *Forroh al Kafi*. Others include *Man la yahduruhu al-Faqih,* by Muhammad ibn Babuya (d. 991); *Tahdhib al-Akhkam,* by Sheikh Muhammad at-Tusi, Shaykhu't-Ta'ifa (d. 1067); and *Al-Istibsar,* by the same author.[8]

SHARI'AH

According to Abu Ameenah Bilal Philips, a leading Western Islamic scholar, *fiqh,* Islamic jurisprudence, literally means 'the true understanding of what is intended', and quotes a *sahih* (sound) *hadith* in support of this.[9] He continues: 'Technically, however, *Fiqh* refers to **the science of deducing Islamic laws from the evidence found in the sources of Islamic law.'**[10] *Shari'ah*, by contrast, in technical terms refers to 'the sum total of Islamic laws which were revealed to the Prophet

Muhammad…and which are recorded in the Qur'aan as well as deducible from the prophet's divinely-guided lifestyle (called the *Sunnah*).'[11] Philips sees the *Shari'ah* as expressly revealed in the *Qur'an* and *Sunnah*, whilst *fiqh* derives from *Shari'ah*, and while *Shari'ah* is usually general, *fiqh* addresses specific situations not directly considered in *Shari'ah*.[12]

Mawdudi states that '*Fiqh* deals with observable conduct…that concerning itself with the spirit of conduct is known as *Tasawwuf* (spirituality/character).'[13] An essential aspect of Islamic ritual and ethics is that of *niyyah*, 'intention'). This becomes especially relevant when considering 'suicide bombings': martyrdom can only be accepted by God if the motive is pure, i.e. to please Allah by fighting the foe. Islamic law largely concerns itself with issues relating to outward obedience. There are two categories of jurisprudence in this regard:[14]

- •**Ibadah:** Essentially, this concerns issues of worship – ritual matters, such as the correct form by which prayers and pilgrimage should be performed.
- •**Mu'amalah:** In this section would be considered what would be seen in the West as 'legal' and political/economic matters – the nature of court testimony, laws on marriage, on divorce, etc.; what one Muslim website defines as 'matters pertaining to man-to-man relationship'.[15]

The essence of Islamic conduct centres on the concepts of *halal* (permitted) and *haram* (forbidden), and so a major function of *fiqh* is to determine the appropriate response to a question concerning practical ethics. As a result, the following categories have emerged: obligatory; recommended; indifferent; disapproved but not forbidden; prohibited.[16] This becomes immediately relevant to the British scene when we consider the permissibility or otherwise of Muslim participation in the electoral process; elements such as HT, the Saved Sect (previously Saviour Sect) and SOS have all declared that 'voting is *haram*'. *Fuqaha* (scholars of *fiqh*) produced the system of legal categories, based on the aforementioned aspects of jurisprudence, that can be summed up by the phrase 'the lawful and the prohibited':[17]

- •*Fard* (**Obligatory**):[18] Failure to fulfil this results in punishment. There are sub-categories:
    - –*Fard 'ayn* – obligation on the *individual*, e.g. prayer[19]

–*Fard kifayah* – obligation on the *community*, e.g. funeral arrangements, or seeking knowledge[20]

–*Wajib* (**incumbent**)[21] – obligatory, because possibly commanded by God or the Prophet, though slightly lower in status than something designated *Fard*, because the evidence is not as strong or direct.[22] However, the evidence 'is strong enough that, practically speaking, this act is also compulsory. One who neglects or rejects such an action is a *fasiq* [sinner] but will not be a *kafir* (disbeliever).'[23]

• *Sunnah* (**Recommended**):[24] Failure to fulfil these acts is not punished, but they bring divine reward if practised. Sub-categories of this division include the following:

–*Mustahabb* (**Prized**)[25]

–*Mandub* (**Preferred**)[26]

• **Mubah** (**Permissible**): This category identifies actions that are permitted, though no sanction or reward is incurred either way.[27]

• *Haram* (**Prohibited**): Conduct of this kind, explicitly proscribed in the *Qur'an* and *hadith*, results in punishment.[28] These punishments are termed *hadd*, and include flogging for drinking intoxicants.[29] It also includes punishing a woman whose claim of rape cannot be substantiated.

• *Makruh* (**Disapproved**):[30] Although not banned, such actions are disliked.[31] Makruh has two further sub-divisions:

–*Makruh tahrimi* – 'that which is nearly unlawful without it being actually so'

–*Makruh tanzihi* – 'that which approaches the lawful'.[32]

• *Mufsid* (**Disturbing/Corrupting**):[33] 'Those things which disturb the devotions, are termed disturbers (*mufsid*) like speaking in prayers; eating and drinking while fasting.'[34]

When we read in Al-Qaida statements that *jihad* is a 'duty', or 'obligatory', they mean it is *fard*: 'The first compulsory obligation after Iman today is defending and fighting against the enemy aggressor...So Jihad today is compulsory on the entire Ummah...'[35] *Fuqaha* are responsible for evaluating issues and supplying directions in the form of a ruling, a *fatwa* – which does not mean 'death sentence', but simply a juridical verdict upon an issue. When the UK *ulama* issued their *fatwa* denouncing 7/7, they referred to certain actions being incumbent (i.e. *wajib*) and stated that pursuing justice for the victims was an obligation (*fard*):

> It is incumbent upon all of us…to help the authorities with any information that may lead to the planners of last week's atrocity being brought to justice. The pursuit of justice for the victims of last week's attacks is an obligation under the faith of Islam.[36]

As a result of this evolution of jurisprudence, three legal principles emerged to establish a court decision:

- *Sahih* – valid[37]
- *Batil* – void[38]
- *Fassid* – irregular.

All Sunni schools of Islamic Law see their basis in the *Qur'an* and the *Sunnah*. Applying these largely centred on the use of *ijma* (consensus). This required theological/juristic effort and examination by scholars, a process called *ijtihad*.[39] The other major principle was that of *qiyas* (analogy), whereby analogical reasoning, based on subjects addressed by the *Qur'an* and *Sunnah*, would be employed to determine the validity or otherwise of an act or proposition.[40] *Qiyas* becomes vital when considering if Islam is compatible with democracy. Participationist groups will often argue that, because Joseph served in a non-Muslim regime (under Pharaoh), it is analogous for British Muslims today to do so in the UK.

Other concepts utilised by one or other of the distinct schools of *fiqh* include *ra'y* 'opinion', as well as the *Sahabah* (Companions of Muhammad) and/or the *fuqahah*. Another means of establishing an opinion that is favoured by some is 'custom' or *'adat*, and customary usage – *'urf* – either of the *Ummah* or, especially, the Caliphs.[41] The particular customs of the people of Medina, as the place of the first Islamic State, are also seen by some jurists as influential.[42] *Istishab* – 'continuity' – is relevant to the issue of apostasy and marriage, where British legislation is at variance with Islamic law.[43] A further principle is *istihsan* or 'preference', over the conclusion that may have been reached by analogy.[44] It is often linked to the concept of 'welfare'.[45] *Istislah* 'welfare' is another category that enables a juristic decision.[46] The 'public interest', especially where issues of finance are concerned, may at times be an overriding concern.[47] These concepts are increasingly used by British and other Western Muslims to address their situation and decide about Muslims' relationship to democracy and participation in majority non-Muslim political systems. For example, scholars such as Dr Azzam Tamimi and his colleague Rachid Ghannouchi have utilised the concept of *maslaha* – 'benefit' or 'welfare' – to justify Islamist involvement in democracy:

> The focus of HT critique of Ghannouchi's *Al-Hurriyat* is the concept of *maslaha* (exigency). Ghannouchi is accused of fabricating and twisting classical *ijtihad*...The HT ideologue concludes that Ghannouchi's book...comes up with a new method for thinking or for legislating based on *maslaha*...[48]

On the other hand, the Saved Sect/Al-Ghurabaa regard this as an illegitimate employment of the concept, attacking 'the false claim of "interests" that MCB and the "Islam channel" call for'.[49] They continue:

> Some people argue that participating in the Kufr parliament is only in order to take it as a platform to call to the Deen of Allah and for the benefit of Islam and the Muslim community. They claim that in order for them to enter, they must ally with the secular people and parties or with the Kufr groups/parties (e.g. Labour, conservative, liberal democrat or respect party etc) in order to gain a political position, claiming that he does so only for the sake of Allah and Da'wah and not for the sake of committing Shirk.
>
> This is one of the arguments that they put forward, to use any means to benefit the Da'wah or for the interests of the people, claiming that they are doing good deeds. That is completely false, misguided and a deviation because of the following contradictions with the Shari'ah,
>
> (i) Allah (swt) says,
>
> *'By your lord, we will account all that they do, so call openly whatever I ordered you and turn away from the mushrikeen, Allah is enough to deal with the mockers.'* [EMQ Hijr: 92–94]

This ayah carries a prohibition from compromising with the Mushrikeen for any political gain or in order to gain some benefit or even for the sake of Da'wah...[50]

Several *madhabs*, i.e. schools of *fiqh*, arose throughout early Muslim history, but only four schools of the Sunni sect continue. These are the Hanafi, Shafi, Hanbali and Maliki schools. Their distinctive features can be presented thus:

HANAFI	SHAFI	HANBALI	MALIKI
Ijma (of the Sahabah)	*Ijma* (of the Sahabah)	*Ijma*	*Ijma*
Qiyas	*Qiyas*	*Qiyas*	*Qiyas*
Ra'y (of the Sahabah)	*Ra'y* (of the Sahabah)	*Ra'y* (of the Sahabah)	*Ra'y* (of the Sahabah)
Istihsan	*'Adat* (of the people of Medina)	*Istishab*	*Hadith Da'if* (a questionable *hadith*)
'Urf	*'Urf* (of the people of Medina)		
	Istislah		

In practice, Shi'ite *fiqh* is little different from its Sunni counterparts.[51] Interestingly, the Islamic Revolution in Iran has led to a more dynamic *ijtihad* and elements of convergence with Sunni *fiqh*. Traditionally, Shia held that during the occultation of the Twelfth Imam, 'civil governmental authority could only derive from common law ('*urf*) rather than from Islamic law'.[52] They also held that the rulings of a dead *mujtahid* were not binding on the living. The elevation of Khomeini to the position of 'Supreme Jurisprudent' and representative of the Hidden Imam transformed the situation. His *fatwa* against Salman Rushdie for blasphemy is 'felt by most Iranian Shi'ites to be irrevocable'.[53]

Khomeini also applied the Sunni principle 'of *maslaha* or state action on behalf of the public good' which previous Shi'ite *fuqaha* had not recognised, and which allows the Islamic Republic to 'do virtually anything and declare it in accordance with Islamic law', on the basis that it benefited the *Ummah*.[54] Naturally, the primary bases of Shia *fiqh* remain the *Qur'an* and *Sunnah*, but therein arises a distinction. Shia Muslims, as we have seen, adhere to their own *hadith* collections and regard many of the Sunni *ahadith* as forged. The division between 'sound' and 'weak' *ahadith* affects the way Shi'ite *fiqh* works:

> ...the Shi'ite 'ulema are of the opinion that only reliable traditions are to be given credence. That is, if the people who make up the chain of narrators, called the musnad, are Shi'ite and just, or at least truthful and reliable, then the Tradition itself can be relied upon.[55]

Two major distinctive features of Shia *fiqh* are the rejection of the *ijma* of *Sahabah* (obviously, since they do not recognise the Sunni *Sahabah* or Caliphs), and the belief that their *fuqaha* can still exercise *ijtihad*, which Sunnis have regarded as a closed science since the Mediaeval Abbasid era.[56] In fact, there is a democratic imperative for all Muslims to learn *ijtihad*:

> We believe that ijtihad in matters of religion is a sufficient necessity (wajib al-kifa'i) for all Muslims in the absence of the Imam, that is to say that should one of them become proficient in ijtihad and become a mujtahid it is enough for them to follow the mujtahid in all the branches of the religion.[57]

The Shia practise *taqlid* – imitating their *mujtahid* (an expert in *ijtihad*, essentially a living Ayatollah) who follows the teaching and practices of the Twelve Imams. The Shia jurists stated that the sources of the *Shari'ah* are four: the Book, the *Sunnah*, *ijma* ('of the 'ulema of the same period as the Prophet or Imams')[58] and *'aql* (reason), emphasis on reason being a major feature of Shi'ism. However, they reject *qiyas* and *ra'y*.[59] The Shia position is that 'Everything that is commanded by reason is (also) commanded by religion.'[60]

An understanding of *fiqh* and *Shari'ah* is important for our subject on several counts, even to the level of recognising that there are different schools of Islamic law. For example, British law now forbids a man to impose his sexual attentions upon his wife if she is unwilling to gratify him – that is, marital rape is recognised as a fact, and is illegal. However, an influential code among the Hanafi school in the subcontinent, and thus relevant to many British Muslims, is *Al-Hedaya*. This contradicts current British law: *Hedaya* Vol. I 3626 (Hanafi Manual): 'where a woman, residing in the house of her husband, refuses to admit him to the conjugal embrace...notwithstanding her opposition...he may...enjoy her by force'. Similarly, the age of consent in the UK is sixteen, but in Islam, girls may have sex (within marriage of course) at nine, because of the *Sunnah*:

> Narrated by Ursa
> Sahih Al-Bukhari 7.88
> The Prophet wrote the (marriage contract) with 'Aisha while she was six years old and consummated his marriage with her while she was nine years old and she remained with him for nine years (i.e. till his death).

Again, British law recognises only monogamy, but Islamic law allows polygamy.[61] Divorce in British law is also at variance with Islamic law, which allows a man to divorce with a three-fold repudiation.[62] If either member of the couple converts from Islam, Islamic law imposes divorce – something not recognised in UK law.[63] Indeed, apostasy and blasphemy are usually considered capital offences.[64] It was this ruling that came to haunt Rushdie. The issue of women's clothing has arisen in European Union countries, notably France, and even in Britain with regard to the *jilbab*. Again, Islamic law is prescriptive on this issue.[65] It can be seen that reconciling obedience to Islamic law with UK legislation can be difficult.

However, understanding *Shari'ah* is also important for comprehending issues such as *jihad*, democracy and involvement in non-Muslim political structures. An important issue in this respect is *ijtihad*. By the Mediaeval period the gates of *ijtihad* were considered by many to have closed, although Hanbalis and some Shafis upheld the prerogative of a jurist to employ 'rational and independent judgment in legal questions'.[66] Most had, however, concluded that *ijtihad* was no longer necessary, since 'all possible issues had already been raised and addressed'.[67] There have been periodic attempts to revive *ijtihad*, essentially to provide answers to new challenges that previous *fuqaha* had not addressed.

In recent years, as large Muslim minorities have arisen in Western lands, this question has become acute. The existence of such *permanent* Muslim minorities in the West resulting from immigration is theologically anomalous and problematic for Islam, a condition for which Muslims have little experience.[68] Islamic theology/jurisprudence prescribes that normally Muslims should migrate *from* non-Muslim lands *to* Islamic countries.[69] Other issues include the relation of Islamic governance to democracy, where some figures associated with the *Ikhwan* (Muslim Brotherhood) have asserted that 'Contemporary *ijtihad* must inevitably arrive at supporting the concept of political pluralism...'[70] Similarly, exposure to the reality of complete religious liberty and the right to convert have led to some scholars like Hassan al-Turabi, Yusuf al-Qaradawi and Azzam Tamimi to question traditional Islamic rulings on apostasy. It can be seen that *ijtihad* and *fiqh* are very relevant to modern Britain.

JIHAD

The Arabic word *jihad* is derived from the root word *jahada*. The latter word has the sense of 'strive' or 'exert'. Firestone observes that *jahada* has been classically defined as 'exerting one's utmost power, efforts, endeavors, or ability in contending with an object of disapprobation'.[71] He continues: 'Such an object is often categorized in the literature as deriving from one of three sources: a visible enemy, the devil, and aspects of one's own self. There are, therefore, many kinds of *jihad*, and most have nothing to do with warfare.'[72] Muslims often distinguish between the 'greater *jihad*' (*jihad al-akbar*) – i.e. by the individual believer against his evil impulses – and the 'lesser *jihad*' (*jihad al-asghar*), involving sacred violence; after 9/11, there was frequent reference to this by Muslim spokesmen. However, with regard to Sunnis, this notion is based upon a *hadith* of questionable provenance, one that presents Muhammad declaring: '"We have returned from the lesser *jihad* to embark on the greater *jihad*." They said: "What is the greater *jihad*?" He said "The *jihad* of the heart, or the *jihad* against one's ego."'[73] Hasan al-Banna, founder of the Muslim Brotherhood, observes that the narration 'is not a *saheeh* (sound) tradition'.[74] Firestone notes that the source for this tradition is usually not given, and that it is absent in the canonical collections.[75] There does seem, however, to be some basis for the concept in Shi'ism.[76] Kohlberg, quoting from the collection *Furu' al-Kafi*, defines the term as a struggle 'against one's own baser instincts (*jihad al-nafs*)'.[77]

The term is broad enough to include any action advancing Islam. The former editor of *Q-News*, Britain's leading Muslim magazine, has stated that: 'For me, *Q-News* is a *jihad*. For me, just going out every day wearing a *hijab* is a *jihad*.'[78] A British Muslim publication states the following on the topic:

> 'The *mujahid* is one who tries to struggle against his self, i.e. evil self.' Ibn Qayyim in his explanation of this aspect of *Jihad* has observed:

> 'The *Jihad* against the enemies of Allah with one's life is only a part of the struggle which a true servant of Allah carries on against his own self for the sake of his Lord. This striving against the evil tendencies which have dominated his mind and heart is more important than fighting against the enemies in the outside world. It is in fact the basis on which the struggle in the path of Allah can be successfully launched.'

> Since *Jihad* is an all-round struggle, a struggle directed to so many channels, it necessitates the employment of different methods to acquit oneself creditably of its wide and varied responsibilities. According to Imam Raghib, a Muslim is required to fight against three foes:
> 1) against the visible enemy,
> 2) against the devil,
> 3) against his self (*nafs*).

> ...In his characteristic style, the Holy Prophet has explained that Jihad consists not only of using the sword, but even when a Muslim used his tongue for protesting against the atrocities of tyrants, he is waging Jihad.[79]

The narration to which the pamphlet refers is the following *hadith*, one that is frequently cited by Muslims today in respect of the political challenges they face in the contemporary period:

Narrated by AbuSa'id al-Khudri
Sahih Muslim 79
I heard the Messenger of Allah as saying: He who amongst you sees something abominable should modify it with the help of his

hand; and if he has not strength enough to do it, then he should do it with his tongue; and if he has not strength enough to do it, (even) then he should (abhor it) from his heart and that is the least of faith.

Mawdudi stated 'To alter people's outlook and spark a mental and intellectual revolution through the medium of speech and the written word is a form of jihad.'[80] In this regard, we should note the observation of al-Banna in regard to the *hadith*, that an act of *jihad* includes reproaching an unjust ruler:

> Narrated by AbuSa'id al-Khudri
> Abu Dawud 4330
> The Prophet (peace be upon him) said: The best fighting (jihad) in the path of Allah is (to speak) a word of justice to an oppressive ruler.[81]

Firestone observes that 'peaceful means of striving for religion' include *jihad al-lisan* ('striving with the tongue'), *jihad al-da'wa* ('striving by propagating the faith'), and *jihad al-tarbiya* ('striving through education').[82] Similarly, the spending of wealth is a form of *jihad*.[83] Raising funds for the propagation of the faith or for guerrillas would, therefore, be covered by this concept, although the idea is not peculiar to Islam. The *Qur'an* specifically links the expending of wealth for the cause of Allah as a form of *jihad*: Surah Tauba 9:41 'Go forth, light armed and heavy armed, and strive (*jahidu*) with your wealth and your lives in the way of Allah!'[84] Since *jihad al-da'wa* is a legitimate expression of *jihad*, and political lobbying, as we shall see, has also been designated as *jihad*, it can be argued that, given the right circumstances, such as the reality of democracy, the empowerment of Muslims in Britain and the West, and a change in Western foreign policy regarding the Muslim world, it might be possible to see the ending of military *jihad*.

The concept of *jihad al-da'wa* is especially important in terms of the conduct of *jihad*, since in offensive *jihad* the call to conversion to Islam is normally supposed to precede the act of war. For example, Taqiuddin an-Nabhani, founder of Hizb ut-Tahrir, elucidated this: 'Therefore, fighting the enemy would not become lawful until the call to Islam had been delivered to the people. The scholars have stressed that it is unlawful for us to fight those who have not received the Islamic call.'⁸⁵ Among the sayings of Imam Ali we find the following fourfold division of *jihad*, demonstrating that *da'wah* (mission) and, by extension, political lobbying and activism can be included in its definition, which has enormous consequences for the future of *jihad vis-à-vis* the West:

> When Imam Ali was asked about Faith in Religion, he replied that the structure of faith is supported by four pillars: endurance, conviction, justice and jihad... Jihad is divided into four branches: to persuade people to be obedient to Allah; to prohibit them from sin and vice; to struggle (in the cause of Allah) sincerely and firmly on all occasions and to detest the vicious. Whoever persuades people to obey the orders of Allah provides strength to the believers; whoever dissuades them from vices and sins humiliates the unbelievers; whoever struggles on all occasions discharges all his obligations and whoever detests the vicious only for the sake of Allah, then Allah will take revenge on his enemies and will be pleased with Him on the Day of Judgment.⁸⁶

Bringing the concept into both the modern age and into Western culture, MPAC defines its lobbying activities as *jihad* – for example, its lobbying of the British Broadcasting Corporation in June 2003 about a two-part programme in a series called *Spooks* that concerned MI5 fighting an extremist British mosque, and that the group, along with most other Muslim organisations, felt was a smear against Islam and British Muslims:

> Well done to those who fought the battle and bothered to protect yourselves... the BBC have been forced to listen to the Muslim community for the first time in history...We are finally standing up for ourselves. Victory is with Allah...Our job is to fight the Jihad.⁸⁷

Traditionally, *fiqh* has divided the world into two main conflicting orbs: *Dar al-Iman* ('Abode of Faith') or *Dar al-Islam*, and *Dar al-Harb* ('Abode of War'). Defensive and offensive *jihad* relate to these two concepts. In Shi'ism, *Dar al-Islam* and *Dar al-Iman* are not necessarily coterminous. The former includes the whole Muslim world that does not accept the rule of the Imams, i.e. the Sunni states.⁸⁸ The rest of the world is *Dar al-Kufr* ('Abode of Disbelief'). It must be emphasised that these are theological *constructs*, not primary sources, as with the *Qur'an* and *hadith*, and, as such, they are not set in stone. Too often, unqualified popular commentators seize on these terms when addressing the subject of *jihad*, without emphasising that they are not binding on all Muslims, are essentially theological *hypotheses*, and can be altered. Tariq Ramadan, a prominent Swiss Muslim influential in UK Islamic circles, emphasises this: '*Dar al-Islam* and *dar al-harb* are two concepts which cannot be found either in the Qur'an or in the *Sunna*...It was the *'ulama* who, during the first three centuries of Islam, by considering the state of the world...started to classify and define the different spaces in and around them.'[89] The definition of *Dar al-Harb* has become increasingly complicated. Traditionally, the concept has been understood in the following terms: 'Dar Al-Harb: Dar is house or home and Harb is war. It is a term used to describe enemy territory or a country that is under the political authority of a non-Muslim government that is in war with the Muslims.'[90]

The Hanafi majority view has been 'that if Friday and the religious holidays can be observed, the land is *dar al-Islam*'.[91] Ramadan notes that, according to the Hanafi *madhab*, '*dar al-harb* is the country where Muslims are neither protected, safe nor at peace. The existence of the abode of war does not necessitate a state of war between the two opposing factions.'[92] Ironically, according to the Hanafi rule, as Ramadan observes, 'the appellation *dar al-Islam* is applicable to almost all Western nations whilst it is not the case for the great majority of the Islamic countries where the populations are overwhelmingly Muslim'.[93] He concludes that, given globalisation and migration movements, and the presence of large Muslim minorities in the West, the terms are no longer relevant.[94] Moreover, the Tunisian Islamist leader Rachid Ghannouchi, who lives in Britain, has suggested that the presence of genuine democracy, with its accompanying features of the rule of law, freedom of thought and expression, negates the ascription of *Dar al-Harb* to the country, since '...the establishment of a secular democratic government which will respect human rights, ensuring security and freedom of expression and belief' are, in fact, the 'essential requirements of mankind that Islam has come to fulfil'.[95] He continues:

> The accomplishment of such important values in any society will immediately transform it, in the Islamic conception, from *darul-*

harb, a land of hostility and war against Islam, to a land of peace and tranquillity. Al-Imam an-Nawawi defines the land of hostility (*darul-harb*) as the country in which the faithful cannot practice their religious duties freely, and consequently emigrating from it becomes an imperative duty. True democracies are not like this; they guarantee the freedom of worship and belief.[96]

Western countries are secular democracies with equal rights for all, so the pre-modern picture of *cuius regio eius religio* confessional states, such as all-Catholic France after the Revocation of the Edict of Nantes or all-Protestant Sweden, facing an Ottoman Caliphate where non-Muslims were unequal *dhimma*, no longer applies: 'The modern world is not the *dar al-Islam* of the middle ages.'[97] The cosmological orbs of *Dar al-Harb* and *Dar al-Islam* are not the only possibilities. *Fiqh* has also presented the option of *Dar al-Sulh*, the 'Abode of Truce' or *Dar al-Ahad*, the 'Abode of Pact', proposed by the Shafi *madhab*.[98] This refers to countries that have signed 'peace or collaboration treaties with one or more Islamic nations'.[99] Sheikh Yusuf al-Qaradawi has also suggested this concept as the 'abode of covenant, the countries that have diplomatic agreements and covenants with the Muslim nation'.[100] Ramadan rejects the hypothesis, ultimately because it only really works if the two other concepts are accepted, and since they are largely irrelevant in the modern world, this one collapses as well.[101] This is realistic: Muslim minorities in the West are usually citizens, and in Britain most have been born in the country. Their presence is not the result of truce or treaty. Ironically, for different reasons, the distinct radicalism of Omar Bakri Muhammad supports the view that there is no *Dar al-Islam* today:

> Dar al-Harb, which is somewhat misleadingly translated 'House of War,' refers to the sphere that wars against God or Muslims. The non-Islamic domain is either at war with Muslims or under treaty. Under Dar al-Ahad – the Domain of Security – the area becomes a suspended Dar al-Harb, because treaty prevents conflict, wherein there is freedom of speech, the right of religious propagation and no military aggression.
>
> Today there is no Dar al-Islam – the whole world is Dar al-Harb because it is the sphere of non-shari'ah. There is Dar al-Harb in terms of military aggression and occupation.[102]

In the pre-modern era, the concepts of *Dar al-Harb* and *Dar al-Islam* were very relevant in regard to the two divisions of *jihad*: offensive and defensive. In past centuries, *offensive jihad* was a very real and often frightening phenomenon for Europeans, as demonstrated by the invasions of Spain, of Constantinople in 1453, of the Balkans and later Vienna in 1683. Al-Muhajiroun, UK supporters of bin Laden, stated this on the topic:

> There is difference of opinion as to whether Jihad is only an offensive duty or whether it can be attributed to both offensive Jihad and defensive Jihad. Al Izz Ibnu Abdul Salaam (Sheikh al Jihad) said that it is only an offensive duty not defensive i.e. Jihad by definition will only be called so if we initiate fighting, the other duty (i.e. defensive Jihad) is called Al Dafa'ah. Defending oneself being instinctive in man just as it is with the animals, not a unique duty like offensive Jihad.
>
> Moreover Ibnu Qayum laid down certain conditions for Jihad:
>
>   i) That the Muslims must start or initiate the fighting.
>
>   ii) That the fighting must be against the kuffar (N.B. fighting the murtadeen (i.e. the apostates) is called Qaatal al Ridda and is implementation of the Islamic penal code, whilst fighting the Baghee (i.e. the rebels) is called Qaatal al Baghee, neither of these being Jihad).
>
>   iii) Al Ma'niyyah – having the intention of fighting Jihad to make Allah's (swt) deen dominant. (N.B. this is not usually the case in defensive Jihad since one usually fights for victory or martyrdom not looking to implement the Islamic ruling system in such circumstances.)
>
> **The divisions of Jihad**
> There are two divisions of Jihad:
> i) Al-Jihad al-Mubadahah – Offensive Jihad
> ii) Al-Jihad al-Dafa'ah – Defensive Jihad.[103]

Shi'ite theology recognises the two forms of *jihad,* with a qualification on the authority to call to military action: 'There are two types of jihad: *ibtida'i* (to be begun by Muslims) and *defa'i* (defensive). In the view of Shi'ite jurisprudence, *ibteda'i* [*sic*] *jihad* can only take shape under the direction of the Holy Prophet or one of the twelve immaculate and perfect Imams, otherwise it is forbidden.'[104]

Hence, offensive *jihad* is inextricably linked to *da'wah*. Offensive *jihad* 'warns' infidels of the coming judgment, and their need to surrender to Islam, either by conversion (obligatory for polytheists or non-Scriptuary believers) or submission to Islamic rule, in the case of Jews, Christians and Zoroastrians.[105] It follows that if the Islamic message can be communicated without hindrance, and Muslims 'empowered' by equal access to power, such as is true of genuinely multi-confessional democracies, the violent aspect of offensive *jihad* can be negated, at least in regard to the views of most Muslims in the West. This is also true of the obligation to fund *mujahidin*: modern *fiqh* recognises that this could be interpreted as financially aiding *da'wah*.[106] Hence, instead of seeking to restrict and marginalise British Muslims, empowering them politically and encouraging their lobbying, especially on foreign affairs, could be a way to keep relations between the Muslim world and the West on a peaceful basis.

It seems virtually certain that the age of *offensive jihad* has passed, which has important consequences for the modern era and Western relations with the Muslim world. This would remain true even if there were a united Islamic Caliphate stretching from Morocco to the Philippines. The reason for this is, quite simply, Western military supremacy. This is not only a matter of practical expediency, but also because the issue has been addressed in Islamic jurisprudence. It has been accepted in the Shafi *madhab* of *fiqh* that if the enemy is too strong, battle should not be pursued.[107] The Shi'ite position is the same.[108] This is based on both the *Qur'an* and the *hadith*.[109]

It can be understood from this presentation of *jihad* that its military *offensive* form is not operative in regard to Britain. The majority opinion is that Muslims are bound by *Islamic* law not to breach *UK* law, as was affirmed by the radical Islamist Kalim Siddiqui when he endorsed Khomeini's *fatwa* against Rushdie, by affirming that 'Muslims in Britain had, under Islamic law, a prior and higher commitment to the law of the land in which they lived as a minority and therefore could not execute the *fatwa* in Britain.'[110] Islamic law has the equivalent of a visa, the *aman*, the guarantee of protection.[111] It should be noted that a Muslim visiting or residing in a non-Muslim country is meant to get an equivalent visa from the Infidel State.[112] Whilst there, he is meant to behave himself in accordance with the laws of the land, and specifically not molest its inhabitants.[113] On this basis, it would appear to be un-Islamic for British Muslims, or for Muslims who have come to the UK for trade, employment or educational reasons, to launch *jihad*. On this basis, it could be argued that the 7/7 bombers, being normally resident in Britain, committed a *haram* act even on this basis alone.

The general ban on attacking one's country of residence even applies to *defensive jihad*, the only form of *jihad* still operative today. *All* Islamist guerrilla groups regard themselves as being engaged in defensive *jihad*. Whereas offensive *jihad* is *fard kifayah*, meaning that only a party of Muslims need perform it, defensive *jihad* is *fard 'ayn*, meaning that it is obligatory on *all* Muslims. This is what complicates matters for British Muslims: they are required by their faith to aid their brethren under attack. Of course, the question is *how* this should be effected. Some have actually fought in places such as Afghanistan, Bosnia, Chechenya, Palestine (two British Muslims died in a 'martyrdom' operation against Israel in Tel Aviv) and Kashmir. For the most part, their contribution is to give moral, political and increasingly *electoral* support.

There are strict rules governing the conduct of *jihad*, and who may be fought. Normally, non-combatants may not be killed. Al-Banna claims that 'It is forbidden to slay women, children, and old people, to kill the wounded, or to disturb monks, hermits and the peaceful who offer no resistance.'[114] This can be observed in both the Sunni and Shia *hadith*:

- **Sunni –**
Narrated by Abdullah
Sahih Al-Bukhari 4.257
During some of the ghazawat [raids] of the Prophet a woman was found killed. Allah's Apostle disapproved the killing of women and children.
- **Shia –**
Related from Imam Saadiq (A) who said:
When the Prophet (S) assigned a leader to an expedition squadron...He would then say: ...Do not use treacherous means, do not plunder and do not mutilate. Do not kill children or hermits and do not set fire to date palms or drown them with water. Do not cut down a fruit-bearing tree and do not burn crops...[115]

However, where women and children are gathered at what can be considered a legitimate military target, such killing of non-combatants is allowed if they are not specifically targeted and it is not deliberate: that is, if it is a question of what the American military have called 'collateral damage'.[116] This is based on a sound *hadith*.[117] Modern Islamists have referred to this as a basis for contemporary martyrdom operations:

> In the case of women and children of the unbelievers, however, they could be fired upon for an expediency of war even if it is not dire necessity, for war may need such action, but the intention should not be specifically to kill the non-combatants. The Prophet (peace and blessings be upon him and his Household) was asked about the pagans being hit by night, and some women and children being killed in the process, and he replied, *"They are from among them."* [Bukhari and Muslim][118]

In fact, this is in no way sectarian: if the enemy attempts to use *Muslims* – including women and children – as human shields, then military action may still be taken against the target.[119] When it was pointed out to bin Laden that among the victims of 9/11 were hundreds of Muslims, his reaction was dismissive, not least because of his view that it is wrong for Muslims to reside permanently in *Dar al-Harb*:

> In my view, if an enemy occupies a Muslim territory and uses common people as human shield, then it is permitted to attack that enemy. For instance, if bandits barge into a home and hold a child hostage, then the child's father can attack the bandits and in that attack even the child may get hurt…The Islamic Shariat says Muslims should not live in the land of the infidel for long. The Sept 11 attacks were not targeted at women and children. The real targets were America's icons of military and economic power.[120]

According to *fiqh*, the defence of the blood and honour of *dhimmis* – non-Muslims living under Islamic rule – is regarded in the same light as that of Muslims.[121] The treaty is binding upon the Islamic State and all Muslims. On this basis, the Al-Qaida attack on a Jewish synagogue in Tunisia in 2002, apparently in retaliation for Israeli actions against Palestinians, but mainly killing German tourists, was sinful (*haram*) according to *fiqh*, because the place of worship was for native *Tunisian* Jews who had *not* 'dispossessed Muslims and Christians in Palestine'. This would also be true of Islamist attacks on Moroccan Jewish properties in 2003 and on Turkish synagogues the same year. Similarly, assaults on Pakistani churches in retaliation for US attacks contradict the *fiqh* of *jihad* because the Pakistani Christians are in no way connected with the US action. For this reason, mainstream Muslim groups had no problems condemning these actions.[122] This needs to be emphasised, because often commentators confuse support for HAMAS and Hezbollah among British Muslims, which is fairly general, with overt support for Al-Qaida, which is limited to elements such as the Saved Sect and SOS. To understand this, we must recognise that the Palestine situation is considered as vastly different from that in Iraq, Kashmir, or America.

This is because Muslims in general do not oppose the Zionist state or Israelis because they are *Jews*, but rather they oppose people who are classified in Islamic law as *aliens* (*harbi*) from outside Palestine who, they believe, have *dispossessed* Muslims and Christians and denied them equal rights. Azzam Tamimi, a prominent member of the Muslim Association of Britain (MAB), expressed this point: '...the Palestinians are simply resisting an occupation of their homes by invaders that came from Eastern Europe, America, S. Africa and many other places...'[123] Because even Israeli women serve in the armed forces on occasion, Muslims usually do not regard them as civilians. *Fuqaha* agree that if women and children engage in military action, they become legitimate targets: '...if a woman fights she can be killed'.[124] Concerning those forced out of their houses, the *Qur'an* enjoins that it is legitimate to physically resist those guilty of attacking people and dispossessing them.[125] This is why British Muslims generally distinguish Israelis from Jews in the Muslim world and US civilians.

There seems widespread theological support from *ulema* for the view that *shahid* (martyr) operations against 'the Zionist enemy' are wholly legitimate, whilst the attack on the World Trade Center was not. Dr M. Sa'id Ramadan Al-Bouti of Damascus University and Oxford Academy draws a distinction between the actions of Al-Qaida and those of the Palestinian Resistance:

> If for instance we said that the people in those buildings had unjustly occupied them, without permission of their owners,

then we could say that humanness justifies that the owners of the buildings take action and avenge this wrongdoing. This example is analogous to the current situation in Palestine. If these tall buildings had been owned by certain individuals, and then were forcibly taken from them and those thousands of men and women inhabited them, we could say that they are occupying buildings that do not belong to them, which is blatant injustice. And we could say that humanness condemn injustice, thus the owners of the buildings are entitled to defend their rights. But this is not the case here, for these people dwell in these buildings rightfully.[126]

Sheikh Yusuf al-Qaradawi, a leading figure in the *Ikhwan* of international reputation, who is increasingly influential in Britain, has vigorously distinguished 9/11 from HAMAS actions, since in the case of 9/11 both the objective and the means – using civilian aircraft full of non-combatants against people not occupying homes taken from Muslims (as in Palestine) and attacking buildings full of innocent people – was totally illegitimate:

Truly, our hearts bleed for the attacks that targeted the World Trade Center (WTC) as well as other institutions in the United States...Even at times of war Muslims are not allowed to kill anybody save the one who is indulged in face-to-face confrontation with them. They are not allowed to kill women, elderly, children, or even a monk in his religious seclusion.

That is why killing hundreds of helpless civilians who have nothing to do with the decision-making process and are striving hard to earn their daily bread, such as the victims of the explosions (in the U.S.) is a heinous crime in Islam.[127]

A strong opponent of al-Qaradawi, Omar Bakri Muhammad, observed the following about Israelis, which is a common view among many British Muslims:

...if children are killed, the fault lies with the adult occupiers who brought them into a battlefield situation. There are two kinds of Jews in Palestine: firstly, the indigenous Palestinian Jews who always lived there with Muslims and Christians, with whom there is no problem unless they support the occupiers, and secondly, the illegitimate European colonists from Poland, Russia, etc., who are legitimate targets in jihad, because they dispossessed Muslims and covenanted [protected, indigenous] Christians.[128]

Generally, it can be said that British Muslims are quite likely to support *jihad* movements in Palestine, Kashmir and some other places, whilst distancing themselves from Al-Qaida – especially when it attacks Britain on our home soil. None of the radical organisations we shall examine support Al-Qaida, except the Saved Sect and SOS. It cannot be assumed that, just because a Muslim supports martyrdom operations in one sphere and by one group, he will support such operations in another arena and by a different organisation. Ultimately, his opinion will be formed by the *fiqh* of *jihad* – as to who is a legitimate target of war. US troops occupying Muslim land will be seen as legitimate targets; US and UK civilians in New York and London not so, and neither will Jewish civilians in Morocco, Turkey or Tunisia, or Christians in Pakistan. That is why many radical Muslims will support HAMAS and Hezbollah, but oppose Al-Qaida.

DEMOCRACY

The question of Islamic radicalism in Britain with regard to democracy reveals a fascinating divergence between Islamic ideologies that had their origins in the Middle East or the subcontinent. Fascinating, too, because those Islamists proposing that democracy is Islamic could be regarded as *radical* rather than traditional. This shows the danger of regarding Islamic radicalism as a monolith. The ideological influences on Islam in Britain increasingly come from three major sources – Ayatollah Khomeini; the Muslim Brotherhood (specifically the teaching of its founder Hasan al-Banna and his successor Sayyid Qutb) and *Jama'at-i-Islami* (specifically the teaching of its founder Abul A'la Mawdudi); and finally, radical Salafi elements. Moreover, in regard to Khomeinism, Qutbism and Mawdudism, it must be recognised that their teachings have been *contextualised* and modified for and by the British situation. In regard to Khomeini and Qutb, these were both revolutionary thinkers and activists, not least because their domestic situations allowed for nothing else, whereas Mawdudi – never as popular or influential in his home setting as these other two figures – was more reformist in approach, again because of the distinct nature of his situation (British India and then Pakistan).

To set this in context, we must understand something of the nature of the relation of Islam to politics. A major difference between Islam and Christianity is that Islam in its full expression requires the existence of a *state*. The very concept of 'law' implies both the presence of government and sanctions, and Islamic law is renowned for its *hudud* punishments, involving the amputation of limbs for theft, or stoning for adultery. Moreover, the concepts of 'government' and 'law' necessarily involve security forces and military policy. The distinction for Islam is that it requires a *religious* state and thus a *sacral* military policy – i.e. *jihad*. The origins of Islamic law go back to the nature of the state created by Muhammad in Medina. Mawdudi emphasised that in Islam, people 'have to follow and obey the laws (*Shari'ah*) given by God through His Prophet'.[129] The *Qur'an* instructs Muslims to obey the divine revelation and the Messenger himself.[130]

Muhammad, after the *hijrah* (the migration of Muslims to Medina from Mecca), was not only a prophet, but also a ruler, exercising administrative, executive and judicial functions. Since Muhammad is the *Uswah Hasanah*, this aspect of his prophetic career is binding on Muslims, and is thus as much a part of Islam as Friday prayers. Thus, an Islamic Government is as essential to Muslim faith as any other feature of Islamic religious practice, as a British Islamist outlines:

> The first Islamic State was set up by the Prophet Muhammad…himself and he was also the head of that State; therefore the State is an integral part of the revealed paradigm of Islam. It can be argued that Islam is incomplete without the Islamic State. Political power, therefore, is an essential component of the Islamic civilization.[131]

Ayatollah Khomeini emphasised this aspect of the *Sirah* (sacred biography of Muhammad):

> The Most Noble Messenger…headed the executive and administrative institutions of Muslim society. In addition to conveying the revelation and expounding and interpreting the articles of faith and the ordinances and institutions of Islam, he undertook the implementation of law and the establishment of the ordinances of Islam, thereby bringing into being the Islamic state. He did not content himself with the promulgation of law;

107

rather, he implemented it at the same time, cutting off hands and administering lashings and stonings.[132]

Thus, the basis for Islamic governance and legislation is the *Qur'an* and *Sunnah* elaborated by *fiqh*. The *Qur'an* and *Sunnah* act as the political constitution of Islam: its equivalent to Magna Carta and the 1689 Act of Settlement, or America's Constitution. The latter is especially relevant. A written constitution, in particular, sets out the limits of legislation and policy. Thus, for example, in America only a native-born citizen can be President. However, it is theoretically possible for a constitutional amendment to change US law on the subject. The distinction with Islam is that, since the *Qur'an* and *Sunnah* are held by Muslims to have been revealed by God, and since God is an eternal being, there is no scope for alteration. The only possibility is that of *re-interpretation*, through *ijtihad*, since religious jurisprudence, unlike the *Qur'an* and *Sunnah*, is not divinely inspired.

The upshot of this is a belief that political sovereignty in a state is the prerogative of *God*, not Man, and herein lies the debate and conflict within Islam – including within the Muslim community in Britain – and indeed between Islamists. One modern Islamist writer comments that in the Islamic State 'sovereignty is invested in the Almighty God whereas authority to run the affairs of the state is delegated to the people'.[133] Qutb asserted that: 'To establish God's rule means that His laws be enforced and that the final decision in all affairs be according to these laws.'[134] The statutes of the State are those revealed by God in the *Qur'an* and *hadith*, and interpreted by Islamic jurisprudence. Many of the Medinan (i.e. later) verses of the *Qur'an* address juridical or constitutional issues:

> Both in the Holy Qur'an and the authentic collections of the Prophet's traditions, one can see clear evidence of the development of a sophisticated administrative organisation of society soon after Hijrah (migration from Mecca to Medinah). Then, the Prophet had two roles: spiritual, in his capacity as the Prophet through whom Divine teachings were revealed to the humans, and political, in his capacity as head and leader of the community.[135]

Essentially, modern Islamism is the belief that the State should be governed by God's revelation in the *Qur'an* and *hadith*, and this naturally rejects the idea that Man is an autonomous being who may initiate laws, although to some extent we enter the area of semantics here, since inevitably Islamic governments *do* initiate laws – although this is usually presented as an extended interpretation of divine legislation. Man is theoretically merely entrusted with the *administration* of divinely instituted legislation. When over 98 per cent of Iranian voters (in an 89 per cent turnout) voted to turn Iran into an Islamic Republic, Ayatollah Khomeini declared 1 April 1979 to be 'The first day of the Government of God'.[136] Mawdudi elaborated the meaning of 'Caliphate':

> *Khilafa* means 'representation'. Man, according to Islam, is the representative of God on earth, His vice-gerent...the authority of *khilafa* is bestowed on the whole of any community which is ready to fulfil the conditions of representation after subscribing to the principles of *tawhid* [oneness of Allah – *my emphasis*] and *risala* [prophethood – *my emphasis*]. Such a society carries the responsibility of the *khilafa* as a whole and each one of its individuals shares in it.[137]

Siddiqui argued that 'The Islamic State was the movement, and the person of the *khalifah* was the centre of allegiance.'[138] The only qualification to this is when the ruler acts contrary to *Shari'ah*, because, as the Muslim Brotherhood reminds people in the light of the *hadith*, 'there can be no obedience to a human in a matter which involves disobedience to the Creator'.[139] Therefore, sovereignty being uniquely *God's* prerogative, to propose *human* sovereignty by some constitutional system – be it liberal democracy, absolute monarchy, military dictatorship or whatever – is to usurp a divine attribute. That being the case, such an action essentially commits what for Islam is the unpardonable sin of *shirk* – assigning 'partners' to Allah.[140] Mawdudi states this explicitly – 'Anyone who claims the authority and power, independent of or in rebellion against God, to lay down the code of life for men in fact claims to be a god, and one who ascribes such power and authority to anyone associates him as a partner with God and commits *shirk*.'[141]

As we shall see, groups like the pro-*Jama'at* network, which played a major role in the formation of the MCB were heavily influenced by figures such as Qutb and Mawdudi. The Muslim Association of Britain was directly influenced by al-Banna and Qutb.

The Islamic Human Rights Commission were influenced by Khomeini. However, and this must be emphasised, all have revised and contextualised their teachings. In order to define and understand British Islamic radicalism, and its relation to democracy, we must investigate the teaching of these figures.

The *Ikhwan al-Muslimeen* (Muslim Brotherhood) was founded in Ismailiya, Egypt, in 1927 by Hassan al-Banna, a teacher. Ismailiya was dominated by the British Suez Canal Company. Al-Banna wrote 'The Europeans worked assiduously...with their corrupting traits...to overwhelm those Muslims that their hands stretched out to.'[142] These 'corrupting traits' included 'imported … semi-naked women … liquors … vices'.[143] He also attacked Europeans for plundering the Egyptian economy.[144] Whereas al-Banna was affected by the Westernisation of Ismailiya, his successor Sayyid Qutb's encounter with it was more direct: he spent two years in the USA from 1948, and was disgusted by its sexual promiscuity.[145] Another cause of his anti-West hostility was the racism he encountered in America; he was quite dark-skinned for an Arab.[146] He was also angered by the support for Zionism and the delight at the execution of al-Banna.[147]

Qutb was a noted *Qur'anic* exegete, whose commentary *In the Shade of the Qur'an* remains very popular, as does his other main work, *Signposts* (sometimes known as *Milestones*), the manifesto of the movement. Qutb supplied a radical new addition to al-Banna's teachings. The central tenet of this was that Islam did not come merely to change people's outlook or belief, but is a revolutionary movement that came to inherit the earth, to remove all the false religions, the false creeds and the false social systems; and it must do so by all means at its disposal, including war. Qutb's view of the nature and purpose of *jihad* in relation to the *Shari'ah*, was that *jihad* 'was a movement to wipe out tyranny and to introduce true freedom to mankind…'[148]

The liberation of human beings, as Qutb developed the idea, means to free them from enslavement by other human beings; the whole mission of Islam is to make everybody worship God uniquely. This involves liberating humanity from worshipping politicians and kings, priests and institutions. Therefore, Islam must try to undermine all other systems – Materialism, Communism, Hinduism, Judaism, Buddhism, Christianity, etc. Qutb quotes Rabaie ibn Amir, Muslim messenger to the Persian court, as stating:

Allah ordered us to set out to save humanity from the worship of creatures and bring it to the worship of Allah alone, to save it from the narrowness of this life so that it may look forward to the broadness of the life hereafter, and from the oppression of other religions so that it may enjoy the justice of Islam.[149]

Not only is God alone to be worshipped in a liturgical fashion, His *will* must be obeyed as the evidence of commitment to Him. This will is revealed in His Law, which concerns political, legal and economic matters as much as specifically 'religious' issues. To set aside that Law, and rule according to some other ideology, is to arrogate to oneself the prerogative of deity:

> The principle on which it (i.e. Jahiliyya) is based is opposition to God's rule over the earth and to the major characteristic of the Divinity, namely sovereignty (al-hakimiyya): instead it invests men with this, and makes some of them gods for the others. This transference of sovereignty does not occur in the primitive manner of the pre-hegira jahiliyya, but by allowing man to unduly arrogate to himself the right to establish values, to legislate, to elaborate systems, and to take positions, all without regard to divine ethics...but rather in accordance with what He has expressly forbidden! Now, to oppose the rule of God in this way is to be the enemy of His faithful.[150]

Therefore, whoever does not obey God's will in the constitutional and cultural spheres has apostatised from Islam. Such rulers are 'false gods' which must be dethroned, and the society purified.

The main strands of Islamic activism in Britain follow ideologies based on the *Qur'an* and *Sunnah*, whose ideologues, in their original oriental settings, demanded the institution of the *Shari'ah* and rule by Islamists. Yet demographic realities make it impossible in the foreseeable future to turn Britain into an Islamic State. The Muslim Parliament of Great Britain (MPGB) accepted this reality: '...we cannot establish an Islamic State in Britain...'[151] Similarly, the Islamic Society of Britain (ISB) does not list among its objectives the establishment of an Islamic State in Britain.[152] Given that the majority of British people are non-Muslims, this means that the process of Islamising the country will be long and gradual. The Mawdudist Young Muslims UK (YMUK) states, under the heading of *tadarruj* (gradualness): '...the Sunnah

(Way) of Allah...necessitates many years of hard work and struggle *before power is given* (2:124)...'[153] YMUK defined itself as being 'Here to help create and maintain in Britain a society where the people rule by Islam'.[154]

For Islamists, divine values are the parameters of legislation. Mawdudi insisted on this point:

> What distinguishes Islamic democracy from Western democracy...is that the latter is based on the concept of popular sovereignty, while the former is based on the concept of popular *khilafa*. In Western democracy, the people are sovereign; in Islam sovereignty is vested in God and the people are his caliphs or representatives. In the former the people make their own laws; in the latter they have to follow and obey the laws (*Shari'ah*) given by God through His Prophet. In one the government undertakes to fulfil the will of the people; in the other the government and the people have to fulfil the will of God.[155]

The Muslim Brotherhood also emphasises this point about the limits of legislative scope:

> The Ummah owes allegiance to Allah alone. It holds the teachings of the Qur'an and the Tradition of the Prophet...as sacred. It believes that the people cannot rule except by what Allah has revealed and in accordance with the Sharee'ah. Hence, it cannot delegate anyone it chooses to rule for it except in matters that the Sharee'ah has permitted. The Ummah has no right to ask its leader to rule in those areas that have already been determined by the Sharee'ah. If the Ummah chooses a ruler then he should deal with matters in accordance with the teachings of Islam because Islam is the basis and the ruler is a mere guardian.[156]

This final point also indicates the constitutional limits within an Islamic State. Neither the Amir nor the *Majlis* may legislate contrary to the *Shari'ah*. The *Ikhwan* state explicitly that the *Ummah* 'cannot delegate anyone it chooses to rule for it except in matters that the Sharee'ah has permitted'.[157] Similarly, Mawdudi emphasised that legislation in the Islamic State may only be effected 'within the limits prescribed by the law of the *shari'a*'.[158]

The nature of the Caliphate in some interpretations may be described as 'Presidential'; to some degree it follows the American model, rather than the British system of parliamentary rule, where the Premier is simply (in theory at least) the leader of the largest group of MPs, and the Crown-in-Parliament is effectively sovereign. In contrast, the caliphate system makes the Amir *de facto* sovereign, in terms of veto.[159] Hence, Ayatollah Khomeini could, without reference to his *Majlis*, freely direct the course of the state, continuing the war against Iraq or threatening Salman Rushdie; and the Taliban in Afghanistan were largely governed by the decrees of their Amir, Mullah Omar. However, this understanding of the relationship between the Amirate and the *Majlis* has been challenged in recent years by radical Muslim thinkers associated with the Muslim Brotherhood tradition. For example, al-Alkim claims that the concept of *Shura* has been misconceived as 'consultation', whereas it actually refers to the 'legislative process whereby the executive authority is obliged to accept the decisions of the legislative authority. It is a divine order since the Almighty God orders his Messenger not to take decisions except through *shura*.'[160] On this basis, the Caliph would be subject to the *Majlis*, which is more in conformity with the British parliamentary system than with America. Al-Alkim sees the scope of legislation as circumscribed only by 'the guiding rule which should neither forbid good nor call for evil'.[161] He also notes that the Islamist view of multi-party democracy that 'is increasingly acquiring prominence in contemporary Muslim political thinking' is that the only condition for non-Islamic parties is that they 'adhere to the state's constitution'.[162] That this is no modern innovation is stressed by Tamimi's historical exploration of Islamist attitudes to pluralism:

> The beginning of modern Islamic thinking in the Arab region is usually traced back to Rifa'ah Tahtawi (1801–1873). In his book *Takhlis Al-Ibriz ila Talkhis Bariz* (1834), Tahtawi compared political pluralism to forms of ideological and jurisprudential pluralism that existed in the Islamic experience. He defined Religious freedom as the freedom of belief, of opinion and of sect provided it does not contradict the fundamentals of religion. The same, he believed, would apply to the freedom of political practice and opinion by leading administrators who endeavour to interpret and apply rules and provisions in accordance with

113

the laws of their own countries. Kings and ministers, he explained, are licensed in the realm of politics to pursue various routes that in the end serve one purpose: good administration and justice.

Muhammad 'Abdu (1849–1905), who was a proponent of parliamentary democracy, defended pluralism and sought to refute the claim that it would undermine the unity of the Umma. He argued that the European nations were not divided by it. The reason, he concluded, was that their objectives had been the same. What varied was the method they pursued toward accomplishing it.[163]

British-based Islamists like Tamimi and Ghannouchi believe that the rejection of democracy by some Islamists is based upon a faulty understanding of the nature and purpose of divine law and government:

> *Hukm –u-llah* is a revolution in the sense that it limits a governor's powers rendering them more executive in nature than legislative. *Hukm –u-llah* does not mean that God comes down and governs humans, but means the sovereignty of law, which, Ghannouchi notes, is a fundamental feature of the modern state, the state of law and order. If, according to this concept, a government in Islam is not to be monopolized by a despot or an oligarchy, it follows that *hukm –u-llah* refers to, and implies, *hukm-ush-sha'ab*, that is the rule of the people or their representatives, who in the Islamic tradition used to be referred to as *ahl-ul-hal wal-'aqd*, whose power is limited by, and derived from, *Shari'ah*.[164]

Just as legislation is enclosed by the bounds of the *Shari'ah*, so are the qualifications for a Caliph or member of the *Majlis*. The usual refrain for the Amir is that he must be 'sane, male and a Muslim'.[165] Mawdudi elaborates on this:

> The basic qualifications for an *amir* are that he should command the confidence of the majority in respect of his knowledge and grasp of the spirit of Islam, that he should possess the Islamic quality of the fear of God and that he should be endowed with qualities of Statesmanship...[166]

Mawdudi seems to imply much the same for members of the *Majlis,* and the exclusion of women and religious minorities from ruling 'the Islamic Emirate of Afghanistan' was a feature of Taliban governance. However, this procedure was not followed in either Sudan or Iran, and the Iranian *Majlis* reserved seats for the Christian, Jewish and Zoroastrian minorities. Clearly, though, it is inconceivable that a woman or a non-Muslim could be ruler of the *Khilafah.* This seems still to be a majority opinion:

> While enjoying full freedom in personal matters, that is matters pertaining to faith, food, drink and marriage, a non-Muslim citizen may still be denied a right enjoyed by a Muslim citizen, that is the right to occupy senior positions in the state – such as the Presidency – that may be considered of significant bearing on the identity of the state.
>
> Scholars and thinkers, both classical and modern, continue to disagree, except with regard to the position of head of state, on which senior positions, or which functions, are denied to non-Muslim citizens in an Islamic state.
>
> Most modern thinkers are of the opinion that dhimmis have the right to participate in elections at all levels and may be nominated for any position apart from that of the head of state, and may therefore be members of nationally or locally elected councils.[167]

However, Tamimi notes that there are moves that question this, such as 'A modern Sudanese ijtihad which grants Christian-majority provinces in Sudan the right to opt for a legal system other than Shari'ah in order to organise their affairs'.[168] Under the Ottomans the various confessions were organised into semi-autonomous *millats* (autonomous units), though not essentially on a geographic basis. Moreover, there are sufficient historical traditions of Grand Viziers being Jews or Christians for creative *ijtihad* to resolve this issue. Iran divides power between the Leader and the President. In the past Egypt and Syria have had Christian prime ministers, and Jews have held ministerial posts in the Iraqi and Moroccan governments. Makrqam Ubeid, the Egyptian Christian leader of the Wafd Party, famously stated 'My homeland is Islam, my religion is Christianity', and Islamist leaders like Adel Hussein have recognised that native Christians and Jews form part of the cultural matrix of Islam.[169]

Divisions within Islam and subsequent internal *jihad* struggles go back to the early days of Islam. The death of Muhammad produced a political/constitutional crisis that is still with us, this being the occasion of the Sunni–Shia divide. Abu Bakr, his father-in-law, became Caliph, by popular acclamation (according to Sunnis). Mawdudi comments on the means by which Abu Bakr became Amir: '…by reason of the Qur'anic teaching that all matters affecting the *Ummah* should be decided by consultation, the Companions rightly deduced that…selection and appointment of the Head of the Islamic State had been left to the elective discretion of the Muslims…The first Caliph, Abu Bakr, was thus elected publicly.'[170] Again we see the combination of popular consensus (*ijma*) and *Qur'anic* constitutionality that Islamists emphasise.

Mawdudi stresses that in the Caliph's Parliament 'there was neither any specific Government Party nor any specific Opposition Party. The whole parliament was his party as long as he kept to the right path.'[171] However, the *Ikhwan* in Egypt have accepted, on the grounds that differences of opinion naturally occur, that plurality of parties should exist, with the proviso that they accept the *Shari'ah*.[172] Iran has allowed divergence of political tendencies.

The Shia position has some distinct nuances. Shi'ism holds that the succession to the Prophet should have gone to his son-in-law Ali, who eventually became the fourth Caliph. Thereafter, it holds that his descendants have the unique right to lead the *Ummah*. Thus, the major point of divergence from the Sunni position had its root in the question of legitimate government. The Shia rejected the first three Caliphs specifically because they questioned the Caliphs' legitimacy as *rulers*, rather than on account of any major theological difference, such as occasioned most of the divisions in Christian history. Khomeini explains how, from the Shi'ite perspective, the Imam or Amir of the *Ummah* had to be appointed by the Prophet:

When the Prophet appointed a successor, it was not for the purpose of expounding articles of faith and law; it was for the implementation of law and the execution of God's ordinances. It was this function – the execution of law and the establishment of Islamic institutions – that made the appointment of a successor such an important matter that the Prophet would have failed to fulfil his mission if he had neglected it.[173]

With the occultation (concealment) of the Twelfth Imam, a constitutional crisis emerged in Shi'ism. From '...late Safavid times [17th to 18th centuries] some *mujtahids* claimed that they had more right to rule than did the impious, wine-bibbing shahs'.[174] This arguably came to its natural conclusion when, following the Iranian revolution, Khomeini established the *Vilayet i-Faqih*, the 'Guardianship of the Jurist'. The theory is that the *ulema* rule, according to *fiqh*, as a 'trust' until the return of the Twelfth Imam. Their Islamic knowledge and *taqwa* permit this, as does their commitment to rule by *Shari'ah*.

The negative implication of both Sunni and Shia theories of government is that those rulers not fulfilling these qualities – such as Ataturk-type secularists or Saudi-style Western 'puppets' – are disqualified. The aim of the Islamic movement is '...to reinstate the Islamic way of life...[T]hese movements have had to confront the westernisation campaigns aimed at undermining Islamic culture and Islamic values.'[175] Rather than having ultra-secularist or puppet regimes, Islamists assert that, given 'a concept for an Islamic government does exist', it follows that 'it is the religious duty of Muslims, both individuals and groups, to work for the establishment of such a government'.[176] Ghannouchi emphasises the constitutional arrangement that Islamists would like to see instead, and once again it mirrors the views of both a Shi'ite Islamist (Khomeini) and a Sunni (Mawdudi); what is important in this respect is that Ghannouchi advocates power-sharing with non-Islamists where a *Khilafah* is not possible for some reason, indicating that any power-sharing is seen as merely a transitional step to a full Islamic State:

> 1. Supreme legislative authority is for the Shari'ah, that is the revealed law of Islam, which transcends all laws. Within this context, it is the responsibility of scholars to deduce detailed laws and regulations to be used as guidelines by judges. The head of the Islamic state is the leader of the executive body entrusted with the responsibility of implementing such laws and regulations.
> 2. Political power belongs to the community (ummah), which should adopt a form of shura, which is a system of mandatory consultation. If this kind of government is possible, it is then the duty of the believers to spare no effort in establishing it.[177]

We should remember that, according to the Sunni *hadith*, the people elect the Caliph, and later scholars upheld this:

> Islamic scholars like ibn Taymiya, ibn Khaldun, Abu Hamid al-Ghazali, al- Mawardi and others, agreed on the principle that the imam or caliph must be chosen by the people. Ibn Taymmia distinguished the caliph from the monarch on the basis of succession to power where the former is elected and the latter is self appointed by coercion. Al-Nassify wrote, in his book 'Al-Aqayd', that Muslims have no choice but to choose the imam who will execute the Islamic laws, defend the national frontiers, build strong armed forces, collect zakat and alms, solve domestic disputes and problems, secure justice, distribute the national income, take care of the elderly and the orphans and engage in jihad (holy wars).[178]

DA'WAH

We have observed the link between *jihad* and *da'wah*, and it is important to recognise how this operates in the UK. The main ideologue of *da'wah* in Britain was the Mawdudist, Khurram Murad. Previously deputy leader of the Pakistani *Jama'at-i-Islami*, he moved to Britain to become Director of the Islamic Foundation.[179] He has been described as 'one of the architects of current Islamic resurgence' on a 'worldwide' scale, who produced an 'action plan' for Britain.[180] YMUK President Zahoor Qureshi described the role Murad performed for Islam in Britain:

> In the words of Larry Poston, a prominent American orientalist, 'What Hasan al-Banna did for Egypt and Mawdudi did for the subcontinent, Khurram Murad did for the West' in that he formulated a strategy and gave a vision for Muslims living in the West and more specifically, in the U.K.[181]

Hence, the 'Islam' Murad proposes for Britain is the ideological Islamism of the *Jama'at-i-Islami*. The Islamic Foundation has not merely acted as a pro-*Jama'at* think-tank: it has played a major role in effecting the contextualisation of Mawdudism in Britain:

> The Islamic Foundation has been a significant spur to young Muslim identity-formation in Britain, with three particularly

important offshoots with influence on university campuses: the student movement, Young Muslims UK; the Islamic Society of Britain; and a newspaper, *Trends*...Murad and his achievement reflect the ideological dynamic of the founder of the movement, the *Jama'at-i-Islami*, with which he was most identified: Seyyid Abu'l Ala Maududi...[182]

Ataullah Siddiqui asserts that the Islamic Foundation is 'a voice which represents an Islam...untainted by cultural accretion'.[183] Geaves comments that the Foundation seeks 'to create an Islam which is suited to the environment of the West without losing the fundamentals of the faith'.[184] He quotes Manazir Ahsan, former Islamic Foundation Director General: 'Of course, there is no British Islam but if we can call it British Islam then it will have independent characteristics and features of its own.'[185] Murad aimed at removing from Islam as practised in Britain all oriental accretions, so that it could be expressed in a *British* cultural form, in the hope that 'British Islam' would win indigenous converts. This involved 'purification' of dogma and practice, that is, adherence to Mawdudi's ideology, using the revived UK Muslim community as the bridgehead to the wider British population and *tabligh*[186] to increase Muslim piety.

Murad's vision has become increasingly successful, since, as well as an intensifying sense of 'Britishness' in the community, there is an increasing trend towards emphasising the *Islamic* component of its identity, focused by the Rushdie controversy: 'Strident commitment to Islamic beliefs and values is indeed increasing among...the younger generation...'[187] One of Britain's most influential mosques is the East London Mosque, closely associated with pro-*Jama'at* groups such as Islamic Forum Europe and the Young Muslim Organisation.[188] By influencing this mosque, Mawdudists are able to influence a substantial proportion of British Muslims.

Murad precipitated developments by organising the very training measures for Muslim youth that his writings advocated.[189] In 1982 Murad formed, under his own leadership, a steering committee of 10 to 15 young people, with the idea of training the youth and imbuing them 'with a vision and knowledge to present Islam to the British population as an alternative way of life'.[190] YMUK was the practical realisation of this vision: 'Thus in 1982, the idea of launching the vehicle to carry out this mission, The Young Muslims UK, was produced. The committee was trained at the Islamic Foundation in Markfield and two years later in 1984, The Young Muslims UK was founded.'[191] Ramadan sees YMUK as a major force combating the ghetto mentality, and one that does so along the lines Murad suggested of political and financial independence from foreign states – an important issue, considering the upsurge in anti-Saudi sentiment among British Muslims since the Rushdie crisis:

> In Britain, faced with influential traditionalist movements (e.g. the *Barelwi* and *Deobandi*), youth associations such as The Federation of Students' Islamic Societies (FOSIS) and the Young Muslim (YM) are combating the ghetto tendency...European Islam also seems to be finding ways of remaining politically and financially independent.[192]

Murad also addressed the issue of Muslim socio-political powerlessness in the West – he rated Muslim influence as 'zero'.[193] We must remember that Murad made this analysis several years before the Rushdie crisis, yet it was precisely this affair that made the issue of powerlessness so immediate to the concerns of the Muslim community as a whole. Again, the fact that Murad's constituency was in some way addressing this concern put them in a position to assume the leadership of British Islam. Murad presented the imperative of mission as a necessity to preserve both Muslim identity and indeed security:

> Indeed, you have only three possible futures. First to be assimilated and absorbed in the secular culture here, receiving in return, a niche where you can practice your private customs and festivals. Second, to face genocide, or extermination, like the Muslims in Spain and Bosnia, and the Jews in Germany. And third, to bring Islam to the West, and the West to Islam.[194]

Similarly, Maulana Ahmed, President of the UK Islamic Mission, stated at its 1988 conference: 'If the Muslim settlers...want to safeguard their progeny...the only way...is to convert the indigenous population to [a] Muslim majority.'[195] These words became very pertinent for British Muslims as they experienced the emergence of modern Islamophobia in the wake of their major crises. However, *da'wah* for Murad is not simply proselytising: '...any act performed in power perspectives – to influence others – is considered a political act...Da'wah, *tabligh*...are, to some extent, political...'[196] Thus, his *organisational* and *missionary* strategies involved redressing Muslim powerlessness. The formation of the UK Action Committee on Islamic Affairs (UKACIA) and the MCB should be viewed in this light, as means to secure the dominance of Mawdudist ideology in British Islam. The Rushdie crisis was the catalyst for realising this goal.

[1] Pickthall, Muhammad Marmaduke, *The Meaning of the Glorious Qur'an* (Amman: Dar al Faihaa, first published in Hyderabad, 1930).

Surah A'la 87:18–19

A'la. Lo! This is in the former scrolls, The Book of Abraham and Moses.

Surah Maida 5:47

It was We who revealed the law (to Moses)...

Surah An-Nisa 4:163

...to David We gave the Psalms.

Surah Hadiid 57:27

...We sent after them Jesus the son of Mary and bestowed on him the Gospel...

[2] Surah Al-i-Imran 3:7

He it is Who has sent down to thee the Book...

[3] Surah Ra'd 13:39

Allah doth blot out or confirm what He pleaseth: with Him is the Mother of the Book.

[4] Mawdudi, S. Abul A'la, *The Meaning of the Qur'an,* vol. IV (Lahore: Islamic Publications Ltd., 1993), p. 172.

[5] Surah Al-Baqarah 2:06

None of Our revelations do We abrogate or cause to be forgotten but We substitute something better or similar; knowest thou not that Allah hath power over all things?

[6] Surah Zukhruuf 43:89

But turn away from them and say 'Peace!' but soon shall they know!

Surah Al-Baqarah 2:190–191

Fight in the cause of Allah those who fight you but do not transgress limits; for Allah loveth not transgressors. And slay them wherever ye catch them and turn them out from where they have turned you out; for tumult and oppression are worse than slaughter; but fight them not at the Sacred Mosque unless they (first) fight you there; but if they fight you slay them. Such is the reward of those who suppress faith.

7 Surah Al-Baqarah 2:8

Of the people there are some who say: 'We believe in Allah and the Last Day' but they do not (really) believe.

8 Momen, Moojan, *An Introduction to Shi'i Islam* (New Haven and London: Yale University Press, 1985), pp. 173–174.

9 Philips, Abu Ameenah Bilal, *Evolution of Fiqh* (Riyadh: International Islamic Publishing House, 1995), p. 1.

Narrated by Muawiya
Sahih Al-Bukhari 4.346

Allah's Apostle said, 'If Allah wants to do good for somebody, he makes him comprehend the Religion (i.e. Islam)...'

10 Philips, *Evolution of Fiqh*, emphasis in original.

11 *Ibid.*, pp. 1–2.

12 *Ibid.*, p. 2.

13 Mawdudi, Abul A'la, *Towards Understanding Islam* (Leicester: Islamic Foundation, 1980; Birmingham: UKIM, 1993, 1998 revised edition), p. 75.

14 Another possible category is *imama,* dealing with the theory of collective organisation: Lapidus, Ira M., *A History of Islamic Societies* (Cambridge: Cambridge University Press), p. 103.

15 'The Philosophy of Takaful';
http://www.cybermelayu.com/insurance/phi_page.htm.

16 Guillaume, Alfred, *Islam* (Harmondsworth: Penguin, 1954, 1978), p. 101.

17 Narrated by Anas ibn Malik
Mishkat Al-Masabih 6111

The Prophet (peace be upon him) said...the one who has most knowledge about what is lawful and what is prohibited is Mu'adh ibn Jabal. Every people has a trustworthy guardian, and the trustworthy guardian of this people is AbuUbayd ibn al-Jarrah.

Ahmad and Tirmidhi transmitted it, Tirmidhi saying this is a hasan sahih tradition. It is also transmitted in mursal form, on the authority of Ma'mar who cited Qatadah as his authority, and it contains the phrase 'The most learned in legal matters is Ali.'

18 Al-Risala (Maliki Manual)
3.03 Purity of Place and Clothes

It is obligatory that the very spot upon which a prayer is to be performed should be clean. Similarly, the clothes in which a person performs a prayer must be clean.

According to an opinion, this obligation of the cleanliness of place and clothes is of the degree of obligation under fard. While another opinion holds the view that it is of the degree of obligation under a sunnah mu'akkadah (strong sunnah).

It is prohibited to perform prayers on the resting place of camels and in the middle of a highway. It is forbidden to perform prayers on the roof of the holy Ka'bah and in the public bath, where one is not sure of the cleanliness of the place. Further it is prohibited to perform prayers at a refuse dump, abattoir, and the cemetery and the place of worship of non-Muslims.

[19] Al-Muwatta Hadith 7.14

The Command to Pray the Witr

Yahya related to me from Malik from Yahya ibn Said from Muhammad ibn Yahya ibn Habban from Ibn Muhayriz that a man from the Kinana tribe called al-Mukhdaji heard a man in Syria known as Abu Muhammad saying, 'The witr is obligatory (fard).'

[20] Fiqh-us-Sunnah

Fiqh 4.26c

Washing the Dead

The majority of jurists are of the opinion that washing the body of a dead Muslim is a fard kifayah or a collective obligation. If some people attend to it, it is done on behalf of all, as commanded by Allah's Messenger, peace be upon him, and practised by the Muslim community.

Fiqh-us-Sunnah

Fiqh 3.80

Giving Charity to Seekers of Religious Knowledge

An-Nawawi holds that if someone is able to earn a suitable living and wants to occupy himself by studying some of the religious sciences but finds that his work will not allow him to do so, then he may be given zakah since seeking knowledge is considered a collective duty (fard kifayah). As for the individual who is not seeking knowledge, zakah is not permissible for him if he is able to earn his living even though he resides at a school. An-Nawawi says: 'As for one who is engaged in supererogatory worship (nawafil) or for one who occupies himself in nawafil with no time to pursue his own livelihood, he may not receive zakah. This is because the benefit of his worship is confined only to him, contrary to the one who seeks knowledge.'

[21] Al-Muwatta Hadith 5.2

Doing Ghusl on the Day of Jumua

Yahya related to me from Malik from Said ibn Abi Said al-Maqburi that Abu Hurayra used to say, 'Doing ghusl as prescribed for major ritual impurity is incumbent (wajib) on the day of jumua on every male who has reached puberty.'

[22] Al-Risala (Maliki Manual)

40.03 The Five Salats

The five daily prayers are obligatory, as is the takbirat al-ihram (the saying of Allahu Akbar, accompanied by raising the two hands upon the point of starting a prayer). However the other takbirs in a ritual prayer are part of the prophetic tradition. Beginning a prayer coupled with intention is obligatory. The recitation of the Fatihah (the first chapter of the Qur'an) in prayer is obligatory, but any addition to that is part of the prophetic tradition and obligatory as well (sunnah wajib)...

[23] Iqra, 'Technical terminology'; http://ccminc.faithweb.com/iqra/articles/prayersm/pm02.htm.

[24] Al-Risala (Maliki Manual)

29.08 'Aqiqa Immolations

It is part of the recommended sunnah or tradition of the Prophet, peace and blessing of God be upon him, that an animal be slaughtered in honour of a baby on its seventh day...

[25] Fiqh-us-Sunnah

Fiqh 2.31

Salatul Duha is a Prized Prayer

Salatul duha is a prized prayer and whoever wishes to earn reward should pray it, while there is no blame upon the one who does not pray it.

Abu Sa'id reports: 'The Prophet sallallahu alehi wasallam would pray duha until we thought he would never abandon it. And he would abandon it to the point that we thought he would no longer perform it.' This is related by at-Tirmidhi who says it is hasan.

[26] Fiqh-us-Sunnah

Fiqh 1.74

She Must Make Ablution for Every Prayer, Menstruating Women

Said the Prophet, 'Make ablution for every prayer.' According to Malik, this is only preferred and not obligatory (unless she nullifies her ablution, of course).

27 Al-Risala (Maliki Manual)

43.01 Greeting

It is obligatory to return a greeting (that is, to acknowledge it and respond). But it is a desirable tradition of the Prophet to greet others first. Greetings shall consist of the following words 'As-salamu alaikum' (peace be upon you). And in return one says, 'Wa alaikum us-salam' (upon you be peace).

Alternatively, the man greeted can say 'Salamun alaikum' (peace be upon you), as was said to him. On most occasions people end their greetings by invoking God's blessings. They say in reply, 'Peace be upon you as well, and the mercy of God and His blessing.' Do not say when replying to a greeting 'God's peace be upon you.' Moreover, if one member of a group performs the greeting, that is enough and there is no need for the rest of them to say anything. Similarly, if a member of a group replies to a greeting, that shall be sufficient.

When a rider and walker meet, the duty to greet first is upon the rider. When a walker comes upon someone sitting down, the duty to greet first is upon the walker. The shaking of hands is a good thing, but Malik considers embracing in a greeting reprehensible. However, another jurist Ibn Uyainah says that embracing in greeting is permissible. Again, Malik considered reprehensible the kissing of hands as a mark of respect, besides he disbelieved the hadith narrated in respect of it.

It is not proper for a Muslim to greet a Jew or a Christian first. But if a Muslim greets a non-Muslim, he does not attempt to retrieve it. And if a Jew or a Christian should say 'Salamun alaikum' to him, all he says in reply is 'alaika'. One can also say 'alaika s-silam' (where 'silam', with the vowel 'i' after 's', means 'stone'). That used to be said by them to Muslims.

28 Al-Muwatta Hadith 25.13

Prohibition Against Eating Animals with Fangs

Yahya related to me from Malik from Ibn Shibab from Abu Idris al-Khawlani from Abu Thalaba al-Khushani that the Messenger of Allah, may Allah bless him and grant him peace, said, 'It is haram to eat animals with fangs'.

29 Al-Muwatta Hadith 42.1

The Hadd for Drinking Wine

Yahya related to me from Malik from Ibn Shihab that as-Sa'ib ibn Yazid informed him that Umar ibn al-Khattab came out to them. He said, 'I have found the smell of wine on so-and-so, and he claimed that it was the drink of boiled fruit juice, and I am inquiring about what he has drunk. If it intoxicates, I will flog him.' Umar then flogged him with the complete hadd.

30 *Al-Hedaya* Vol. IV (Hanafi Manual)

Book XLIV

Of Kiraheeat or Abominations

Difference of opinions concerning the extent of the term Makrooh

The author of the Hedaya remarks that our doctors have disagreed concerning the extent in which the term Makrooh *(Makrooh is the participle passive of Kuriha, to abominate; this word is frequently taken in a milder sense; and may relate to anything improper or unbecoming) is to be received. Mohammed was of opinion that everything Makrooh is unlawful; but as he could not draw any convincing argument from the sacred writings in favour of this opinion, he renounced the general application of unlawfulness, with respect to such articles, and classed them under the particular description of Makrooh; or abominable. It is recorded, on the other hand, from Haneefa and Aboo Yoosaf, that Makrooh applies to anything which, in its qualities, nearly approaches to unlawful, without being actually so. This article is comprehended under a variety of heads or sections.

[31] Fiqh-us-Sunnah

Fiqh 3:81 3:82

Zakat: Distribution: (3/4) Local versus Non-local

Zakat: Zakat Al-Fitr: (1/6) Local Distribution

The jurists agree that zakat can be transferred from one city to another provided the needs of the city residents whom the zakat was originally derived from have first been satisfied...The Hanafi scholars hold that transferring zakat is disliked (makruh) except when:

- it is for needy relatives and serves the ties of blood, or
- the needs of a group of Muslims are more pressing than those of the locals, or
- it is tied to the general interests of the Muslims, or
- it is sought from a country at war against the Muslims to the land of Islam, or
- it is intended for a scholar, or
- zakat is paid before the completion of the year (hawl).

In such cases, transferring zakat is not disliked (makruh)...

[32] Fiqh-us-Sunnah

Fiqh 4.71

Prohibition on Sitting, Leaning, and Walking on Graves

It is not permissible to sit on a grave, or lean on it, or walk over it...The majority of scholars hold that such an act is merely disapproved. An-Nawawi said: 'Ash-Shafi'i (See Al-Shafi'i's work Al-Umm) and the companions mentioned in various narrations disapprove of sitting on a grave, holding it to be makruh tahrimi, (Makruh is divided into makruh tahrimi "that which is nearly unlawful without it being actually so," and makruh tanzihi "that which approaches the lawful.") a term well-known to jurists. The majority of scholars including An-Nakha'i, Al-Laith, Ahmad, and Daw 'ud hold this view. They also disapprove of reclining or leaning on a grave.'

[33] Fiqh-us-Sunnah

Fiqh 2.72a

Begging in the Mosque

Shaikh al-Islam Ibn Taimiyah says: 'Begging is forbidden whether it is in the mosque or outside it, unless there is a real need for it. If necessary, one may beg in the mosque as long as one does not harm anyone and does not lie in begging, or disturb the people by stepping over them or with one's loudness, for instance, when the people are listening to the Friday khutbah, and one distracts them by one's voice.'

[34] http://www.diyanet.gov.tr/english/ch.htm.

[35] Al-Qaida, 'Exposing the new Crusader War', February 2003.

[36] MCB, Ulama statement.

[37] Al-Majalla (The Ottoman Courts Manual (Hanafi)) 188

In the case of a sale concluded subject to a condition sanctioned by custom established and recognised in a particular locality, both sale and condition are valid.

Example: The sale of a fur subject to a condition that it shall be nailed to its place; or of a suit of clothes subject to the condition that they shall be repaired. In these cases the condition must be observed in carrying out the sale.

Fiqh-us-Sunnah

Fiqh 1.91

About Praying at Sunrise, Sunset and While the Sun is at its Meridian

The Hanifiyyah are of the opinion that prayer during such times is not valid, regardless of whether the prayer was obligatory or voluntary, or if one was making up a prayer or fulfilling a requirement. But, they make an exception for the afternoon prayer of that particular day and the funeral prayer (if the funeral is at any of these times, the funeral prayer is still to be made). They also permit the prostration in response to Qur'anic recitation if the respective verses were recited at such times. Abu Yusuf also makes an exception for voluntary prayers on Friday while the sun is at its meridian. The Shariyyah say that voluntary prayers which are not offered for a particular reason are disliked at such times. Obligatory prayers, voluntary prayers because of some occasion, voluntary prayers on Friday when the sun is at its meridian and the prayer of the circumambulation of the Ka'bah are all permissible at such times without any disliked aspects. The Malikiyyah say that voluntary prayers during sunrise and sunset are forbidden, even if there is some occasion for them. The same applies to a prayer that was vowed, prostration owing to Qur'anic recitation, and the funeral prayer (unless they fear some decay or alteration in the deceased). But they always allow prayer, voluntary or obligatory, at the time when the sun is at its meridian. Al-Baji wrote in his commentary to al-Muwatta, 'In al-Mubsut it is related from Ibn Wahb that Malik was asked about praying at mid-day and he said, "I found the people praying at mid-day of Friday. Some hadith do not consider it desirable (to pray at such times), but I do not stop the people from praying. I do not like to pray at that time because it is not desirable to do so.'" The Hanbaliyyah say that no voluntary prayers should be made during such times, regardless of whether or not there is a reason for such prayers, and regardless of whether it is Friday or not, save for the prayer of salutations to the mosque on Friday (they allow this without any dislike for it while the sun is at its meridian or while the imam is making his address). They also say that the funeral prayer is forbidden at that time, unless there is a fear of alteration or decay in the corpse. They allow the making up of missed prayers, the vowed prayers and the prayer of the circumambulation of the Ka'bah (even if it is voluntary) at any of these three times.

[38] Al-Majalla (The Ottoman Courts Manual (Hanafi)) 189

In the case of sale subject to a condition which is not to the benefit of either party, the sale is valid, but the condition is voidable.

Example: The sale of an animal subject to a condition that it shall not be sold to a third party, or that it shall be put out to graze. In such a case the sale is valid, but the condition is of no effect.

Narrated by Umm Habibah daughter of Jahsh
Abu Dawud 0305

Ikrimah said: Umm Habibah daughter of Jahsh had a prolonged flow of blood. The Prophet (peace be upon him) commanded her to refrain (from prayer) during her menstrual period; then she should wash and pray, if she sees anything (which renders ablution void) she should perform ablution and pray.

Fiqh-us-Sunnah
Fiqh 3:57-a
Zakat: Payment (Timing): (4/4) Delayed
Delaying of zakat (payment) does not void it:

Shafi'i holds that anyone who does not pay zakat for a number of years must pay it all together. Whether or not he is aware of its obligation or he happens to be in a Muslim or non-Muslim land, makes no difference.

Based on the opinion of Malik, Shafi'i and AbuThawr, Ibn al- Mundhir says: 'When unjust people rule a country and the people of that country do not pay their zakat for a number of years, then their new leader should take it from them.'

Fiqh-us-Sunnah

Fiqh 3.138

Actions that Void the Fast

The actions that void the fast may be divided into two types:

1. those which void the fast and require that the day be made up later, and

2. those which void the fast and, in addition to being made up, also require an act of expiation.

[39] Narrated by Mu'adh ibn Jabal

Abu-Dawud 3585

Some companions of Mu'adh ibn Jabal said: When the Apostle of Allah (peace be upon him) intended to send Mu'adh ibn Jabal to the Yemen, he asked: How will you judge when the occasion of deciding a case arises? He replied: I shall judge in accordance with Allah's Book. He asked: (What will you do) if you do not find any guidance in Allah's Book? He replied: (I shall act) in accordance with the Sunnah of the Apostle of Allah (peace be upon him). He asked: (What will you do) if you do not find any guidance in the Sunnah of the Apostle of Allah (peace be upon him) and in Allah's Book? He replied: I shall do my best to form an opinion and I shall spare no effort. The Apostle of Allah (peace be upon him) then patted him on the breast and said: Praise be to Allah Who has helped the messenger of the Apostle of Allah to find something which pleases the Apostle of Allah.

[40] Fiqh-us-Sunnah

Fiqh 3.29

Zakah on Kharajiyyah Land

Land subject to tax is divided into two categories:

…Just as zakah is payable on 'ushriyyah, so it is paid on kharajiyyah when the inhabitants of the latter accept Islam or when a Muslim buys it. In that case, both the tithe and the kharaj become due, and neither of them will negate the application of the other.

Ibn al-Mundhir witnesses: 'This is the view of most of the scholars, including 'Umar ibn 'Abdulaziz, Rabi'ah, az-Zuhri, Yahya al-Ansari, Malik, al-

Awzai, ath-Thauri, al-Hasan ibn Salih, Ibn Abu Layla, al-Layth, Ibn al-Mubarak, Ahmad, Ishaq, Abu 'Ubaid, and Dawud.' Their opinion is derived from the Qur'an, the Sunnah, and the exercise of their intellect – that is, by means of analogical reasoning or qiyas.

The Qur'anic verse referred to is: 'O you who believe! Spend of the good things which you have earned and of that which We produce from the earth for you' [al-Baqarah 267]. Sharing the produce of one's land with the poor is obligatory, whether the land is kharajiyyah or 'ushriyyah. The Sunnah referred to is: 'From what the heavens water, a tithe [is due].' This hadith encompasses in its general meaning both the kharaj and the 'ushriyyah land.

As to the analogical reasoning (qiyas), both zakah and kharaj are a kind of obligation (haqq), each based on a different reason, and one does not nullify the other...

[41] Narrated by AbuHurayrah

Al-Muwatta 6.1.2

The Messenger of Allah, may Allah bless him and grant him peace, used to exhort people to watch the night in prayer in Ramadan but never ordered it definitely.

He used to say, 'Whoever watches the night in prayer in Ramadan with trust and expectancy, will be forgiven all his previous wrong actions.'

Ibn Shihab said, 'The Messenger of Allah, may Allah bless him and grant him peace, died while that was still the custom, and it continued to be the custom in the Khalifate (period) of AbuBakr and at the beginning of the Khalifate (period) of Umar ibn al-Khattab.'

Fiqh-us-Sunnah

Fiqh 3.49a

The Location of Rikaz

Rikaz might be found in the following places:

...In a barren land, a land of unknown ownership, or in an intractable road, or ruined village. In that case, khums has to be paid, and the one who found it may keep the other four-fifths for himself. This is based on a report from an-Nasa'i on the authority of 'Amr ibn Shu'aib from his father and from his grandfather, who said that when the Messenger of Allah, upon whom be peace, was asked about a lucky find (al-luqatah), he responded: 'For anything along a tractable road or in an inhabited village, its ownership is determined by established custom...'

Al-Majalla (The Ottoman Courts Manual (Hanafi)) 36

Custom is an arbitrator; that is to say, custom, whether public or private, may be invoked to justify the giving of judgment.

Al-Majalla (The Ottoman Courts Manual (Hanafi)) 41
Effect is only given to custom where it is of regular occurrence or when universally prevailing.

Fiqh-us-Sunnah
Fiqh 2.98
Smiling or Laughing During the Salah

Ibn al-Mundhir records that there is a consensus of opinion that laughing (during the salah) invalidates the prayer. An-Nawawi says: 'This is the case if one laughs aloud, and produces sound. Most of the scholars say that there is no problem with smiling. If one is overcome by laughter and cannot control it, his salah will not become invalid if it is of minor nature. If it is a hearty laughter, it will invalidate the salah. Custom would determine whether it is a major or a minor laughter.'

[42] Fiqh-us-Sunnah
Fiqh 1.146
Sunnah Acts of Prayer, Reciting Behind an Imam

One's prayer is not accepted unless al-Fatihah is recited in every rak'ah. But, one who is praying behind an imam is to keep quiet while the imam is reciting aloud, as Allah says in the Qur'an, 'When the Qur'an is recited, listen and remain silent that you may attain mercy.' The Prophet, upon whom be peace, also said, 'When the imam makes the takbir, (you too) make the takbir. When he recites, be silent.' (Related by Muslim.) One hadith states, 'Whoever is praying behind an imam, the imam's recital is his recital. If the imam reads quietly, then all of the followers must also make their own recital. If one cannot hear the imam's recital, he must make his own recital.'

Commenting on this subject, Abu Bakr al-'Arabi says: What we see as the strongest opinion is that one must recite during the prayers in which the imam's recital is subdued. But, during the prayers where the imam recites aloud, one may not recite. This is based on the following three proofs:

1. this was the practice of the people of Madinah,

2. it is the ruling of the Qur'an, as Allah says, 'When the Qur'an is recited, listen and remain silent,' and

3. this is supported by two hadith: one from 'Imran ibn Hussain states, 'I know that some of you compete with me (in my recital...),' and 'If it is recited, you should listen.' The preceding hadith is the weightiest position according to the

following argument: If one cannot recite along with the imam, then when can one recite? If one says, 'While he is silent,' then we say, 'It is not necessary for him to be silent,' so how can something that is obligatory be dependent on something that is not obligatory? But we have found a way in which the person may 'recite' with the imam, and that is the recitation of the heart and of concentrating on what is being recited. This is the method of the Qur'an and the hadith, and the way the worship has been preserved. It is also part of following the Sunnah. One is to act by what is the strongest (opinion). This was also the choice of az-Zuhri and Ibn al-Mubarak, and it is a statement from Malik, Ahmad and Ishaq. Ibn Taimiyyah supports it and shows it to be the strongest opinion.

[43] Al-Risala (Maliki Manual)

32.11 Effects of Change of Religion

If either of a couple apostatises, the marriage shall be judicially dissolved by a divorce. But according to the view of other jurists, such a marriage is to be dissolved without a divorce. If a non-Muslim couple embrace Islam, their marriage shall continue to subsist. But if only one of them accepts Islam, such a marriage is to be dissolved without a divorce. Supposing it is the wife who embraces Islam and the marriage is subsequently so dissolved and she starts to observe the iddah, then if the husband follows suit during the iddah, he will have claim on her.

If the husband accepts Islam, while the woman is either a Jewess or a Christian, he has the permission to retain her. But if the husband accepts Islam, while the woman was a Magian and she also immediately accepts Islam after him, they can then continue as husband and wife; but if she does not accept Islam immediately then they are separated.

When a polytheist accepts Islam at a time when he is married to more than four wives, he must choose four out of them and separate from the rest of them.

[44] Al-Majalla (The Ottoman Courts Manual (Hanafi)) 46

When Prohibition and Necessity Conflict, Preference is Given to the Prohibition Consequently, a person may not sell to another a thing which he has given to his creditor as security for debt.

Fiqh-us-Sunnah

Fiqh 3:76-a

Zakat: Distribution: (2/4) Who is to Distribute Zakat

The Messenger of Allah used to send his authorised agents to collect zakat. He would then distribute it among the deserving people. AbuBakr and Umar did the same. There is no difference between unhidden wealth (i.e. plants, fruit, cattle and minerals) and hidden wealth (i.e. trade goods, gold, silver and treasure).

When Uthman became Caliph, he followed this practice for a while. Later on, when he saw that the hidden wealth was tremendous and that pursuing it embarrassed the community and while checking it harmed its owners, he left the payment of zakat on such property to the individual's discretion.

Jurists agree that the owners themselves should assume the distribution of zakat, especially when it is for hidden wealth.

As-Sa'ib ibn Yazid reported: 'I once heard the Messenger of Allah, upon whom be peace, say: "This is the month of your zakat. If any one of you still owes a debt, let him pay it off so that your properties become free from debts. Then, you can pay the zakat on them."'

(H1: Bayhaqi reports it with a sahih chain.)

Nawawi says that some scholars agree with this practice.

Whether it is Preferable for Owners to Distribute the Zakat Due on Their Hidden Wealth, or to Let the Leader Distribute it

The preferred choice among the Shafi'i scholars is that zakat be paid to the government, especially when it is a just government.

According to the Hanbali scholars, it is preferable that the zakat payer distribute it himself, even though it is permissible to give it to the ruler.

Malik and the Hanafi scholars however hold that if the wealth is unhidden, the Muslim leader and his agents have the authority to ask for and take their zakat.

The opinion of the Shafi'i and Hanbali scholars concerning unhidden wealth is similar to that on hidden wealth.

[45] Fiqh-us-Sunnah

Fiqh 5.110

The Best Animals for Sacrifice

There is consensus among scholars that a sacrifice must be of one of the animals, and that the best of these are, camels, then cows, then sheep and so on, for a camel is more beneficial for the poor because of its great size (more can benefit from its meat), and similarly a cow is more useful than a sheep.

There is disagreement, however, as to what is best for an individual to offer in sacrifice, a camel or a cow sharing one seventh of their price, or a sheep. Apparently the preference in this regard is to what is more useful and beneficial for the poor and the needy.

[46] Al-Majalla (The Ottoman Courts Manual (Hanafi)) 58

The exercise of control over subjects is dependent upon the public welfare.

[47] Fiqh-us-Sunnah

Fiqh 3.71a

The Preference of the Majority Opinion Over That of Ash-Shaf'i

The author of ar-Rawdah an-Nadiyyah says: 'Distributing all of the zakah to one group is more benefiting to the realization of the word of Allah.'

There is not a single case in the entire corpus of hadith literature which could be used to make the distribution of zakah to all groups of people obligatory...In this case, any transfer of the share of one group to another, even if the group concerned was for some reason non-existent, will not be permissible. Such an approach will be contrary to the consensus of Muslim scholars. If we accept that, then the deciding factor for the sadaqah's distribution is the leader's wish rather than, and not the specific categories of, eligible people. Thus, there is no evidence that makes division obligatory, and it is consequently permissible to give some sadaqah to those eligible people and some to other groups. Indeed, when the leader collects all the sadaqat from his people and all eight categories are eligible to receive them, each group has the right to claim its share. However, he does not have to divide the collected sadaqat among them equally or distribute it without any distinction, for he can give any amount to any group or groups that he wants to, or he can give some without giving the rest if he thinks it is in the interest of Islam and its people. For example, if the sadaqah was collected and then a jihad was announced, meaning that it would become necessary to defend the territory of Islam against the unbelievers, the leader can give some or all of it to the deserving warriors. This also applies to other concerns if the interest of Islam necessitates it.

[48] Tamimi, Azzam, *Rachid Ghannouchi: A Democrat within Islamism* (Oxford and New York: Oxford University Press, 2001), p. 184.

[49] Al-Ghurabaa, 'Al Masaalih Al Shirkiyyah: The juristic limits of benefit and interests in Islam'; http://www.al-ghurabaa.co.uk/Deen/tawhid1/masaalihshirki.htm.

[50] *Ibid.*

[51] Guillaume, *Islam*, p. 103.

[52] Cole, Juan, *Sacred Space and Holy War: The Politics, Culture and History of Shi'ite Islam* (London and New York: I. B. Tauris, 2002), p. 194.

[53] *Ibid.*, p. 195.

[54] *Ibid.*, pp. 195–196.

[55] Mutahhari, Murtada, *Jurisprudence and Its Principles,* trans. Salman Tawhidi, ed. Laleh Bakhtiar; http://www.al-islam.org/jurisprudence/title.htm.

[56] Guillaume, *Islam*, p. 103.

[57] Al-Muzaffar, Muhammad Rida, *The Faith of Shi'a Islam*; http://home.swipnet.se/islam/shia-faith.htm.

[58] Mutahhari, *Jurisprudence and Its Principles*.

[59] Mutahhari, Murtada, *The Role of Ijtihad in Legislation*, translated from the Persian by Mahliqa Qara'i, Vol. IV, No. 2; http://www.al-shia.com/html/eng/books/al-tawhid/ijtihad-legislation.htm.

[60] Al-Musawi al-Din, '*Abd al-Husayn Sharaf, The Right Path*, trans. Muhammad Amir Haider Khan (Blanco: Zahra, 1986), p. 345.

[61] Al-Risala (Maliki Manual)
32.08 Number and Condition of Wives
Both a freeborn man and a slave have permission in law to marry concurrently a maximum of four freeborn Muslim women or four freeborn women belonging to the People of the Book. Further, a slave has permission to marry concurrently a maximum of four Muslim slave-women.

[62] *Al-Hedaya* Vol. I (Hanafi Manual)
Talak Hoosn
The Talak Hoosn, or laudable divorce, is where a husband repudiates an enjoyed wife by three sentences of divorce, in three Tohrs...

[63] Al-Risala (Maliki Manual)
32.11 Effects of Change of Religion
If either of a couple apostatises, the marriage shall be judicially dissolved by a divorce...If a non-Muslim couple embrace Islam, their marriage shall continue to subsist. But if only one of them accepts Islam, such a marriage is to be dissolved without a divorce...

[64] *Al-Hedaya* Vol. II (Hanafi Manual)
Of the Laws Concerning Apostates
An exposition of the faith is to be laid before an apostate;
When a Muslim apostatises from the faith, an exposition thereof is to be laid before him, in such a manner that if his apostasy should have arisen from any religious doubts or scruples, those may be removed. The reason for laying an exposition of the faith before him is that it is possible some doubts or errors may have arisen in his mind, which may be removed by such exposition; and as there are only two modes of repelling the sin of apostasy, namely, destruction or Islam, and Islam is preferable to destruction, the evil is rather to be removed by means of an exposition of the faith; but yet this exposition of the faith is not incumbent*, (according to what the learned have remarked upon his head,) since a call to the faith has already reached the apostate.

* That is, it is lawful to kill an apostate without making any attempt to recover him from his apostasy.

Al-Risala (Maliki Manual)

37.19 Crimes Against Islam

A freethinker (zindiq) must be put to death and his repentance is rejected. A freethinker is one who conceals his unbelief and pretends to follow Islam. A magician also is to be put to death, and his repentance also is to be rejected. An apostate is also killed unless he repents. He is allowed three days' grace; if he fails to utilise the chance to repent, the execution takes place. This same also applies to women apostates. If a person who is not an apostate admits that prayer is obligatory but will not perform it, then such a person is given an opportunity to recant by the time of the next prayer; if he does not utilise the opportunity to repent and resume worship, he is then executed. If a Muslim refuses to perform the pilgrimage, he should be left alone and God himself shall decide this case. If a Muslim should abandon the performance of prayer because he disputes its being obligatory, then such a person shall be treated as an apostate – he should be given three days within which to repent. If the three days lapse without his repenting, he is then executed.

Whoever abuses the Messenger of God – peace and blessing of God be upon him – is to be executed, and his repentance is not accepted.

If any dhimmi (by 'dhimmi' is meant a non-Muslim subject living in a Muslim country) curses the Prophet – peace be upon him – or abuses him by saying something other than what already makes him an unbeliever, or abuses God Most High by saying something other than what already makes him an unbeliever, he is to be executed unless at that juncture he accepts Islam.

The property of an apostate after his execution is to be shared by the Muslim community.

[65] Al-Risala (Maliki Manual)

12.01 Clothing

The minimum dress which is sufficient for a lady to say prayer in is a thick chemise which covers down to the back of her feet; that is a gown and a thick veil.

Fiqh-us-Sunnah

Fiqh 1:111

Prayer Prerequisites: General: Clothing One's Nakedness (Covering the Awrah; (Un)covering the Head)

...The Awrah of Women

There is no such dispute over what constitutes a woman's awrah. It is stated that her entire body is awrah and must be covered, except her hands and face…

[66] Lapidus, *A History of Islamic Societies*, p. 193.

[67] Philips, *Evolution of Fiqh*, p. 105.

[68] Siddiqui, Dr Kalim, *Generating 'Power' without Politics* (London: Muslim Institute, 1990), p. 3.

[69] Lewis, Philip, *Islamic Britain* (London: I. B. Tauris, 1994), p. 50.

[70] Al-Awa, Muhammad Salim, 'Political pluralism from an Islamic perspective' in Tamimi, Azzam (ed.), *Power-sharing Islam?* (London: Liberty for Muslim World Publications, 1993), p. 74.

[71] Firestone, Reuven, *Jihad: The Origins of Holy War in Islam* (New York and Oxford: Oxford University Press, 1999), p. 16.

[72] *Ibid.*, pp. 16–17.

[73] Al-Banna, Hassan, *Jihad* (London: International Islamic Forum, 1996 edition), p. 34.

[74] *Ibid.*

[75] Firestone, *Jihad*, p. 140n (19).

[76] Imam Ja'far al-Sadiq (a) said: 'The Prophet (s) of God dispatched a contingent of the army (to the battlefront). Upon their (successful) return, he (s) said: "Blessed are those who have performed the minor *jihad* and have yet to perform the major *jihad*." When asked, "What is the major *jihad*?" the Prophet (s) replied: "The *jihad* of the self (struggle against self)."'
[Al-Majlisi, *Bihar al-Anwar*, vol. 19, p. 182, hadith no. 31]

[77] Kohlberg, Etan, 'The development of the Imami Shi'i doctrine of *jihad*', *Zeitschrift der Deutschen Morgenländischen Gesellschaft* (Wiesbaden: AHCI, 1976), p. 66.

[78] McRoy, Anthony, 'Interview with Shagufta Yaqub', *Third Way*, March 2003, p. 20.

[79] Islamic Propagation Centre International (UK), *Jihad in Islam* (Birmingham: IPCI, n.d.), pp. 3–4.

[80] Mawdudi, Abul A'la, *Jihad fi Sabilillah* (Birmingham: UK Islamic Mission, 1997), p. 4.

[81] Al-Banna, *Jihad*, p. 35.

[82] Firestone, Reuven, 'Conceptions of Holy War in Biblical and Qur'anic tradition', *Journal of Religious Ethics*, No. 21.1, Spring 1996, p. 108n.

[83] Mawdudi, *Jihad fi Sabilillah*, p. 4.

[84] Narrated by Abu Wail

Sahih Al-Bukhari 6.41

Hudhaifa said, 'The Verse:

"And spend (of your wealth) in the Cause of Allah and do not throw yourselves in destruction," (2.195) was revealed concerning spending in Allah's Cause (i.e. Jihad).'

85 An-Nabhani, Taqiuddin, *The Islamic State* (London: Al-Khilafah Publications, 1998), p. 144.

86 Nahjul Balagaha 30 (*Peak of Eloquence* – Sayings of Imam Ali).

87 Muslim Public Affairs Committee, 'MPAC challenges executive producer of *Spooks* live on air', 9 June 2003; www.mpacuk.org.

88 Kohlberg, 'The development of the Imami Shi'i doctrine of *jihad*', p. 69.

89 Ramadan, Tariq, *To Be a European Muslim* (Leicester: Islamic Foundation, 1999), p. 123.

90 Tamimi (ed.), *Power-sharing Islam?*, p. 181.

91 Lewis, *Islamic Britain*, p. 51.

92 Ramadan, *To Be a European Muslim*, p. 126.

93 *Ibid.*, p. 127.

94 *Ibid.*, pp. 127–128.

95 Ghannouchi, Rachid, 'The participation of Islamists in a non-Islamic government' in Tamimi (ed.), *Power-sharing Islam?*, p. 60.

96 *Ibid.*

97 Lewis, *Islamic Britain*, p. 51.

98 Ramadan, *To Be a European Muslim*, p. 127.

99 *Ibid.*, p. 127.

100 Khalil, '*Dar Al-Islam* and *Dar Al-Harb*: its definition and significance'; http://bismikaallahuma.org/History/dar_islam-harb.htm.

101 Ramadan, *To Be a European Muslim,* p. 128.

102 McRoy, Anthony, 'There can be no end to Jihad', interview with Omar Bakri Muhammad, *Christianity Today*; http://www.christianitytoday.com/ct/2005/105/22.0.html.

103 Al-Muhajiroun, *Jihad*; http://www.almuhajiroun.com/islamictopics/islamicissues/jihad.html.

104 Mutahhari, Martyr Ayatullah Murtada, *Jurisprudence and Its Principles* (New York: Tahrike Tarsile Qur'an); http://www.al-islam.org/jurisprudence/index.htm.

105 Al-Misri, Ahmad ibn Naqib, *The Reliance of the Traveller*, Manumission (Delhi: Aamna Publishers, 1991, 1994). Book O: Justice Chapter O-9.0: Jihad;

O-9.9: The caliph fights all other peoples until they become Muslim (O: because they are not a people with a Book, nor honored as such, and are not permitted to settle with paying the poll tax (jizya) (n: though according to the Hanafi school, peoples of all other religions, even idol worshippers, are permitted to live under the protection of the Islamic state if they either become Muslim or agree to pay the poll tax, the sole exceptions to which are apostates from Islam and idol worshippers who are Arabs, neither of whom has any choice but becoming Muslim (al-Hidaya sharh Bidaya al-mubtadi' (y-21), 6.48-49)).

[106] Fiqh-us-Sunnah

Fiqh 3.69

Sadaqah for the Cause of Allah

Fee sabil lillah means for the sake of Allah – that is, making use of knowledge and deeds to attain Allah's pleasure. Most scholars understood this phrase as fighting for the cause of Allah. Part of zakah designated for the cause of Allah is given to volunteer fighters, especially those who are not on the payroll of the state, regardless of their financial status.

The hadith of the Messenger of Allah, stated elsewhere, also confirms it: 'Sadaqah is not permitted to the rich except to the following five: the warrior (ghuzi) for the cause of Allah . . . and so on.'

As to the pilgrimage (hajj), it does not fall under the zakah designated for the cause of Allah because it is an obligation for one who can afford it. Commenting on the issue, the authors of al-Manar say: 'Spending of this portion on securing the routes of the pilgrimage and for providing water, food, and health services for the pilgrims is permissible if funds from other sources are not available.'

Included in the share designated 'for the cause of Allah' are those spendings in the interest of the common good that pertain to both religious and secular matters. The foremost is the preparations for war, including buying arms, food supplies for soldiers, means of transportation, and equipment for warriors. However, the supplies for warriors are to be returned to the treasury after the war. This applies especially to unconsumable items such as weapons, horses, and so on. A warrior does not always possess such items, for he uses them in the cause of Allah only when necessary. This is not the case, however, with other recipients of zakah, such as zakah collectors, debtors, people who received money under the expense account 'reconciliation of hearts,' and the wayfarers. They do not have to return the zakah, even if they are no longer entitled to it.

Also included in the expense account 'for the cause of Allah' are projects such as establishing military hospitals, paved and unpaved roads, the extension of military (not commercial) railway lines, and the building of cruisers, warplanes, fortresses, and trenches. An important item in this category could be the preparation of Muslim missionaries and sending them to non-Muslim countries to spread Islam, just as non-Muslim missionaries are now spreading their religions in Islamic countries. Also falling under this heading would be school expenses to prepare adequate courses in religious sciences and in other areas of public interest. Teachers involved in such programmes should be given sadaqah as long as they continue to perform their assigned jobs without resorting to other means of income. Scholars who are rich should not be paid for their work, despite their obvious benefits to the people.

[107] Al-Misri, *The Reliance of the Traveller*, Book O: 'Justice', Chapter O-9.0: Jihad O-9.2, p. 601:

Jihad is personally obligatory upon all those present in the battle lines (A: and to flee is an enormity…) (O: provided one is able to fight. If unable, because of illness or the death of one's mount when not able to fight on foot, or because one no longer has a weapon, then one may leave. One may also leave if the opposing non-Muslim army is more than twice the size of the Muslim force).

[108] Khadduri, Majid, *War and Peace in the Law of Islam* (Lanham: University Press of America, 1981), p. 67.

[109] Surah Al-Anfal 8:65–66

O Prophet! Exhort the believers to fight. If there be of you twenty steadfast they shall overcome two hundred, and if there be of you a hundred steadfast they shall overcome a thousand of those who disbelieve, because they (the disbelievers) are a folk without intelligence.

Now hath Allah lightened your burden, for He knoweth that there is weakness in you. So if there be of you a steadfast hundred they shall overcome two hundred, and if there be of you a thousand (steadfast) they shall overcome two thousand by permission of Allah. Allah is with the steadfast.

Narrated by Ibn Abbas
Sahih Al-Bukhari 6.176

When the Verse: 'If there are twenty steadfast amongst you (Muslims), they will overcome two-hundred (non-Muslims),' was revealed, it became hard on the Muslims when it became compulsory that one Muslim ought not to flee (in war) before ten (non-Muslims). So (Allah) lightened the order by revealing: '(But) now Allah has lightened your (task) for He knows that there is weakness in you. So if there are of you one-hundred steadfast, they will overcome two-hundred (non-Muslims).' (8.66) So when Allah reduced the number of enemies which Muslims should withstand, their patience and perseverance against the enemy decreased as much as their task was lightened for them.

[110] Muslim Parliament of Great Britain, *Kalim Siddiqui: A Life in the Islamic Movement* (London: Open Press, 1996), p. 20.

[111] *Al-Hedaya* Vol. II (Hanafi Manual) 3821

Case of Whoredom Committed Between Infidel Subjects and Aliens

If an alien should come into a Muslim state under a protection, and there commit whoredom with a Zimmeea, or female infidel subject, or if a Zimmee or male infidel subject should so commit whoredom with a female alien, punishment is to be inflicted upon the infidel subject, (according to Haneefa) but not upon the alien. This also is the opinion of Mohammad with respect to an infidel subject, where he is guilty of whoredom with a female alien; but if an alien be guilty of whoredom with a female infidel subject, in this case he holds that there is no punishment for either party. There is also an opinion recorded from Abu Yusuf to this effect; but he afterwards delivered another opinion, that punishment is incurred by all the parties concerned, both the alien, and female infidel subject – and also by the male infidel subject; and the female alien – for he argues that an alien under protection, during the time that he continues in a Muslim territory, subjects himself to all the ordinances of the temporal law, in this same manner as an infidel subject does for life, whence it is that punishment for slander may be inflicted on an alien under protection, and that he may also be put to death in retaliation: contrary to punishment for drinking wine, as in his belief the use of wine is allowable. The argument of Haneefa and Mohammad is that a protected alien does not come into a Muslim state as a resident, but is only brought there occasionally, from some particular motive, such as commerce, and the like, and therefore is not to be considered as one of the inhabitants of a Muslim country; (whence it is that he is at liberty to return into the foreign country, and also that if a Muslim or an infidel subject, were to murder a protected alien, no relations would be exacted of them;) now a protected alien subjects himself to such of the ordinances of the law only as he himself derives an advantage from; and those are all such as respect the rights of individuals; for where he is desirous of obtaining justice for himself from others, he also subjects himself to justice being exacted on him in behalf of others; and retaliation* and punishment for standard are among the rights of individuals, but punishment for whoredom is the right of the law. The argument of Mohammad is that in whoredom the man is the principal, and the woman only the accessory, according to what was before stated; now the prevention of punishment in respect to the principal occasions the prevention of it in respect to the accessory, but the prevention of punishment with respect to the accessory does not occasion the prevention of it with respect to the principal; as in a case, therefore, where a protected alien commits whoredom with a female infidel subject, there is no punishment for the alien, so neither is there any for the infidel subject; but where an infidel subject commits whoredom with a female protected alien, punishment is to be inflicted on the subject, but not upon the alien; and the remission of punishment in respect to the alien does not occasion its remission with respect to the infidel subject, because the woman is only an accessory. – Correspondent to this is the case of a man committing whoredom with a girl who is an infant, or with a woman who is insane, where punishment is inflicted upon the man, but not upon the infant or the lunatic; whereas, if a woman admit a boy or an idiot to commit whoredom with her, neither of the parties is liable to punishment. The argument of Haneefa is that the act of the protected alien is whoredom, because he is equally with Muslims called to the observance of certain commands and prohibitions, on account of the torments and chastisements of a future state, (according to the Mazhab-Saheeh,) although he be not called to the religious observances of the LAW; but the woman's admitting him to commit the fact is the occasion of punishment to her:- contrary to the case of the boy or the idiot, for they are not called, nor under any constraint. A difference similar to this obtains in the case of a man, who being possessed, or under the influence of magic, commits adultery with a woman not under such influence; that is to say, according to Haneefa, punishment is inflicted; but according to Mohammad it is not inflicted on either of the parties.

* This is an apparent contradiction, as it is said above that there is no retaliation for the murder of an alien: it is to be considered, however, that although a Muslim, or an infidel subject, be not liable to retaliation for the murder of an alien, yet the alien would be so for the murder of a Muslim, or an infidel subject.

[112] *Al-Hedaya* Vol. II (Hanafi Manual) 4080

No Decree Can be Passed in a Muslim Court Respecting Transactions Between a Muslim and an Alien (or Between Two Aliens) in a Foreign Country

If a Muslim, having procured a protection, should go into a foreign country, and there purchase goods of an alien upon credit, or dispose of his goods to the alien upon credit, or usurp the property of an alien, or an alien usurp his property, and he afterwards return into the Muslim territory under a protection, in none of these cases is the Qazi to pass any decree against one of those in favour of the other: - not in the first instance, because the validity of a decree of the Qazi rests upon his authority, and here the Qazi was possessed of no authority whatever at the time of the debt being contracted, with respect to either the debtor or the creditor, on account of separation of country; - neither is he possessed of any authority with respect to the protected alien at the time of the decree, as the alien has not undertaken to submit to the Muslim laws with regard to acts done in time past, he undertaking only for the future, that is, from the period of his being admitted to protection : - nor in the second instance, because the property usurped has become the property of the usurper, as the usurper's acquisition of power over what he has usurped is an acquisition of power over neutral property, according to what has been before stated. – If, moreover, both of those persons were aliens, and one of them should act by the other as above described, and they both afterwards come, under a protection, into the Muslim territory, the rule is the same, for the reasons here mentioned: - but if both become Muslims, and then come into the Muslim territory, in this case the Qazi may pass a decree with respect to the debt, because the debt of the one to the other is a lawful debt, as having been voluntarily engaged in; and the authority of the Qazi exists with respect to both at the time of the decree, as they have then both submitted to the laws of Islam, by embracing the faith. – If, however, one of them should have usurped property belonging to the other, in this case the Qazi cannot pass any decree whatever, according to what was before observed, that 'the usurper becomes proprietor of what he has usurped.'

[113] *Al-Hedaya* Vol. II (Hanafi Manual) 4079

A Muslim Residing Under a Protection in a Hostile Country Must Not Molest the Inhabitants

If a Muslim go as a merchant into a hostile country+, it is not lawful for him to molest the inhabitants either in person or property, because he, in his acceptance of a protection, has undertaken to observe this forbearance towards them; any molestation of them afterwards would therefore be a breach of agreement; and a breach of agreement is prohibited. – It is therefore unlawful for him to molest them in person or property, unless where the sovereign of the country breaks the engagement with respect to him, by seizing his property, or throwing him in prison, – or where others do so with the sovereign's knowledge, he not preventing them, – in which case it is lawful for the merchant to molest them in person and property, as here the breach of contract is on their part. It is otherwise in the case of a captive, to whom it is lawful to molest them in person and property, although they should release him of their own accord, because a captive is not under protection. – It is proper, however, to observe that if the merchant break his agreement with the people of the country, and seize any of their property, and bring the same into the Muslim territory, he becomes the proprietor, because his acquisition of power over

143

neutral property is established; – but yet in his possession of it there is an abomination, because the property has been obtained by a breach of treaty, and this is the occasion of abomination with respect to that property; and hence the merchant must be directed to bestow it in alms.

+ Arab. Dar-al-harb: meaning, any foreign country under the government of infidels. The translator generally renders it foreign country.

[114] Al-Banna, *Jihad,* p. 33.

[115] Shirazi, Imam Muhammad, *War, Peace & Non-Violence: An Islamic Perspective* (London: Fountain Books, 2001), pp. 28–29.

[116] Peters, Rudolph, *Jihad in Classical and Modern Islam* (Princeton: Markus Wiener Publishers, 1996), p. 13.

[117] Narrated by As Sab bin Jaththama

Sahih Al-Bukhari 4.256

The Prophet passed by me at a place called Al-Abwa or Waddan, and was asked whether it was permissible to attack the pagan warriors at night with the probability of exposing their women and children to danger. The Prophet replied, 'They (i.e. women and children) are from them (i.e. pagans).'

[118] 'The Islamic Ruling on the Permissibility of Martyrdom Operations'; http://www.geocities.com/jihadfiles/operationallowed.htm.

[119] *Al-Hedaya* Vol. II (Hanafi Manual) 3998

The Use of Missile Weapons is Allowable, Although There Be Muslims Among the Infidels

It is no objection to shooting arrows, or other missiles, against the infidels, that there may chance to be among them a Muslim in the way either of bondage or of traffic; because the shooting of arrows and so forth among the infidels remedies a general evil, in the repulsion thereof from the whole body of Muslims; whereas the slaying of a Muslim slave or trader is only a particular evil; and to repel a general evil a particular evil must be adopted; and also, because it seldom happens that the strongholds of the infidels are destitute of Muslims, since it is most probable that there are Muslims residing in them, either in the way of bondage or of traffic; and hence, if the use of missile weapons were prohibited on account of these Muslims, war would be obstructed.

Al-Hedaya Vol. II (Hanafi Manual) 3999

Or, Although the Infidels Place Muslim Children or Captives Before Them, as Shields, in Fight

If the infidels, in time of battle, should make shields of Muslim children, or of Muslims who are prisoners in their hands, yet there is no occasion, on that account, to refrain from the use of missile weapons, for the reason already mentioned. It is requisite, however, that the Muslims, in using such weapons, aim at the infidels, and not at the children or the Muslim captives; because, as it is impossible, in shooting, to distinguish precisely between them and the infidels, the person who discharges the weapon must make this distinction in intention and design, by aiming at the infidels, and not at the others, since thus much is practicable, and the distinction must be made as far as is practicable. There is also neither fine nor expiation upon the warriors on account of such of their arrows or other missiles as happen to hit the children or the Muslims, because the war is in observance of a divine ordinance, and atonement is not due for any thing which may happen in the fulfilment of a divine ordinance, for otherwise men would neglect the fulfilment of the ordinance from an apprehension of becoming liable to atonement. It is otherwise in the case of a person eating the bread of another when perishing for hunger, as in that instance atonement is due although eating the bread of other people, in such a situation be a divine ordinance*; because a person perishing for hunger will not refrain from eating the provision of another, from the apprehension of atonement, since his life depends upon it; whereas war is attended with trouble, and dangerous to life; whence men would be deterred, by apprehension of atonement, from engaging in it.

*That is to say, is enjoined and authorised in the sacred writings.

[120] Mir, Hamid, interview with bin Laden, 9 November 2001, 'Osama Bin Laden claims he has nukes', *DAWN*; http://www.jihadunspun.net/BinLadensNetwork/interviews/index.cfm.

[121] *Al-Hedaya* Vol. II (Hanafi Manual) 3994

And, If They Refuse the Faith, to Pay Tribute

If they do not accept the call to the faith, they must then be called upon to pay Jizyat, or capitation-tax*; because the prophet directed the commander of his armies so to do; and also, because by submitting to this tax, war is forbidden and terminated, upon the authority of the Koran...If those who are called upon to pay capitation-tax consent to do so, they then become entitled to the same protection, and subject to the same rules as Muslims, because Allah has declared 'Infidels agree to a capitation-tax only in order to render their blood the same as Muslim blood, and their property the same as Muslim property.'

*Tribute from the person, in the same manner as Khiraj is tribute from lands.

Al-Misri, *The Reliance of the Traveller,* Book O: Justice Chapter O-11.0: 'Non-Muslim Subjects of the Islamic State (Ahl Al-Dhimma)', O-11.8, p. 609:

It is obligatory for the caliph (def: o-25) to protect those of them who are in Muslim lands just as he would Muslims, and to seek the release of those of them who are captured.

[122] MCB press release, 'MCB condemns attack on church in Pakistan', 18 March 2002; 'MCB condemns bombings in Istanbul', 21 Nov 2003.

[123] Tamimi, Azzam, 'Anti-Semitism or just Jews behaving badly?'; http://www.ii-pt.com/web/articles/anti.htm.

[124] Al-Risala (Maliki Manual)

Chapter 30: A Chapter on Jihad or Holy War
30.01 How And When Obligatory

…Women and children are not to be killed. Muslims must avoid the killing of monks and learned men except where these fight them. Similarly, if a woman fights she can be killed…

[125] Surah Al-Baqarah 2:191–194

And slay them wherever ye find them, and drive them out of the places whence they drove you out, for persecution is worse than slaughter…Such is the reward of disbelievers.

And fight them until persecution is no more, and religion is for Allah. But if they desist, then let there be no hostility except against wrongdoers.

The forbidden month for the forbidden month, and forbidden things in retaliation. And one who attacketh you, attack him like manner as he attacked you. Observe your duty to Allah, and know that Allah is with those who ward off (evil).

Surah Al-Mumtahina 60:8–9

Allah forbiddeth you not those who warred not against you on account of religion and drove you not out from your homes, that ye should show them kindness and deal justly with them. Lo! Allah loveth the just dealers.

Allah forbiddeth you only those who warred against you on account of religion and have driven you out from your homes and helped to drive you out, that ye make friends of them. Whosoever maketh friends of them – (All) such are wrong-doers.

[126] Al-Bouti, M. Sa'id Ramadan, 'The American tragedy: a scholar's opinion', *Q-News,* No. 336, October 2001, p. 16.

[127] Al-Qaradawi, Yusuf, 'Fatwa on 9/11';
http://islamonline.net/fatwa/english/FatwaDisplay.asp?hFatwaID=49756.

[128] McRoy, 'There can be no end to Jihad'.

[129] Mawdudi, Abul A'la, *Human Rights in Islam* (Leicester: Islamic Foundation, 1976, Second Edition 1980), p. 10.

[130] Surah An-Nisa 4:59

O ye who believe! Obey Allah, and obey the Apostle, and those charged with authority among you. If ye differ in anything among yourselves, refer it to God and His Apostle if ye do believe in Allah and the Last Day: that is best and most suitable for final determination.

[131] Siddiqui, Kalim, 'The global Islamic movement: outline of a grand strategy' in *In Pursuit of the Power of Islam* (London: Open Press, 1996), pp. 42–43.

[132] Khomeini, Ayatollah, *Islamic Government*, trans. Hamid Algar (Tehran: The Institute for Compilation and Publication of Imam Khomeini's Works [International Affairs Division]), p. 18.

[133] Al-Alkim, Hassan, 'Islam and democracy: mutually reinforcing or incompatible?' in Tamimi (ed.) *Power-sharing Islam?*, p. 81.

[134] Qutb, Sayyd, *Milestones* (Delhi: Ishaat-e-Islam Trust, 1981 edition, 1996 reprint), p. 104.

[135] Tamimi, 'Introduction' in *Power-sharing Islam?*, pp. 9f.

[136] Hiro, Dilip, *Islamic Fundamentalism* (London: Paladin, Revised Edition 1989), p. 169.

[137] Mawdudi, *Human Rights in Islam,* pp. 9–10.

[138] Siddiqui, Kalim, 'The struggle for the supremacy of Islam – some critical dimensions' in *Issues in the Islamic Movement 1981–82* (London and Toronto: Open Press, 1983), reproduced in *In Pursuit of the Power of Islam*, p. 185.

[139] Muslim Brotherhood, 'Shura and the multiparty system in Islam' in *Three Essays: The Role of Muslim Women in an Islamic Society; Shura and the Multiparty System in Islam; Our Testimony,* (London: International Islamic Forum, 1996; MB essay, March 1994), p. 29.

[140] Surah An-Nisa 4:48

Allah forgiveth not that partners should be set up with Him...to set up partners with God is to devise a sin most heinous indeed.

[141] Mawdudi, Abul A'la, *The Islamic Movement: Dynamics of Values, Power and Change*, ed. Murad, Khurram (Leicester: Islamic Foundation, English version, 1984), p. 86.

[142] Al-Banna, Hasan, *Between Yesterday and Today* (London: International Islamic Forum, 1996), p. 22.

[143] *Ibid.*

[144] *Ibid.*

[145] Ali, Ahtsham, 'Sayyid Qutb', *Trends,* Vol. 7:3, 1977, p. 28.

[146] Haddad, Yvonne Y., 'Sayyid Qutb: ideologue of Islamic revival' in Esposito, J. L. (ed.), *Voices of Resurgent Islam* (New York: OUP, 1983), p. 69.

[147] *Ibid.*

[148] Qutb, *Milestones,* p. 111.

[149] Qutb, Sayyid, *In the Shade of the Qur'an,* Vol. 30 (London: MWH London Publishers, 1979, 1981 reprint), pp. 305–306.

[150] *Ibid.,* pp. 44–45.

[151] Muslim Parliament of Great Britain, *Majlis al-Shura: A Political System of Islam in Britain* (London & Manchester: Muslim Parliament of Great Britain, January 1997), p. 2.

[152] Islamic Society of Britain, *Islamic Awareness Week* Broadsheet (Leicester: Islamic Society of Britain, September 1997), p. 11.

[153] Young Muslims UK, *The Characteristics of the Islamic Movement*; http://www.idiscover.co.uk/ymuknet/ym-info/i-move.htm (my emphasis).

[154] YMUK advert, *Trends,* Vol. 5:2, p. 25.

[155] Mawdudi, *Human Rights in Islam,* p. 10.

[156] Muslim Brotherhood, 'Shura and the multiparty system in Islam', p. 29.

[157] *Ibid.,* p. 29.

[158] Mawdudi, *Human Rights in Islam,* p. 13.

[159] *Ibid.*

[160] Al-Alkim, 'Islam and democracy: mutually reinforcing or incompatible?', p. 81.

[161] *Ibid.*

[162] *Ibid.,* p. 85.

[163] Tamimi, Azzam, 'Political pluralism in modern Arab Islamic thought'; http://www.ii-pt.com/web/papers/pluralism.htm.

[164] Tamimi, *Rachid Ghannouchi,* p. 185.

[165] Mawdudi, Sayyid Abul A'la, *The Islamic State: An Outline of the Fundamental Principles,* trans. Khurshid Ahmad (Birmingham: UK Islamic Mission Dawah Centre, 1994), p. 21.

[166] Mawdudi, *Human Rights in Islam,* p. 13.

[167] Tamimi, Azzam, 'Islam and human rights'; http://www.ii-pt.com/web/papers/islam&h.htm.

[168] *Ibid.*

[169] Burgat, François, *Face to Face with Political Islam* (London: I. B. Tauris, 2003), pp. 88–89.

[170] Mawdudi, *The Islamic State*, p. 24.

[171] *Ibid.*, p. 29.

[172] Muslim Brotherhood, 'Shura and the multiparty system in Islam', pp. 31–32.

[173] Khomeini, *Islamic Government,* p. 18.

[174] Keddie, N. K., *Roots of Revolution* (New Haven: Yale University, 1981), p. 18.

[175] Tamimi, 'Introduction' in *Power-sharing Islam?,* p. 11.

[176] Ghannouchi, Rachid, 'The participation of Islamists in a non-Islamic government', p. 51.

[177] *Ibid.*

[178] Al-Alkim, 'Islam and democracy: mutually reinforcing or incompatible?', p. 82.

[179] Poston, Larry, *Islamic Da'wah in the West: Muslim Missionary Activity and the Dynamics of Conversion to Islam* (New York: Oxford University Press, 1992), p. 82.

[180] Taylor, Jenny, 'An Islamic vision for Britain?'in Newbigin, Lesslie, Sanneh, Lamin, and Taylor, Jenny, *Faith and Power: Christianity and Islam in 'Secular' Britain* (London: SPCK, 1998), p. 109.

[181] Qureshi, Zahoor, 'Building foundations in the West', *Q-News*, No. 251–254, February 1997, p. 21.

[182] Taylor, 'An Islamic vision for Britain?', p. 111.

[183] Geaves, Ron, *Sectarian Influences within Islam in Britain,* Community Religions Project (Leeds: University of Leeds, 1996), p. 204.

[184] *Ibid.*, p. 205.

[185] *Ibid.*

[186] *Tabligh* – 'Preaching', aimed at increasing piety. Often understood as making Muslims truer to the practice of the faith.

[187] Gardner, Katy and Shakur, Abdus, 'I'm Bengali, I'm Asian and I'm living here' in Ballard, Roger (ed.), *Desh Pardesh: The South Asian Presence in Britain* (London: C. Hurst & Co., 1994), p. 162.

[188] *MuslimLife* (London: Young Muslim Organisation, summer 1999), p. 15.

[189] Qureshi, 'Building foundations', p. 21.

[190] *Ibid.*

[191] *Ibid.*

[192] Ramadan, *To Be a European Muslim*, p. 253.

[193] Murad, Khurram, *Islamic Movement in the West: Reflections on Some Issues* (London: Islamic Foundation, 1981), p. 7.

[194] Islamic Society of Britain, *Islam – a Vision for Britain* convention brochure (Leicester: Islamic Society of Britain, 1995), pp. 8–9.

[195] Lewis, *Islamic Britain,* p. 102.

[196] Editorial comment by Khurram Murad in the Introduction to Mawdudi, *The Islamic Movement*, p. 36.

PART THREE

ISLAMIC ORGANISATIONS IN BRITAIN

(A) PARTICIPATIONIST GROUPS

ISLAMIC HUMAN RIGHTS COMMISSION

The diversity of Islamic radicalism and the dangers of seeing it as an unchanging monolith are best illustrated by a study of the Islamic Human Rights Commission (IHRC). The IHRC essentially began life when it split off from the Muslim Parliament of Great Britain (MPGB), which had been founded by Kalim Siddiqui. Siddiqui's death allowed tensions to rise within the MPGB and led to disastrous rifts. One such rift saw the defection of the MPGB's Human Rights Committee with its leader, Massoud Shadjareh, who then founded the IHRC. Shadjareh is a Shi'ite of Iranian origin, and his wife, Arzu Merali, British-born of Gujerati heritage, is Director of Research and is respected in her own right as an effective researcher and spokeswoman on Islamic women's issues.[1] Under Siddiqui, the MPGB adopted an often confrontational approach to the Government: 'Had it not been for the Rushdie affair, it would not have been possible to convince British Muslims that they live in a country whose Government, political system and media are inveterately hostile to Islam and Muslims.'[2] The same was true of its attitude to other Muslim groups: Siddiqui stated that he was not going 'to go cap in hand' to existing organisations that were 'alienated' from him; it was better 'they remain out'.[3] As a result, the Government ignored the body, and Home Office Minister Patten dismissed the venture, expressing the hope that all law-abiding Muslims would reject such 'nonsense'.[4] The isolation of the MPGB was even apparent at what was, arguably, the high point of the movement – the 1993 MPGB Bosnia conference, with 3,000 people in attendance, enjoying speakers from even pro-*Ikhwan* elements around the world; yet UMO, Muslim Aid, Bradford Council of Mosques, UKIM and the Islamic Foundation 'all boycotted the event'.[5] One unnamed Muslim leader explained why – it 'would only have given Dr Kalim Siddiqui precisely the credibility he doesn't deserve'.[6] Moreover, his championing of Islamic Iran was something that many Sunni Muslims, who frequently regard Shi'ism as a theological aberration, could not accept.[7]

The IHRC has moved away from the confrontational nature of the MPGB and has been quite successful in fulfilling its mandate. The group, whilst attracting many Shia, is firmly interdenominational. It also has a good record of collaboration with people of other faiths that share its perspective on human rights, such as the Sikh Human Rights Group or the anti-Zionist Orthodox Jewish group *Neturei Karta*. For example, in June 2005, it staged a conference on the theme 'Towards a New Liberation Theology: Reflections on Palestine', which aimed 'to discuss the role religion plays in the lives of peoples' [*sic*] struggling for justice, looking at other liberation struggles as well as the Palestinian cause.'[8] Speakers included an Evangelical Anglican vicar, an Irish Catholic priest, Orthodox rabbis, an Israeli lecturer, a Greek Orthodox priest, and an American Sunni imam. Unlike the MPGB in its heyday, the IHRC has managed to establish good relations with other Muslim groups, so that the conference was backed by the Friends of Al-Aqsa and the Muslim Association of Britain. It also participated in a 'Muslim Unity' march in April 2005 that included a plethora of Muslim organisations.[9] The IHRC has also, again unlike the MPGB, won recognition from public institutions:

> IHRC was recognised as an international NGO by The Commonwealth back in 1997 and has since received recognition for its work and accreditation as an international NGO from many fora including the International Relations and Security Network and various EU and UN agencies. We were accredited to consultative status with the United Nations Department of Political Affairs in 2002...
>
> Our work is widely used: from the United Nations Special Rapporteur on Religious Freedom, the European Union Monitoring Centre to the Commission for Racial Equality, Amnesty International, International Helsinki Federation and the House of Commons Research Library.[10]

At its foundation, the IHRC described itself as 'an independent organisation, with no affiliation to any other organisation, or to any government. Our team works in areas to do with the rights of Muslims both in the UK and abroad, in accordance with Islamic teaching and doctrine.'[11] The IHRC has produced reports on various international and domestic issues, many of them, like 'War Crimes Watch' (which deals with the Bosnian conflict), continuing campaigns that were initiated with the MPGB. One IHRC aim is to 'look into discrimination cases in Britain, as part of our campaign to make religious discrimination illegal'.[12] In this regard, the IHRC achieved something Siddiqui never managed, when it secured publication of its report on religious discrimination, *Anti-Muslim Discrimination and Hostility in the United Kingdom, 2000*. It was launched by Lord Ahmed at a meeting in the House of Lords that was addressed by Home Office Minister Mike O'Brien. The launch of this report marked an end to the lack of access to the Government that had hindered the MPGB. Notably, the report concerned what was arguably the most immediate problem confronting British Muslims: domestic Islamophobia – something the isolation of the MPGB never allowed it to address in any practical or effective way.[13]

The IHRC has produced reports on *The Oldham Riots* (2001) and the BNP (*Islamophobia – The New Crusade* [2002]). It has also conducted a strong campaign for 'Prisoners of Faith', i.e. Muslim political prisoners around the world, including those at Guantanamo Bay.[14] An intriguing and popular IHRC activity is the 'Annual Islamophobia Awards', a tongue-in-cheek Oscars take-off, where public figures in politics, religion and the media are given 'awards' for their 'contribution' to Islamophobia (the 2004 winner of 'Islamophobe of the Year' was President Bush).[15] However, an interesting aspect of IHRC radicalism is that the group does not restrict criticism of human rights abuses to *Western* governments, such as France on the *hijab* issue, or liberal Muslim states such as Turkey on similar matters; it also condemns 'militant' Islamic regimes, such as Sudan for human rights abuses in Darfur – a fact that makes its work more credible.[16] It comments: 'The situation in Sudan has been a crunch issue for Muslims everywhere. The initial silence from Muslims...evidenced a combination of a lack of knowledge of the situation, a reluctance to take a stance when Muslims are oppressors...'[17] Shadjareh expounded the IHRC view on the relationship between Islam and human rights and democracy in a presentation in 2000:

> Some Muslim groups have said that there is no such thing as human rights in Islam...What we talk about when we talk about rights from an Islamic perspective is Justice, including 'adl (justice), insaaf (fairness), mizaan (balance, proportion), ihsaan (goodness, virtue), karaamah (nobility of spirit, chivalry), murrawah (generosity, magnanimity), and many more such words...
>
> Perhaps the most important element for our meaning of Islamic Human Rights is standing against oppressors

(mustakbirin), whoever they are and wherever they are, even when this means standing witness against ourselves and our own people (Al-Qur'an 4:135). This is the key in our present situation, when Muslims the world over, and numerous non-Muslims too, are confronted with an oppressive and exploitative western civilization, and are ruled by repressive governments who put the interests of that civilisations [*sic*] before the rights and concerns of the people that they rule. In this situation, the responsibilities of Muslims can be seen in an ayah from the Qur'an:

'And what reason have you that you should not fight in the way of Allah and of the weak among the men and the women and the children, (of) those who say: Our Lord! Cause us to go forth from this town, whose people are oppressors, and give us from Thee a guardian and give us from Thee a helper.' 4:75

The whole of shari'ah law deals with the question of implementing justice and mizaan (balance).[18]

It should be noted that, whilst much of what Shadjareh stated is true of Islam in general, Shi'ism places a particular emphasis on justice and on resisting oppressors: 'This emphasis on divine justice has influenced not only the theoretical aspect of Shi'ism, for the Shi'a regard justice as such so fundamental an aspect of Islam that they have often called for its implementation in society.'[19] Surprisingly, there is no reference to Khomeini's theory of the *Vilayet i-Faqih* in IHRC discourse. A paper by Saied Reza Ameli for an IHRC conference criticised not democracy, but its use as a slogan to justify American domination.[20] As a human rights advocacy group, the IHRC does not usually engage in abstract theological/ideological brainstorming, but rather addresses subjects from a *practical* perspective. For example, a study by Ameli and Merali on how British Muslims viewed the Government revealed this:

The Muslim respondents in this survey viewed democratic and parliamentary processes as legitimate vehicles to safeguard individual and community rights. That belief and expectation is not only conducive to social cohesion but a prerequisite to establishing the well-being of the nation state.[21]

The IHRC approvingly reproduced an interview with Sheikh Ibraheem Zakzaky who asserted that 'Islamic law is not meant to be practised under an un-Isamic [*sic*] system.'[22] He warned about the abuse of *Shari'ah* to oppress people: 'But when they find that he establishes himself above the Sharia and use the Sharia to oppress people, they would come to realise that it is not anybody who can implement Sharia. [*sic*]'[23] The IHRC has even supported calls for Iran to improve its treatment of religious minorities:

> The Minorities' Committee of the Organization for Defending Victims of Violence would like to commend the government of the Islamic Republic of Iran for the efforts that have been made through debates in the Islamic Parliament towards the improvement of the situation of the religious minorities of Iran.
>
> However, we...would like to urge and remind the Islamic Republic's authorities and officials that they still have a long road ahead of them and must continue their efforts towards the full realization of the human rights of the religious minority citizens of the country as stated in the Universal Declaration of Human Rights and all other declarations, covenants and treaties that fully recognize the rights to religion.
>
> ...[I]t is naturally and rightfully expected for this group to have equal opportunities and enjoy all the rights and benefits as the rest of the society that they are a part of do.[24]

With regard to *jihad*, the choice of the specific *Qur'anic* verse as a motto reveals that the IHRC views itself as being in a political *jihad*, even if it does not explicitly state this. It condemned 9/11 unreservedly: 'The Islamic Human Rights Commission (IHRC) unequivocally condemns the attacks on innocent civilians in America by as yet unidentified terrorists yesterday 11 September 2001. IHRC gives its condolences to the surviving victims of the attacks, their families and the families of those who have lost their lives or are missing.'[25] However, whilst the IHRC condemns Al-Qaida, in common with other British Muslim groups it draws a distinction between it and what it sees as legitimate resistance movements. Though it does not list these, the fact that one of the speakers at the Palestine conference mentioned above was part of the political wing of Hezbollah indicates who is meant. Its own contribution to the Palestinian struggle has led the IHRC, in collaboration with other Muslim groups, to picket the Zionist

157

Federation's 'Celebration of Israel'.[26] It has also taken part in other pro-Palestinian events, and was active in the Stop the War rallies.

MUSLIM ASSOCIATION OF BRITAIN

One of the most recently established but enormously successful bodies in British Islam is the Muslim Association of Britain (MAB). Founded in 1997, it represents a break from the subcontinent-originated bodies, such as those in the pro-*Jama'at* network, in that it was largely founded by people of Arab ethnicity. Its quick rise to prominence is explained by the personalities involved, and, partly, by its strategy. The chief ideologue of the MAB is the Palestinian-born Azzam Tamimi, an Islamist intellectual. Tamimi runs a London-based Islamic think-tank, the Institute of Islamic Political Thought, which has its own website (www.ii-pt.com) that mainly addresses issues relating to the Middle East, especially Palestine, but also tackles the relationship of Islam to democracy – a subject on which Tamimi is an acknowledged expert. His two principal works – *Power-sharing Islam?*, which he edited, and *Rachid Ghannouchi: A Democrat within Islamism*, a study of the exiled Tunisian Islamist leader (whose daughter is a prominent leader of the MAB youth wing) – both centre on this topic. The other major individual of note is Anas Altikriti, son of an exiled Iraqi politician. At one time President of the group, until he stood down to run as a RESPECT candidate in the 2004 European elections, he remains one of its chief spokesmen. Having been raised in Britain, he speaks unaccented English and normally gives a polished and accessible performance, which is combined with a personable approach that represents his brand of Islam well.

The MAB has experienced two major episodes of controversy. Louise Ellman, Labour/Co-op MP for Liverpool Riverside and a member of the 'Labour Friends of Israel' used the protection of parliamentary privilege to attack the MAB, accusing its leading members of 'anti-Semitism' and terrorist links. She stated in Parliament: '...the House should not adjourn until it has debated the important issue of the role Islamicist [sic] organisations play in inciting racial hatred in the United Kingdom through propagating anti-Semitism under the guise of anti-Zionism...It is time that the spotlight fell on the Muslim Association of Britain, particularly the key figures, such as Azzam Tamimi, Kamal El-Helbawy, Anas Al-Tikriti and Mohammed Sawalha. All of them are connected to the terrorist organisation,

Hamas.'[27] This led to furious denunciations not only by the MAB figures involved, but also by the Muslim Council of Britain, which 'rejected utterly' Ellman's comments:

> MAB...are well-known for their balanced views and admirable work in the Muslim community. They have also been working with mainstream groups on issues of common national concern. We wonder whether perhaps the true reason that the MAB have incurred Mrs Ellman's wrath is the crucial role they have played in drawing public attention to the illegal and quite brutal Israeli occupation of Palestinian lands...[28]

In a letter to the *Guardian*, Altikriti stated:

> For Louise Ellman to use parliamentary privileges to mount an attack on the Muslim Association of Britain is a sign that she would rather use the immunity of parliament than risk making such slanderous remarks in public...Her quotations from Dr Azzam Tamimi are either completely false or taken out of context. The Muslim Association of Britain is not a supporter nor a condoner of terrorism. It has constantly been at the fore of the battle against extremism and terrorism of all kinds, especially that perpetrated by states such as Israel. MAB is transparent about supporting all oppressed people and has never shied from criticising states and individuals who create death and wreak havoc. Among our many supporters and sympathisers are Jews with whom we are proud to be working.[29]

The MAB gave concrete expression to the last clause during the 2005 general election when it supported Mark Krantz, RESPECT candidate for Stretford and Urmston:

> This is the first time that the Muslim Association of Britain (MAB) has backed a Jew as a parliamentary candidate. Anas Altikriti, a national MAB spokesperson, said: 'That Mark Krantz who is a Jew, is standing for Respect, and I, a Muslim, give him my full support, shows that what really matters is showing respect for people here and around the world. What matters is what is in the heart of people, whatever religion they come from.'...It was Mark Krantz's record as a local campaigner

against the war in Iraq and his commitment to the cause of the Palestinians that won their support.[30]

The other major row that engulfed the MAB was the visit by Sheikh Yusuf al-Qaradawi, arguably the most influential Sunni scholar in the world. When he arrived in Britain for a series of meetings the *Sun* newspaper ran the headline: 'The Evil Has Landed'. At the MAB conference Tamimi observed 'the negative publicity that had bedevilled Shaikh Qaradawi's visit to the UK, in a campaign initiated by the Board of Deputies and faithfully executed by politicians such as Michael Howard and Louise Ellman, and media such as the Sun and the Daily Mail'.[31] The controversy largely surrounded his support for Palestinian and Iraqi insurgents, though, as we have seen, he distinguishes their *jihad* from that of Al-Qaida, which he denounces.

Many MAB founders were connected to the *Ikhwan*, but they have contextualised their beliefs and praxis for the UK situation. It is vital to recognise this in order to understand their policy and strategy. In a statement replying to an attack on the group by Anthony Browne in *The Times* of 11 August 2004, the MAB referred to the intellectual pedigree of the group, and specifically its links to the ideology of the Muslim Brotherhood:

> MAB is proud of the diversity its membership profile displays in terms of origins, cultures, traditions, schools of thought, ages, skills, educations and specialties. Amongst its members are those who, back in their original countries, were members of the Muslim Brotherhood, and they were found to be of a level of awareness, understanding, skill and ability, that would serve MAB and what it aims for. One of these founding members, and not 'the founder' as Browne claims, is Dr. Kamal Al-Helbawi...He was elected as the first president of MAB in 1997 for two years in free elections, which Anthony Browne seems to think are not applicable for Muslims![32]

One of the major flaws in Browne's article was the presumption that the MAB simply reproduces the thought of Qutb because of its ideological link to the *Ikhwan*. What Browne failed to note, however, was that Qutb's ideology is not held to be sacred even by the *Ikhwan* in Muslim countries. For example, when we speak of 'Qutbists' in Egypt, there are those who have taken up *jihad* against the regime, whereas the more mainstream Brotherhood eschews this and, as we have seen, speaks of inter-confessional respect and democracy. It might be better to refer to 'revisionist Qutbists' or 'post-Qutbists'. It should also be remembered that Qutb himself revised some of the teachings of al-Banna, so we should not view Qutb's thought in its purity or entirety as the definitive ideology of the movement. Rather, the MAB has a dynamic attitude to ideology that is also governed by its concern to contextualise Islam in the British sphere. The group had this to say about its attitude to Qutb:

> Qutb was one of the most prominent Muslim thinkers and intellects of his time. His writings were diverse and touched on various aspects of life, including art, aesthetics and literature. His commentary on the Holy Quran is amongst the most wide-spread in the entire world and has been translated into dozens of languages. Despite the high stature Qutb occupies in the hearts and minds of hundreds of Millions Muslims world-wide, no one will argue that his statements, stands, views or opinions are a forgone conclusion and cannot be disputed. In Islam, no one enjoys such a status but the Holy Prophet Mohammed. Therefore, many scholars and latter day thinkers and intellects disagreed with Qutb on a variety of issues.[33]

The MAB explained its relationship to the *Ikhwan* thus:

> MAB enjoys good relation with every mainstream Islamic orgnisation [*sic*] in the UK and abroad among them is Muslim Brotherhood which is well respected not only by the common people on the street throughout the Arab and Muslim countries but also by politicians, intellectuals and opinion-makers in most Arab countries. Prominent within their ideology is the urging of dialogue with others, the rejection of terrorism and respecting those whom differ in views or opinions. As any organization that exists, especially for such a considerable amount of time and through such troublesome events, a plurality of opinions and initiatives may exist.
>
> MAB reserves the right to be proud of the humane notions and principles of the Muslim Brotherhood, who has proven to be an inspiration to Muslims, Arab and otherwise for many decades.

We also reserve the right to disagree with or divert from the opinion and line of the Muslim Brotherhood, or any other organization, Muslim or otherwise on any issue at hand.[34]

The MAB also effectively acknowledges an ideological affinity in some respects with *Jama'at* figures such as Mawdudi and Murad, as well as al-Banna and others.[35] In practice, the Islamic radicalism represented by the MAB is a divergence from traditional, folk religion, an activist approach to political involvement, and linked to this, a determination to change UK policy on the Muslim world. If there is one thing that distinguishes the MAB from other groups, it is its emphasis on political activism and interaction with the wider civil society of Britain. The MAB defines its objectives and methodology as follows:

- ...to promote and propagate the principles of positive Muslim interaction with all elements of society to reflect, project and convey the message of Islam in its pure and unblemished form.
- Part of the wider British Islamic movement and a supporter of all other ventures that agree on the proper principles of Da'wa and human collaboration.
- Affirmed the principles of Muslim citizenship and the firm and undeniable roots of Islam and Muslims within British society...

What do we want?
- For British Muslims to act as the first line of defence for Islam and Muslims all over the world.
- For a constructive religious and civilisational dialogue to be initiated between Muslims and elements of modern society for the betterment of all concerned.
- For Muslims to become involved in the making of laws, the shaping of political and social decision-making procedures and the installation of government.[36]

This being the case, we can understand why the MAB interacts not only with other Muslim organisations (for example, it is a member of the MCB) but also with non-Muslim groups. In this it has been so spectacularly successful that, in just a short time and despite initially springing from a minority ethnic group among British Muslims, it has become well-known and influential, punching above its weight of about 1,000 members.[37] Apart from the leadership qualities of its staff, two men in particular are responsible for its rise – Bush and Blair: as well as outraging many Britons from the wider community, the decision to invade Iraq galvanised the British Muslim community. Both these factors are essential in understanding the success of the MAB. Its strategy of forming cross-confessional alliances placed the group in an advantageous position to reap the harvest of disaffected activism. The MAB became an important member of the Stop the War coalition, with Tamimi being one of the major speakers at its rallies, and Altikriti chairing them. This central involvement was the best publicity the organisation could have, since it naturally associated them with the amazingly successful mobilisation of the masses for the anti-war demonstrations. A further development related to this was the emergence of a Muslim–Leftist alliance in the shape of the RESPECT coalition. At first glance this is an unlikely marriage of convenience between Islamists and the traditionally ultra-secularist, even atheist Left. The latter is usually associated with support for abortion and homosexuality, whereas Muslims emphasise traditional family values, and it remains to be seen whether the tactical alliance can be maintained after the dust of the Iraq war has settled. The MAB supported George Galloway's election bid in East London (it should be noted that Galloway opposes abortion), and advised people how to vote in other seats, listing the supported candidates on the following basis:

> MAB wishes to affirm that any sitting MP who voted against the recently proposed Anti-Terror legislation and against war and calls for immediate withdrawal of British troops in Iraq must be supported for re-election, regardless of their party.
>
> Any sitting MP who voted with the anti-terror legislation and voted for and continues to support war in Iraq should not be supported for re-election.[38]

Of course, as with the advice and involvement of other Muslim groups, it is impossible to ascertain what impact this had on the community, but the cumulative effect of public disaffection and the voting guidelines from the MCB and MAB, actually naming candidates who should be supported, probably did contribute to the outcome. It should be understood that this was simultaneously an expression of the MAB's commitment to involvement in 'political and social decision-making procedures and the installation of government', as well as an act of *da'wah*, in that it propagated the Muslim position to the wider community, and, furthermore, was a contextualised act of *jihad*. The group was acting as 'the first line of defence for Islam and Muslims all over the world' – i.e. *defensive jihad*. By mobilising the masses – Muslim and non-Muslim – against the Iraq war, and by translating this into the electoral realm, it acted as peaceful *mujahidin* against the invader. The MAB approvingly quoted the words of Salma Yaqoob about her involvement in the anti-war movement: 'I actually saw it as our jihad really.'[39]

Furthermore, this enabled the MAB to consolidate the political power of the Muslim community, and specifically around its vision. It also provides a point of contact with the current strategy of the *Ikhwan*, as Tamimi illustrates in a study of the Egyptian movement and its 'adoption of the strategy of peaceful and gradual reform of society and state. This trend considers democracy to be compatible with Islam, and accepts the principle of power-sharing.'[40] It should be remembered that Ikhwan ideology has influenced the Egyptian Labour Party, which is on record as supporting the Iraqi insurgency, so the Muslim–Left alliance in this respect is no innovation, but has a precedent in recent Islamist history.[41] A revealing comment comes from a MAB article about RESPECT candidate Salma Yaqoob, concerning her creditable performance 'in Birmingham Sparkbrook and Small Heath, where Labour's incumbent Roger Godsiff, while retaining the seat he has held for some 12 years, saw his majority smashed from over 16 000 to just around 3000 as a result of a 27% swing from Labour to Salma Yaqoob…'[42] The MAB referred to her campaign as a:

> …display of people-power, real democracy in action. Because the most amazing thing about Salma Yaqoob's campaign wasn't the result, it was the manner in which her campaign seemed to usher in a new era in politics for the people of her constituency, a form of politics with greater involvement from the youth and women, in which people felt they could speak and vote out of conscience rather than out of traditional tribal or religious ties. This wasn't just tactical voting, or coming out in support of one of one's own, this was a real movement for change.[43]

Deconstructing this in the light of the writings of Tamimi and indeed the Ikhwan heritage, we can see the emphasis on mobilisation of the masses, on a turning away from traditional patterns, and on democracy. This demonstrates Ghannouchi's thesis that democracy is a vehicle for establishing Islam.

In regard to *jihad*, the MAB as such has not expressed support for particular movements or actions. However, Tamimi has described himself as a 'sympathiser and supporter' of HAMAS.[44] His papers include an examination of the *jihad* of HAMAS, including 'martyrdom operations':

> Deriving justification of armed resistance from Islam, the movement declares in its charter: The day the enemies usurp a Muslim land, Jihad becomes fard-u-'ayn (compulsory) upon every single Muslim...In recent times, Hamas' military wing, the Brigades of Martyr 'Izziddin Al-Qassam, planned and carried out a number of what Hamas calls 'amaliyyat Istish-hadiyah (martyrdom operations). These are usually described in the Western media as suicide operations. These operations, which target civilians, are considered an aberration from Hamas' fundamental position of hitting only military targets. Hamas officials insist that these operations represent an exception necessitated by the Israeli insistence on targeting Palestinian civilians and by Israel's refusal to agree to an understanding prohibiting the killing of civilians on both sides; an understanding comparable to the one reached between Israel and Hezbollah in southern Lebanon.[45]

Similarly, he wrote a laudatory examination of Hezbollah's victory against Israeli occupation, remarking that 'The Israeli humiliating defeat at the hands of Hizbollah has proven beyond doubt that the Hebrew state understands no language but that of force.'[46] As previously noted, support for the anti-Israeli resistance is widespread among British Muslims. However, again like most in the community, Tamimi strongly condemned 'the atrocities committed in America on 11 September', and rebuked those Muslims 'whose hatred for America prevents them from recognizing the savagery and inhumanity of this attack'.[47] To understand this dichotomy, we must think back to who, according to *fiqh*, is considered a legitimate target in *jihad*. Likewise, the MAB, whilst opposing the occupation of Iraq, unreservedly condemned the killing of British hostage Ken Bigley by insurgents.[48]

The MAB, which has both Sunni and Shia members, has been strongly condemned by the Saved Sect as *munaafiqeen* – 'hypocrites', i.e. false Muslims – because of its interactive approach to British society and politics.[49] The difference – indeed the rivalry – between the variant forms of radicalism is best expressed by the way Finsbury Park Mosque, long a hub of Salafi militancy under its imam Abu Hamza, was taken over by supporters of the MAB in 2005.[50] Far from being a monolith, Islamic radicalism in Britain is often not only diverse, but sometimes mutually antagonistic.

MAWDUDIST NETWORK

The Mawdudist network in Britain comprises the following bodies: the UK Islamic Mission (UKIM), Dawatul Islam, Islamic Foundation, Islamic Society of Britain (ISB), Islamic Forum Europe (IFE), East London Mosque, Young Muslims UK and Young Muslims Organisation (YMO). We have already looked in some depth at the influence of Mawdudists on the radicalisation of British Muslims, so this study of their groupings will necessarily be shorter than that of other bodies. Mawdudi saw himself as a *mujaddid*, a reformer or renewer, based on a prophecy that in every century God would send someone to restore the pristine purity of the faith and excise any accretions:[51]

> Narrated by AbuHurayrah
> Abu Dawud 4278
> The Prophet (peace be upon him) said: Allah will raise for this community at the end of every hundred years the one who will renovate its religion for it.

Mawdudi stood out against 'traditional' Islam, and wanted the faith purified.[52] We have seen that Khurram Murad's missiology adapted this to the UK scene. Mawdudi also sought to 'insulate Muslims from Western influences', a major concern of British Muslims during the Rushdie crisis, involving particularly the fear of degenerating into 'brown Sahibs'.[53] Later, he decided to 'infiltrate' the *ulema*, and the process of creating mosques through UKIM and Dawatul Islam continues this strategy in Britain.[54] He placed great emphasis on Islamic education (which involved wide-scale publishing and *da'wah*), and he established an institution (*Daru'l Islam*) to this end. We can see how the Islamic Foundation continues this emphasis, especially since Mawdudi sought 'to train a cadre of men who would be able to operate in the political arena', which reminds us of how the Islamic Foundation spawned YMUK.[55] In a sense, the ISB, IFE and their youth wings perform a role in Britain that is analogous to that of the *Jama'at-i-Islami* in the subcontinent – the political vanguard.[56] Mawdudi believed in Islamic revolution, not in the insurrectionist sense, but rather as a 'gradual and evolutionary process of cultural, social and political reform', occurring through Islamic education/propagation, just as YMUK have declared their commitment to 'gradualism' in the process of Islamisation.[57] The final end, of course, was the Islamic State, which he saw as a 'democratic caliphate', and 'theo-democracy'.[58]

The parent Mawdudist group in Britain is UKIM, founded in 1962 – i.e. almost at the start of the permanent subcontinental Muslim settlement in Britain. It claims 'over 30 centres and 45 branches located across the British Isles'.[59] A major emphasis is placed on *da'wah* to non-Muslims, and it is also sensitive to the image of Islam, offering a free book by Khurram Murad, *Islam and Terrorism*, and Mawdudi's book on *jihad*. The Bangladesh war of independence led to ethnic tensions in the Muslim community, and in 1978 a more specifically Bengali group, Dawatul Islam, was formed. A former Amir, Abdus Salam, explains:

> During the struggle to establish Bangladesh, the Hindu and secular elements found a chance to infiltrate the mainstream Bengali Muslims in the U.K. A general antipathy grew against Islam, while Pakistan was taken as an enemy country...[T]here was mass infiltration of Hindu culture in our community...In any programme, if it was organised by the Mission, then an ordinary Bangladeshi would not like to join as Pakistanis were there...[I]t was decided that a separate organisation to provide Islamic da'wah to the Bangladeshi community would be the right solution.[60]

Its emphasis is indistinguishable from UKIM's, and it boasts the prestigious East London Mosque in Whitechapel, a hub of Islamic leadership. In 2004 a major annexe, visited by Prince Charles, was opened. Another major step forward was the establishment of the Islamic Foundation in 1973, a major intellectual think-tank, educational and publishing institution. It also includes a 'New Muslim Unit' that deals with converts. By means of conferences, the use of prestigious scholars such as Ataullah Siddiqui, and an enormous output of literature with a Mawdudist/Qutbist emphasis, the Foundation has managed to influence the progress of British Islam.

The next link in the chain is YMUK, the brainchild of Murad. YMUK exemplifies the radical attitude of British Muslim youth to 'corrupt tyrants' who rule the modern Muslim world, and most specifically the Saudi regime. In the leaflet *For All Nations, For All Times* YMUK stated: 'Our hearts are being torn out by the oppressors of the ummah. Our limbs are being torn apart by the treachery of King Fahd.' In another leaflet, *The Islamic State of Sudan*, it lauds the Sudanese Islamist regime and attacks the Saudis, associating them with the Zionist enemy: '...both the Israeli and Saudi governments have been shipping arms to the rebel SPLA'. In the leaflet *Muslims Must Help Save Chechenya*, which dealt with the first Chechen independence war from 1994 onwards, YMUK lambasted the failure of Muslim states to come to the assistance of the Chechen Muslim insurgents: 'Chechenya's struggle for independence should be supported by all freedom-loving peoples...The response of the so-called Muslim governments has been the usual big zero.' YMUK unequivocally supports both *jihad* and the restoration of the *khilafah,* observing that the Islamic Movement

> ...deals with the issue of jihaad by either sending mujaahideen or supporting the mujaahideen (according to hadeeth, these two actions are equivalent) in various areas of the world. In fact the Islamic Movement has been the main force behind the jihaad against the kuffaar in Kashmir, Afghanistan, Palestine, Bosnia etc...[and] strives internationally to re-establish the Khilaafah...[61]

The YMO is essentially the equivalent group for Bangladeshis. The two parent groups, the IFE and ISB, bring the call to older Muslims. The IFE was founded in 1988 and is mainly Bengali in leadership. Although it does not refer to specific *jihadi* groups, the fact that it carried a news article about a Hezbollah operation against the Israelis indicates its sympathies.[62] It takes a positive stance on democratic participation as a way of empowering Muslims, as evidenced by the 2005 general election, and it rejected allegations of racism in Oona King's defeat in Bethnal Green and Bow:

> The Islamic Forum Europe (IFE) ran a successful campaign to encourage Muslims to use their vote and participate in the political process, pointing out that Islam expects Muslims to do whatever they can to establish justice and to better society.
>
> IFE strongly opposed the war in Iraq, along with the majority of British people. The election results, particularly in constituencies like Bethnal Green and Bow, show that the

Labour party cannot take the Muslim vote for granted... IFE condemns those politicians and commentators who dismissed the importance of the Iraq issue, and rejects as unfounded the idea that anti-war candidates in Tower Hamlets or anywhere else were exploiting racial tensions.[63]

The ISB, founded in 1990, has played a major role in the indigenisation of Islam in the UK. In 1995 it was the main organiser of the 'Islam – A Vision for Britain' Convention which proposed a way of harmonising Islam with British life. Significantly, the convention brochure quoted from the writings of Rachid Ghannouchi in *Power-sharing Islam?*, which upheld democracy, arguing that Islamists could legitimately participate in a non-Muslim government.[64]

MUSLIM COUNCIL OF BRITAIN

Following a meeting in Birmingham on 30 April 1994 the National Interim Committee on Muslim Unity (NICMU) was formed to address the issues of how to co-ordinate Muslim activities and provide effective representation. The Muslim Council of Britain (MCB), which was the fruit of these discussions, describes the outcome in its *Invitation* document:

> A country-wide process of consultation followed. A Consultation Paper was printed and circulated to Muslim organisations, mosques, Islamic centres and institutions and individuals active in the community...Members of the NICMU working party had meetings with all the major Muslim organisations in the country and with prominent persons.[65]

According to the document, the consultations enjoyed broad support and led to the establishment of the MCB:

> The NICMU Survey has been described as 'broad-based and representative'. It was the first of its kind to poll Muslim opinion across the whole of the United Kingdom...The consultation process provided a clear signal from the community. It showed that the majority of Muslims in Britain felt that there is a need for greater co-ordination and unity...In the light of these findings, NICMU continued the process of consultation and was required to draft a Constitution to give shape to the consensus

that emerged. Many meetings were held in various parts of the country. The Muslim Council of Britain is a practical outcome of this process of consultation...[66]

In its document *Seeking the Common Good*, the MCB justifies its existence in tones almost of alarm: 'Increasingly, coordination and unity is now seen as a question of the very survival of the community.'[67] We should understand this not merely as a propaganda tactic, but also as a consequence of contemporary Islamophobia and the corresponding fears it raised, especially in the light of Bosnia, and in relation to the anxieties aroused by the Rushdie affair. This is confirmed by an obvious reference to *The Satanic Verses* and subsequent crises (presumably the Gulf war and Bosnia):

> ...events like the publication of grossly abusive and sacrilegious material have shown the need and the value of greater coordination within the Muslim community. But issue after issue and crisis after crisis continue to emphasise that Muslims are not at all well-prepared to deal with these issues and crises, much less even to think of long-term needs and objectives.[68]

The Rushdie connection was even more explicit at the inaugural conference of the body in 1997:

> Mr Sacranie outlined the issues they would tackle. The Government's support for the Satanic Verses, which has caused 'deep hurt and offence to Muslims' was one of the examples he enumerated. Other examples Mr Sacranie gave were the refusal of the Government to fund Muslim schools 'in line with opportunities enjoyed by other communities', and rejection of outlawing of religious discrimination.[69]

At a meeting in Bradford on 25 May 1996, the formal decision was taken by representatives of various Muslim groups to form the Muslim Council of Britain. The MCB rejected any idea of a ghettoised existence, insisting that '...Muslims must be concerned with the wider society in which we live'.[70] This immediately identifies the MCB as a participationist grouping. One proposed MCB activity was to be 'effective public campaigning on issues of shared concern, so that there is never any doubt that the million Muslims or more in Britain, can, when necessary, be mobilised'.[71] The MCB was determined to establish a distinct, united *Islamic* identity for Muslims in Britain: 'to create more avenues for Muslims of all cultural backgrounds to associate and interact to remove racial, ethnic and national barriers and develop true Islamic identity and strength on the basis of that identity'.[72]

The influence of UKACIA in the MCB is obvious, not least in the fact that Iqbal Sacranie, UKACIA Joint Convenor, was the first MCB Secretary General.[73] UKACIA was one of the bodies that took part in NICMU.[74] Some of the MCB's phraseology displays the influence of UKACIA,[75] and the latter's agenda is clearly reflected in the MCB's programme. For example, UKACIA was impatient with the practice of racial classification. After pointing to the multi-ethnic origins of Britain's Muslim community, and observing that most are now British-born, it wrote '...British Muslims do not perceive themselves to be an ethnic or racially-categorised community.'[76] This point received further emphasis in a statement by the group on the inclusion in the 2001 census of the question of religious affiliation. This was seen as important to the Muslim community, whereas 'The question on ethnicity in the 1991 Census is increasingly irrelevant [to] Muslims in Britain as our identity is linked to our faith rather than ethnic origin.'[77] Lobbying the Government for a question on religious affiliation in the census was a major MCB concern, and even its terminology echoes UKACIA: 'British Muslims, particularly British-born Muslims, identify themselves on the basis of faith rather than ethnicity or national origin.'[78] We have previously seen how the MCB has issued statements on international issues, often very impassioned in tone. This is a recognition that the affairs of the *Ummah* impact on the lives of British Muslims. The view that British Muslims belong to the *Ummah* is demonstrated by this statement from UKACIA:

> ... Britain's foreign policy, especially in relation to the Muslim world and even Islamic issues seems still to be informed by the advice of its orientalists and its old-school experts...In Bosnia, Cyprus, Palestine and Kashmir and Sudan and Algeria to name only a few, British policy lacks transparency and credibility.[79]

The influence of UKACIA brings us back to one of the issues in the Rushdie crisis – the power struggle between the different factions in British Islam. UKACIA's formation was a major step forward for Mawdudist elements in this regard, and the NICMU project was a vital event in bringing Muwdudists to the leading position within British

Islam. One of the most revealing comments resulting from the study was the reference to existing Muslim representative organisations. According to the MCB, there were three options before NICMU:

> 1. A Do-Nothing Option; 2. Adapt an existing national body option and 3. Inaugurate a new national body option. The do-nothing option was obviously discarded. The second option was examined in detail but proved to be unacceptable. The majority felt that a new national representative body should be inaugurated.[80]

It is the second option that is important in this regard. Although not explicitly stated, it is not unreasonable to infer that the 'existing national bodies' in question were UMO and the MPGB. The MCB was able to avoid the weakness UMO demonstrated during the Rushdie crisis, thanks to its superior intellectual resources, manifested especially in the Islamic Foundation, as well as its activist youth constituency in the form of YMUK and YMO. It was also able to overcome the inadequacies of the MPGB, which lacked firm local bases and open channels to the Government. Sacranie described the MCB as a means through which to 'deal directly with the government' on 'religious discrimination'.[81] The fact that the doors are open to the MCB has raised the prospect of some progress being made in this area, and the proposed Religious Incitement Bill is an indication of this. Furthermore, through the mosque network of UKIM and Da'watul Islam, the MCB already possessed a local mosque base, which has been augmented as other bodies, including Shia, have joined.

Q-News noted that pro-*Jama'at* elements dominate the MCB: 'A closer look at the CWC [Central Working Committee] shows that the majority belong to or have sympathies with a UK organisation which is a side-kick of the Jamat-e-Islami in Pakistan.'[82] Certainly, a considerable number of organisations affiliated to the body are *Jama'at*-related, such as UKIM, Da'watul Islam, the Islamic Foundation, IFE, YMO, YMUK and ISB. The UKACIA connection was explicitly revealed in a dispassionate *Muslim News* article:

> In April 1994, UK Action Committee on Islamic Affairs set up a committee called National Interim Committee on Muslim Unity (NICMU). This was in response to the demand by Michael Howard, the then Home Secretary, in March 1994, to form a

representative body which he would then support and recognise...In May, 1996, at the meeting of NICMU in Bradford, it was felt by those present that they had sufficient mandate to proceed to form a national body, which was named the Muslim Council of Britain.[83]

In the light of this, we might infer that the creation of the MCB was something of a 'palace coup' in British Islam by Mawdudists. However, it would be unfair to view the MCB as *wholly* Mawdudist; the diversity of its affiliates precludes its being depicted as a pro-*Jama'at* front. Although not every mosque is affiliated to the MCB, the fact that it is effectively recognised as the principal representative of British Muslims by both the Government and the secular media (which rarely, if ever, mention UMO) suggests that it has set the course for the development of the Muslim community in Britain, as it is increasingly the port of call for Muslims concerned about specific issues, both individual and communal. Moreover, given the pro-*Jama'at/Ikhwan* ascendancy in the MCB, the character of British Islam is likely to reflect, albeit in a contextualised way, the thought of radical Islamist ideologues such as Mawdudi, Qutb and al-Banna.

Hence, British Islam is likely to be more *ideological* in nature than the traditionalist/ritualist South Asian variety brought over by the first migrants. Moreover, the crucial role of Khurram Murad in the development of Mawdudist ideology at the Islamic Foundation, and of institutions such as the YMUK, and indeed his vision of a Muslim Federation like the MCB itself, also implies that Islam in Britain is likely to develop according to his strategy. That is, not only will it purge South Asian/Arab cultural elements that cannot be supported by what Mawdudists/Qutbists see as 'true Islam', but it will deliberately indigenise and contextualise its message and presentation according to British cultural norms. This will lead to the emergence of a specific 'British Islam' and a Muslim community whose culture owes more to London than to Islamabad or Sana'a.

One problem the MCB faces is that it must tread a fine line between being too close to the Government on the one hand, and too receptive to radical voices in its community on the other. The MCB cannot afford to ignore grass-roots feeling, and at times this can lead to confrontation with the Government, especially on international issues. It is significant that, almost immediately after its foundation, it departed from the stance UKACIA took on overseas concerns (other than on Bosnia), and began to confront the Government on issues like Iraq and the US bombings of Sudan and Afghanistan. The MCB has formed an 'International Affairs Committee' to address overseas issues. In the light of the Chechen war and purported human rights abuses by Russian troops, it strongly condemned Blair's reception of Russian President Vladimir Putin in April 2000, and even announced that it was joining a demonstration against the visit.[84] On 10 September 1999, Sacranie wrote to the Foreign Secretary, urging that the FCO 'should marshal its diplomatic strengths, and through the EU particularly, ensure that the status of Jerusalem is not altered. The British Government should further ensure that no country should relocate its embassy to Jerusalem. It should also dissuade the US from doing so out of unprincipled opportunism.'[85] These developments serve to demonstrate how far the impact of the three major crises that British Muslims had faced – Rushdie, the Gulf war and Bosnia – had radicalised the community.

Essential to the MCB's credibility is official recognition of its role as the primary representative of British Muslims: since the body enjoys access to the Government, it is thus able to raise issues of concern.[86] Perhaps the most obvious indication of this role is that, when the Government was making arrangements with the Association of British Hujjaj (pilgrims to Mecca) for a temporary consulate in the Holy City, it suddenly decided to alter the composition of the delegation handling consular representation 'to allow MCB general secretary Iqbal Sacranie to be joint head', rather than just have it led by Lord Ahmed of Rotherham.[87]

The MCB also requires credibility within the Muslim community – it must not merely be assertive about particular concerns, but must actually remedy them. The very existence of the body asserts that the centre of Muslim self-identity in Britain is faith, rather than race, and this has led, partly as a result of MCB lobbying, to the Government agreeing to include a religious question in the census, reflecting communal self-perception.[88] The Crime and Disorder Bill was amended to include religion as an element in racially motivated crime.[89] The MCB has addressed Islamophobia in the media, for example when it managed to pressure the *Daily Express* into apologising for the headline 'Moslem Plot to Bomb London', and to get the BBC World Service to commit itself to cease coupling the words 'extremist/terrorist' with 'Muslim/Islam'.[90] Success in changing both government domestic and international policy is essential to the MCB's credibility among its constituency. Failure will leave it exposed to the charge that it is ineffectual, and will leave the door open for more confrontational elements – especially among the youth, which leaders such as Lord Ahmed acknowledge is alienated.[91]

Sir Iqbal Sacranie has negotiated the often stormy waters of relations with the British Government, wider UK society and the competing voices in the Muslim community with considerable skill. He combines an intelligent public image, not least on TV, with a personable, friendly manner, and both characteristics have been essential in what, since 9/11, has been one of the most testing periods in the history of British Muslims. He has also led the MCB in establishing good relations with other communities. The MCB expressed very deep condolences over the death of Pope John Paul II (2 April 2005 – 'The Pope's Death is a Loss for All of Us'), and when Yousuf Bahilok was Secretary General, a strong condemnation was issued on 21 October 2001 over 'the slaughter of innocent worshippers at St Dominic's Catholic Church' in Pakistan ('MCB Condemns Killing of Christians in Pakistan'). At times, community relations have been tested, especially over Palestine, which is arguably the central Islamic concern. For example, Sir Sigmund Sternberg from the 'Three Faiths Forum' retracted the Sternberg Interfaith Prize just days before it was due to be presented to Sacranie, after an MCB press release (21 May 2004) decrying Israeli military actions in Gaza as 'ethnic cleansing' and 'creeping genocide', and referring to Ariel Sharon's 'murderous leadership', all of which Sir Sigmund found 'unhelpful'.[92] Sacranie amicably but firmly declined to back down, and as a result there was a general Muslim boycott of the awards ceremony.

Relations with the Government and the Labour Party were severely tested by the Iraq war, as was demonstrated by the MCB press release 'UK Muslims Reject Neo-Conservative/Zionist Plans For Iraq' (11 April 2003), and the MCB was prominent in opposing the conflict, with Sacranie speaking at various anti-war rallies. Whilst the MCB does not usually refer to *jihad*, nor express support for *jihadi* operations, its fierce condemnation of the Israeli assassination of HAMAS leader Dr Abdul Aziz al-Rantisi may indicate support if not for military resistance, then at least for the aims of HAMAS to some degree, which, as we have seen, is the general sentiment among British Muslims. By contrast, the MCB has unconditionally condemned Al-Qaida actions wherever they have occurred. Two MCB officials, Dr Daud Abdullah and Dr Musharraf Hussain, even travelled to Iraq in an unsuccessful attempt to secure the release of British hostage Ken Bigley.

The MCB is committed to democracy in a very practical way, and we have seen how it called on Muslims to vote in 1997, 2001 and 2005. Sacranie argued that electoral participation by Muslims was not only an expedient course, but also a religious obligation, again using both the experience of Joseph and the *Sirah* as a basis and guide:

> The story of the Prophet Yusuf (upon whom be peace) is told in great detail in the Quran...he took charge of the most important office in the pagan Pharaoh's government. He did not wait for the ruler and people to renounce their paganism before acting...We look also to similar examples in the life of the Prophet Muhammad (peace be upon him)...When the Prophet (peace be upon him) arrived in predominantly non-Muslim Yathrib after the hijrah, his first instruction to his Companions was to spread the greetings of peace and attend to the welfare of the people.[93]

MUSLIM PUBLIC AFFAIRS COMMITTEE

The Muslim Public Affairs Committee (MPAC) is one of the most interesting radical groups in Britain, for the simple reason that, unlike the others, no major external ideological influence on its aims and strategy can be discerned. That is, its ideology and tactics are wholly domestic.[94] It has no HQ and is essentially a cyber-group, centring on its website. MPAC explains its origins thus:

> Originally set up as a web-based media monitoring e-group, MPACUK's first mission was to fight the bias in the media and to re-dress the balance...Rather than being a concentrated group of activists, funded by the community, MPACUK aim to give the power to the community. A system of media monitoring, political lobbying and grass-roots community and institutional activism to allow the individual and the community the ability to change their own situation and the situation for Muslims at large.[95] [sentence *sic*]

The very fact that it describes its function as 'lobbying' demonstrates its participationist approach to British society and politics. Its expression of Islamic radicalism is its head-on engagement with British society to empower the Muslim community. It does not describe its aim as the Islamisation of Britain or the restoration of the Caliphate and its extension to Britain, but rather the transformation of what it sees as negative UK domestic policy, and especially foreign policy, notably on Palestine:

> How many times are Muslims made to feel as if Britain has done them a great favour by allowing them to live and work here – when many Muslims in Britain today were born here, and many others have reverted to Islam, either way we are British citizens and we live and work and bring revenue in and pay taxes. Muslims are law-abiding citizens and as such have a right to be heard, a right to be listened to and a right to be taken seriously. It is the aim of MPACUK to change the situation for Muslims in Britain and throughout the rest of the world.[96]

Examples of this lobbying for Palestine have included mass emailing and telephoning of Bradford Chamber of Commerce to persuade it not to do business with Israeli firms, and of Watford FC to dissuade it from leasing its ground to the Israeli soccer squad:

> After hundreds of you emailed and called in, The Bradford Chamber of Commerce has retreated, and will no longer be organising a trade mission or encouraging business with Israel. In short this is the biggest Victory in MPAC's history.[97]

Or again:

> **'After being approached to host Israel's home European Championship matches at Vicarage Road, MPAC launched an offensive to stop them. Today Watford have officially written to the Israeli FA to turn down the request.'(Watford FC)**
>
> MPAC has taken on israel [sic] yet again and won. Only days after MPAC buckled the Bradford Chamber of Commerce, we launched a campaign against Watford FC to stop it from allowing the Israeli Football Team to play in their grounds. Today Watford turned down the Israeli football team...
> **MPAC IS LIVING PROOF LOBBYING WORKS**[98]

Whereas Islamic groups usually start by drawing on some person or event in Muslim history as their example – Muhammad himself, the Righteous Caliphs, the *Muhajirun* in Abyssinia, or Hussein the son of Ali – the model MPAC proposes as a way to alter what it sees as the depressed condition of British Muslims is both contemporary and ironic – 'the Zionist lobby':

> Compare [*sic*] with the Zionist lobby groups, there are over 100 members of the Friends of Israel lobby in the Labour party alone. This gives them a very loud voice simply because they are active, each and everyone is giving and working for the good of their community. If the Muslims could learn from their example we would never have to suffer in silence again.[99]

MPAC is by no means unique in referring to the influence of the pro-Israeli lobby, but it places a greater emphasis on adapting their strategy. The reference to this lobby demonstrates the *practical* and *activist* emphasis of MPAC, as opposed to what could be characterised as abstract theological/ideological justification. This lobby is seen as paradigmatic of what can be accomplished by successful organisation and mobilisation within a minority community in Britain, even if certain aspirations are rejected by members of that community (that is, not all Jews support the views of the pro-Israel lobby, just as not all Muslims identify with MPAC or other groups). Asghar Bukhari, MPAC Chief Executive, told a group of US evangelical students how MPAC had 'ironically...learnt their tactics which they successfully employed in the Brent East by-election from the American-Israel Public affairs Committee [*sic*]...'[100] This involved tactics it has employed subsequently, namely canvassing, leafleting outside mosques and homes, and 'aiming to telephone every Muslim household'.[101] Unlike the MCB, its attitude to the Government is confrontational:

> Tired of the governments [*sic*] attitude of being merely interested in using Muslim groups and individuals to support its policies, rather than taking account of the Muslim voice. In response MPACUK are aiming to politicise the Muslims and encourage them to get to know their Member of Parliament, and to feel confident in raising issues with them – it is after all their job to look after the interests of their constituents.[102]

It can be seen that MPAC also adopts a confrontational approach to certain Muslim leaders. Whereas other Muslim groups might criticise certain leaders on essentially doctrinal grounds, MPAC's approach is directly practical and uncompromising. For example, during the 2005 election, it lambasted Ibrahim Masters, Chairman of the Lancashire Council of Mosques, for supporting Foreign Secretary Jack Straw, Blackburn's MP, despite what MPAC saw as his negative stance on Iraq and Palestine. Masters was quoted as saying:

> ... the contact we have had with Mr Straw has resulted in many improvements for Muslims in Blackburn...We do not want to burn our bridges and ruin the work of 20 years just because of what is happening in Iraq and Palestine.

MPAC saw this as a selfish and indeed treacherous attitude, and were not coy about expressing this:

> Ibrahim Master [sic] Head of the now disgraced Lancashire Council Of Mosques openly states he sold out Palestine for 20 years with the Labour party and a few Mosques...[T]he traitor has no shame and the Lancashire Council of Mosques no honour. He must be sacked...Both Hazrat Abu Bakr and Hazrat Umar ibn Al-Khattab (rtz) Caliphs of Islam, reflected the notion of accountability in their inaugural addresses when they said to their community, 'If I follow the right path, follow me. If I deviate from the right path, correct me so that we are not led astray.'[103]

Their description of Masters as a 'traitor' rather than 'apostate' is significant, evidencing the cultural Britishness of the group. However, their Britishness does not mean an abandonment of Islam; their reference to the Righteous Caliphs demonstrates that their criticism of this official, whom they regard as deviant, is based on the *Sunnah*. Their attack on him is typical of their criticisms of many mosque leaders for compromise, passivity or irrelevance: '1500 pathetic mosque leaders do nothing to mobilise Muslims...[V]ote in next mosque elections so we can get better men running them!'[104] Moreover, lest anyone imagine that MPAC is simply a militant group intent on attacking traditional Muslim leaders, it should be recognised that it also regularly criticises groups like HT. The main criticism levelled at it is essentially the same as that meted out to traditional leaders – that its passive approach to British society undermines the interests of the Muslim community, both in the UK and abroad. HT's rejectionist approach, if followed by all Muslims, would prevent the community from having any influence on government policy:

> Ask them though what we should do and they will collectively shout 'Establish the Khilafah!'
>
> Well yes agreed, but your [*sic*] in England, what shall we do tommorow?[*sic*] Talk about establishing the Khilafah, and the day after?, 'Talk about establishing the Khilafah' and the day after that? Talk about establishing the Khilafah...for how many years will we be talking...Ask these chaps to help in...anything...remotely practical and your [*sic*] talking to a brick wall...I doubt you could find one true Member who actually has done anything practical to help Palestine, Kashmir in-fact anywhere. And their reason? Too busy trying to create Khilafah by, yes you have guessed it, by talking about it...Voting according to them is HARAM, for some reason despite knowing this will destroy the Muslim influence and give total control of Parliament to the Zionist and Indian Lobby.[105]

Similarly, MPAC has been dismissive of Omar Bakri and his supporters for, in its eyes, damaging the image of Muslims in Britain, for example after a British Muslim performed a 'martyrdom operation' in Palestine:

> As if Muslims were not demonised enough but this fool and the baboons who follow him had scored another goal for the Zionists...A British Muslim killed himself to protect the Palestinians, only to have his life wasted by the damage this maniac and his group have done again to the Palestinian cause...Omar Bakri is one man, when he called for Muslims to attend his lunatic rally in trafalger [*sic*] Square no more then [*sic*] 50 people turned up. It is said he has even less support now then [*sic*] he did then, and yet the Media give him more airplay then [*sic*] any other Muslim. Why?[106]

Likewise, it denounced Abu Hamza for essentially the same reasons:

...Abu Hamza Almasri the Finsbury Park mosque cleric with alleged ties to Al-Qaida bombers will be appearing on Radio *Talk Sport*...Abu Hamza has said nothing to support our position in the west with his rhetoric...he cannot make a logical argument stand on any interview and always utters mindless remarks that make us all look stupid and ignorant.[107]

MPAC is committed to democracy, but its approach is based firstly on practical realities (the need for Muslim community empowerment) and only then does the group present theological justification for participation in a non-Muslim majority democracy. Its own activist defence of participation is suggestive of the character of the group:

> The freedoms and benefits that are enjoyed by other British citizens are being denied to the Muslim population...We are determined to counter this through the process of democracy and by holding those in power accountable to their electorate. They are enjoying the power that they gained partly through the Muslim vote so it is up to Muslims to ensure that their rights are not trampled upon and that they have a greater voice in this country.[108]

As for theological justification, MPAC is on familiar territory in Islamist circles, identifying democracy with *Shura*, and thus indicating its compatibility with Islam:

> Democracy is not a separate or superior ideology from Islam. In fact democracy is very much there in Islam. When we analyse what democracy is We come to the conclusion that it is nothing but the sense of Responsibility and Accountability. The absolute system of governing, which Islam presents totally based [*sic*] upon three golden fundamentals i.e. Consultation, Responsibility and Accountability...The political system of Islam totally depends upon Shooraiat (consultation). The significance of consultation in governance proves by this that a complete surah in Quran is named 'Al-shoorah' (consultation). It is ordered in the 38th verse of this surah that you must consult with each other in dealing the problems and matters of people.

This verse is the base and essence of the Islamic political and governing system...Hazrat Abu Bakar didn't decide many major problems of politics, or cases, without consultation...

[I]n the era of Khulfa-e-Rashideen a scene of peoples' [*sic*] government appears before our eyes, whose leader was a politically elected Ameer. He had limited sovereignty and powers.[109]

With regard to *jihad*, MPAC members regularly describe themselves as *mujahidin*, but their *jihad* is non-violent. They describe it as a *political jihad*, employing the weapons of political activism to overcome the enemies of Islam. In this sense, emails, leaflets and the ballot box replace the Kalashnikov:

MPACUK refer to Media and Political Jihad and would like to provide an explanation of the meaning of Jihad...Need for Muslims to be pro active, not always reactive. This should be in all spheres of life.

Allah put mankind on this earth as His vice-regent. We have a responsibility to take care of our people/environment and bear witness the Truth of Islam...The Holy Prophet Mohamed (Peace Be Upon Him) said: 'The best fighting (Jihad) in the path of Allah is (to speak) a word of justice to an oppressive ruler.' {Sunan of Abu Dawood Hadith 4330, Narrated by Abu Said al-Khudri (RA)}

A Muslim is only permitted to take up arms in two main instances. Firstly, against an oppressive government. Secondly, in self defence.[110]

MPAC does not generally express sympathy for specific guerrilla organisations, but neither does it condemn groups such as HAMAS and Hezbollah, and its strong emphasis on Palestine, together with its recognition of *jihad* as effectively the 'Sixth' Pillar of Islam, leaves little doubt of its attitude. Its attitude to Al-Qaida was displayed when MPAC supported the Islamic Society of Britain's 9/11 commemorative event in 2002 (which rivalled that at Finsbury Park) and condemned the killing of innocents:

The Event will show the Media exactly how we feel about Sept the 11th and will comemorate [*sic*] those who died in Sept the

11th...If no one turns up the column inches will be filled by Omar Bakri and Abu Hamza's event on the same day...[S]how them Muslims care for human life more then [*sic*] they often do, we care for both sides, not just one.[111]

MPAC has made great strides since its foundation. Its website claims millions of hits, and it has been the subject of an objective TV programme, *Operation Muslim Vote*.[112] This showed it in action in the run-up to the 2005 general election, trying to unseat Blackburn's Jack Straw and Rochdale's Lorna Fitzsimmons, both Labour MPs. Straw made two gaffes about MPAC, firstly confusing them with the Saviour Sect, and secondly claiming that they were well funded, which allowed Bukhari to point to his less than abundant possessions. Controversy followed MPAC twice during the campaign. The first was when Bukhari and Project Manager Muddassar Ahmed were physically attacked by supporters of Labour peer Lord Adam Patel in Blackburn, actions caught on film. The second concerned Lorna Fitzsimmons. A local group that MPAC was working with during the election incorrectly identified her as Jewish, which led to accusations of anti-Semitism by certain media and obliged MPAC to issue the following statement:

> It has come to our attention that leaflets written and distributed by the Rochdale Association of Muslims and sponsored by MPACUK describe Lorna Fitzsimons [*sic*] as a 'Jewish Zionist'. We unequivocally apologise to Lorna Fitzsimons for this inaccurate statement and sincerely regret this mistake.
>
> MPACUK will continue to campaign against MPs such as Lorna Fitzsimons on the basis of their policies. Lorna Fitzsimons is an active member of the pro-Israeli lobby group 'Labour Friends of Israel' and has been funded by this group on visits to Israel. Her record as representative of her Rochdale constituency (which includes a large Muslim community) shockingly illustrates her pro-Israeli bias. We believe that she should be held accountable for these policies in this election.[113]

MPAC carried on campaigning against her, and, whilst it cannot be proven that its intervention was decisive, the combination of anti-war backlash, MCB direction to vote for candidates on specific policies, and the on-the-spot canvassing by MPAC may have contributed to her defeat, an outcome triumphantly celebrated by MPAC as a *jihad* victory:

> ...we printed thousands of graphic leaflets of the dead and dying in Iraq and Palestine ensuring Lorna remained linked with the death of innocent people...Lorna was defeated, and MPACUK made British history as the only Muslim group in the country to unseat an MP.
>
> We did it for the children of Palestine, Iraq and Afghanistan, and most of all we did it for our faith in God...
>
> [A]ll the brothers and sisters who helped us in the campaign...truly showed they were Mujahids...[as did] all those who voted against Lorna in this Political Jihad...[114]

Cock-a-hoop about the election results, MPAC made clear that its political *jihad* is centred on Palestine, as well as on domestic anti-Muslim prejudice, and that its campaign would intensify through the elaboration of a strategic plan over the next few years that would, by implication, attack traditional Muslim leaders:

> The message is simple; 'Hold your leaders to account, by getting involved in the political system.' MPACUK are educating Muslims to understand how the election process works and when a politician doesn't represent our views or follows policies counter to our interests, we at the very least vote against them. In other words to vote along policy and not party lines. The other part is to hold self styled community leaders to account for not using their influence to benefit the community they pretend to serve and represent...
>
> So the fight against Zionism and Islamophobia is being lead [*sic*] by young men and women in their early to mid twenties, who spend out of their own pockets and work in their spare time. It seems ironic that Britain's biggest website, the Western world's first Muslim lobby which has managed to remove a pro war, pro Israeli MP is filled with young girls and boys who have taken the mantle of political Jihad for Palestine as their responsibility.[115]

MPAC is perhaps an indication of how the British-born generation of UK Muslims views concepts like democracy and *jihad*, and, more importantly, of how it puts its ideas into practical action within the UK context, in terms of empowering British Muslims and influencing overseas issues. The more British the Muslim community becomes, the more radical will be its expression of Islam.

(B) REJECTIONIST GROUPS

HIZB UT-TAHRIR

Hizb ut-Tahrir (Party of Liberation) was founded in Palestine in 1953 by Sheikh Taqiuddin an-Nabhani, and belongs to the rejectionist brand of Islamic radicalism. Its central thesis is that the depressed political condition of Muslims in the contemporary era is a result of the abolition of the Caliphate in 1924, and thus it believes the way to revive their glory is to reconstitute the *Khilafah*. The essential ideas of Hizb ut-Tahrir (HT) can be found in an-Nabhani's book *The Islamic State*. The book does not uphold the Ottoman ('Uthmani) Caliphate as the ideal state; in fact, it points to several weaknesses in its regime, even at the height of its military power:

> The 'Uthmani *Khilafah* united most of the Muslim lands under its leadership. They initiated *Jihad* throughout Europe and resumed the conveyance of the Message of Islam. However, this outburst in activity was only backed by the solid *Iman* [belief] of the first 'Uthmani *Khulafah* and the military might of the army, and not on a clear understanding of the Islamic concepts and comprehensive implementation of Islam...Consequently, the State soon waned, eventually collapsing until it finally ceased to function.[116]

From this we can see that HT is concerned to effect the institution of a pure *Khilafah* in every respect. An-Nabhani condemns the Ottoman regime for its intellectual stagnation, which involved closing the doors of *ijtihad* and neglecting the Arabic language, and for its failure to understand the 'intellectual and legislative side of Islam' – something that led to perplexity when the Industrial Revolution and democratic ideas transformed Europe.[117] There were two reactions to this transformation: either to denounce Westernisation/modernisation as unbelief, or to try to harmonise it with Islam, which essentially led to the jettisoning of the latter.[118] It is clear that he has in mind secularists such as the Young Turks and Arab nationalists, but he also devotes three chapters to nineteenth-century Western Christian missionary activity in importing such ideas, although he avoids sectarian hostility towards Arab Christians. Mustafa Kemal, who abolished the Caliphate and secularised Turkey, is viewed with vehement antagonism. From this we can infer that all forms of secular ideology are rejected by HT – including democracy.

An-Nabhani insists on the *Khilafah* not primarily as expedient necessity, but as a Scriptural injunction – 'The appointment of the *Khilafah* is an obligation upon the Muslims.'[119] By 'obligation' he means it is *fard* – and thus something which, if not done, has negative eschatological consequences. He continues: 'The obligation of appointing a *Khalifah* has been confirmed by the Qu'ran [*sic*], *Sunnah* and the general consensus of the *Sahabah*.'[120] He cites Surah Al-Maidah 5:48: 'So judge between them by what Allah has revealed, and follow not their vain desires' (which, if we did not realise it already, is seen as evidence by rejectionist Islamists of the fallacy of 'man-made law'); and he also quotes various *ahadith*, including the narration noted by 'Ahmed and al-Tabarani' that they 'extracted from the Hadeeth of Mu'awiyah', which reads 'The Messenger of Allah said, "Whoso dies while there was no *Ba'yah* [*sic* – oath of allegiance to the Caliph] on his neck dies a death of *Jahiliyyah* [Era of (pagan) Ignorance]."'[121] Finally, he observes support from 'the '*Ijma*' of the *Sahabah*', who 'made the appointment of a *Khalifah* their top priority in the wake of the departure of the Messenger of Allah'.[122] The reference to *Jahiliyyah* – the time of 'ignorance' in Arabia before Islam – is a warning that failure to establish the *Khilafah* (or at least to try) gives one the same status as pagans.

The conditions for being a Caliph are that he must be sane, male and Muslim, which immediately excludes women and non-Muslims, and thus places the *Khilafah* at odds with modern democracy.[123] The structure of the state resembles more the US Presidential system than Britain:

> The structure of the Islamic State is based on seven pillars: the *Khalifah*; the Assistants; the Commander of *Jihad*; the Judiciary; the *Wulaa*'; the Administrative System; and the *Majlis Al Ummah*...As for the principles of the ruling system in the Islamic State, there are four:
>
> 1. The sovereignty belongs to the *Shari'ah*.
> 2. The authority belongs to the *Ummah*.
> 3. The appointment of **one** *Khalifah*.
> 4. The *Khalifah* alone reserves the right to adopt the *Shari'ah* rules, i.e. to enact them as laws.[124]

The emphasis on a single Caliph also shows that the party aims at a united pan-Islamic State, rather than several Muslim entities. Unlike SOS and the Saved Sect, HT accepts both Sunni and Shia members. The way to establish the *Khilafah* is through *da'wah*, and Muslims must work to change '...their land where Islam is not implemented, and which is considered as *Dar al-Kufr*, into *Dar al-Islam*'.[125] An-Nabhani regards it as an obligation for the Islamic State to perform offensive *jihad* to conquer and 'liberate' non-Muslim states on the basis of Surahs 8:39, 2:193 and 9:29.[126]

HT has spread to other countries, especially Central Asia, and there have been claims of involvement in the protests that shook Uzbekistan in 2005. Apparently, 'there are more HT prisoners in Central Asia's prisons than those of any other movement...'[127] It is also banned in Germany. It was established in Britain by a Palestinian, Fuad Hussein, and was later headed by Sheikh Omar Bakri Muhammad. HT first leapt to public notice during the Gulf war, when some members visited the Iraqi embassy to urge Saddam to 'announce his acceptance of the office of Caliph'.[128] LeBor quotes Zaki Badawi of the Muslim College as stating that HT 'appeared after the Gulf War, after the delegitimisation of the regimes in the Gulf, which all appeared to be paper regimes, unable to defend themselves'.[129] Taji-Faruki also observes that Omar Bakri 'first shot to notoriety in Britain at the height of the Gulf War, when, in line with the Amman spokesman [of HT], he urged Muslims to attack British, American and French interests worldwide'.[130]

The Gulf war and its many complications helped to provide a springboard for the emergence of HT. Taji-Faruki observes the main attraction of HT: 'The simple message that the answer to all problems lies in the resurrection of the Caliphate is expressed with a relative intellectual sophistication which appeals in particular to young Asian Muslims...'[131] LeBor notes that the party's 'biggest triumph was the *Khilafah* Conference in August 1994, held at Wembley Arena. Thousands of Muslims jammed the aisles to hear the usual rhetoric against radical Islam's *bêtes noires*: Israel, the Middle East regimes – condemned as creations of imperialism...'[132] Taji-Faruki estimates that 'Seven thousand people, mostly young British Muslims, gathered to hear Islamic religious leaders and intellectuals...'[133] The conference called 'for the overthrow of the existing order in the Muslim world and the establishment of a single Islamic Caliphate which would come to the defence of Muslims whenever they faced danger'.[134] Taji-Faruki also notes:

> It has been observed, for example, that the Wembley conference brought together diverse anti-MB [Muslim Brotherhood] elements, all sharing a revolutionary ideology and a willingness to adopt an anti-Saudi stance. In fact Zaki Badawi, a veteran voice of Islamic moderation in Britain, has remarked that Wembley marked 'the final blow to all Saudi efforts to control Muslims in Britain'.[135]

Further notoriety for HT arose in *student* politics. The strong stance of HT on Palestine and homosexuality, its perceived negative attitude towards other communities, and its arguably inflammatory rhetoric have fuelled condemnation from the National Union of Students (NUS), as have allegations of violent threats. For example, a Sikh welfare officer, speaking at the 1995 NUS conference, claimed to have received 'death threats' from HT.[136] A Jewish student, speaking at the 1996 NUS conference, claimed to have failed her end of year exams 'due to consistent harassment by members of HT...'[137] Although the complaint of intimidation is frequently voiced, there does not appear to be any presentation of concrete, objective evidence other than uncorroborated accusations against the group. *Q-News* observed that *Campuswatch*, 'a high profile anti-racism hotline initiated jointly by the Union of Jewish Students and the NUS', was based on 'anecdotal reports, none of which were independently verified'.[138] Most corroborated accusations relating to HT or Al-Muhajiroun campus activity concern 'inflammatory' leaflets, rather than physical intimidation; for example, a leaflet accusing the NUS of being a 'tool of gays and Israelis'.[139] The April 1994 NUS annual conference committed the union to combating HT on campus, accusing the party of being a threat to Jews, Hindus and homosexuals, and furthermore attacked it for being racist.[140]

After the departure of Omar Bakri, HT became less public for a while, but its stance remained unchanged. In 2003 it organised a conference in Birmingham, which attracted 8,000 people, under the title 'British or Muslim?' Reprising its original UK emergence, it came to public attention once again through the rallies protesting at the prospect of the Iraq war, with tables at Hyde Park and local rallies pushing its literature. However, it came in for some derision when, during the anti-war campaign, it distributed stickers and leaflets that urged 'Don't stop the war – except through Islamic politics'. These emphasised the importance of avoiding *kufr* politics, and instead advised UK Muslims to demand of the Qatari and other Muslim embassies that their countries prevent the Americans launching war from their soil. Their next major appearance came with the *jilbab* episode, when 16-year-old Shabina Begum won her High Court case for the right to wear this Islamic attire. Her victory speech was very political, referring to 'a world where Muslim women, from Uzbekistan to Turkey, are feeling the brunt of policies guided by western governments', and declaring that her triumph was a 'victory for all Muslims who wish to preserve their identity and values' in the face of 'an atmosphere that has been created in western societies post-9/11, an atmosphere in which Islam has been made a target for vilification in the name of the "war on terror".'[141] The reference to Uzbekistan might seem unusual, until we consider that her brother was said to be an HT supporter, and HT confirmed that it had advised Shabina.[142] This was perhaps an unusual move for a group that opposes 'man-made law', and it was criticised by the Saviour Sect for this very reason.[143]

The move reflects the more open stance of HT's new leadership under Jalaluddin Patel, a young IT consultant. Patel has called for 'interaction with the wider community which allows us to present our values as well as trying to engage with various public bodies in society without compromising our ideals'.[144] Patel has stated that HT in Britain is led by 'an executive committee...and elections are held to determine the composition of this committee. The elections take place every two years and the entire membership...takes part in these elections.'[145] HT has also become more open to collaboration with other Islamist groups, especially in regard to anti-war rallies or against anti-terror laws.

However, its attitude towards participation in UK elections remains the same: utter rejection. During the 1997 election, Farid Kassem, then a leading HT member, argued on the basis of the *Sirah* against voting, using the argument that Muhammad had rejected the offer of the Quraish to become king, and had thus refused to join a *kufr* political system.[146] Kassem also noted the experience of the *Sahabah* in Abyssinia, who remained aloof from that kingdom's politics, adopting a neutral position during political upheavals in the country (although, in critique of Kassem, it should be questioned how far this was because of theological reasons, rather than the *pragmatic* considerations of a relatively small refugee community). Kassem's conclusion was that, if they voted in British elections 'The Muslims by doing so would be voting for *taghut*.' During the 2005 elections HT ran a campaign against voting, but this was couched in more accessible terms than the terminology used by other rejectionist groups, since it called for activity 'outside the corrupt party political electoral process'.[147] The alternative it put forward was to strengthen the community's Islamic identity and *da'wah* to non-Muslims. It rejected the three main parties as all possessing views that 'erode' Islamic values, because of their policies on the war (noting that the Lib Dems supported the invasion of Afghanistan) and on family values, and it also rejected RESPECT, despite its acknowledged opposition to the occupation of Iraq and Palestine, because of its policies on homosexuality and abortion, and because it did not support the establishment of an Islamic State in Iraq and Palestine.[148] Unusually, it opposed the proposed Religious Incitement Bill, since it held that a resulting Act could be used against Muslims.[149]

In terms of democracy as a concept, HT is unequivocal. Democracy is rejected as an infidel system, and only the *Shari'ah* should be implemented:

> The basis of the democratic system is that people possess the right of sovereignty, choice and implementation...[I]t is a *Kufr* system because it is laid down by man and it is not from the Shari'ah Laws. Therefore to rule by democracy is to rule by disbelief...Therefore to call for it is prohibited and to take from it is prohibited under all conditions. This democratic system is against the laws of Islam, because Muslims are ordered to perform their actions by the laws of Islam...The matter which controls the choice of the Ummah is the Shari'ah because to it alone belongs sovereignty. The Ummah, therefore, does not possess the right of legislation because Allah (swt) is the Legislator...However, Allah (swt) has given the authority i.e. of rule, and the implementation to the Ummah and therefore given it the right to elect or appoint a ruler.[150]

However, HT does allow for plurality of parties, with the proviso that they must all be established by Muslims and be committed to Islam.[151] On these two bases alone, it can be seen why from a *theological*, as opposed to a merely pragmatic basis, it rejects participation in the democratic British system. In regard to *jihad*, it is obligatory [*fard*] on Muslims under pain of sin if neglected:

> Jihad originally is *fard kifayah* (a collective duty to be fulfilled by a sufficient number of Muslims) but when the enemy attacks it becomes an individual duty for all Muslims. The meaning that jihad is *fard kifayah* originally is that we begin fighting the enemy even if he did not start fighting us. If no one from the Muslims begins fighting in any period of time, all Muslims then would have committed a sin by leaving jihad. And therefore jihad is not a defensive war; it is in fact a war to raise the Word of Allah (swt), and it is compulsory originally in order to spread Islam and to carry its message even if the disbelievers did not attack us.[152]

However, it must be understood that HT is not advocating a violent overthrow of the British State; rather, it hopes to convert Britain by *da'wah*, and this is its chosen method for all countries. In fact, it states bluntly: 'No-one is seriously attempting to re-establish the Khilafah in the UK. The role of the Muslims in Britain and other Western countries is to support the work of the Muslims in the Muslim lands.'[153] Essentially, this involves contacting family and friends in the Muslim world, but some have done more: 'Indeed Muslims of Britain have already participated in helping the work for Khilafah in many Muslims countries [*sic*] including Pakistan, Egypt and Syria just to name a few.'[154] It should be noted that in 2002 three British HT members were arrested in Egypt. If *da'wah* ever succeeded in turning Britain into a Muslim-majority country, HT would implement its three-stage plan to bring about the *Khilafah* here:

> **The First:** The stage of culturing; this involves finding and cultivating individuals who are convinced by the thought and method of the party...
>
> **The Second:** The stage of interaction with the *Ummah* (nation) in order to encourage the *Ummah* to work for Islam and to carry the *Da'wah* as if it was its own, and so that it works to establish Islam in life, state and society.
>
> **The Third:** The stage of taking the government and implementing Islam completely and totally, and carrying its message to the world.[155]

This involves seeking *nusrah* ('help'), in the sense of protection, just as the Ansar in Medina provided such to Muhammad.[156] In practice, this is usually sought in the army, with the hope that a military coup will hand over power to the party. However, HT has expressed support for HAMAS in the past, and Patel has stated in relation to Afghanistan and Iraq that 'Islam permits Muslims to resist the occupation of their land...Jihad as a defensive enterprise can be undertaken with or without an Amir and with or without an Islamic State. This is because it is the duty of every Muslim to defend his land and property.'[157] Offensive *jihad*, however, requires the authorisation of the *Khilafah*. This does not apply to 9/11; Patel condemned it as 'not condoned by the Shari'ah'.[158]

In response to the London bombings, the Government suggested the proscription of HT, even though no evidence was presented of a link between the group and the bombers. HT condemned the proposal, seeing it as an expression of the 'government's fanaticism and extremism to curtail legitimate Islamic political debate in Britain, for their own political ends. This is a clear proof of the government's failure to face the political opinions of the party through rational debate and discussion and a desperate attempt to prevent the British public hearing the opinions of the Muslim community...Hizb ut-Tahrir has in explicit terms stated that Islam forbids the killing of innocent civilians and expressed its denunciation of the killing of 58 innocent individuals on 7th July 2005 in London.'[159] The Muslim Council of Britain expressed 'concern and alarm' at the move:

> 'The MCB holds no brief for Hizb ut-Tahrir...However, banning Hizb ut-Tahrir is certainly not the solution and may well prove to be counterproductive. We understand that Hizb ut-Tahrir in the United Kingdom are an avowedly non-violent group. If there are groups that are thought to be contravening our laws, then they ought to be prosecuted in courts of law, not driven underground. Our democratic values need to be upheld, not undermined,' said Sir Iqbal Sacranie, Secretary-General of the Muslim Council of Britain.[160]

Similarly, MAB opposed the ban: 'MAB also [*sic*] extremely concerned by the decision of the Prime Minster to ban Hizb ut-Tahrir. Despite the fact that MAB has constantly had major disagreement with Hizb ut-Tahrir, banning HT will serve no cause and could prove counter productive.'[161] The MAB statement was particularly significant because of the ideological and historical links between MAB and the Muslim Brotherhood, who have had serious differences with HT over democracy, political participation, and jihad.

SUPPORTERS OF SHAREE'AH

Supporters of Sharee'ah (SOS) are a small Salafi group characterised by its uncompromising opposition to the British state, US foreign policy, mainstream Muslim groups such as the MCB, and democracy, and support for *jihadi* movements such as Al-Qaida. Its leading figure is Abu Hamza, born in Egypt, but a UK citizen by virtue of marriage to a Briton. SOS has worked closely with followers of Sheikh Omar Bakri Muhammad, and on the first anniversary of 9/11 formed the 'Islamic Council of Britain' with Al-Muhajiroun, as a conscious Salafi alternative to the MCB. SOS first came to public notice – and notoriety – when a group of young British Muslims in Yemen, allegedly associated with SOS, were arrested for terrorist offences.[162] SOS is believed to have only about two hundred members, but as with most groups, no exact figures have ever been presented: 'We don't keep track or records of members, both for their own security and because we are not a fundraising organisation.'[163] The description of how to become an SOS member implies a very loose, diffuse group linked more by ideology than actual organisation.[164]

Further notoriety attached itself to SOS when anti-terrorist police raided Finsbury Park Mosque in January 2003, though nothing substantial was found. The mosque was then closed for many months. The raid was condemned by SOS and Muslims across the spectrum, who noted that no Catholic church was ever raided during the Northern Ireland Troubles.[165] Abu Hamza himself was arrested on terrorism charges in 2004, and the Home Secretary indicated that he would use changes in the law to strip the Sheikh of UK citizenship. SOS alleges that he has been tortured and abused in Belmarsh Prison.[166]

SOS is explicitly Salafi in its theology, and equally explicit in its support for Al-Qaida (although on more than one occasion Abu Hamza has denied Al-Qaida responsibility for 9/11, blaming instead a Zionist plot; his supporters blamed his arrest in 2004 on an American government conspiracy: 'the US Government wanted Shaykh Abu Hamza silenced').[167] It opposes any integration with the British state and society. Interviewed by *Q-News*, Abu Hamza rejected the idea of being a 'British' Muslim, opposed involvement in the UK political system, and even advocated *hijrah* to Muslim lands, warning Muslims 'Not to melt in this society', instead urging them to preserve their Islamic identity, emigrate to Muslim lands, and avoid voting in British elections:

> Treat this country for what it is: a vampire land which is thoroughly anti-Islam and Muslims. We need to give them an invitation to Islam and this does not mean that just because we are in their land, we do not enjoin what is good and right and forbid what is evil and wrong...
>
> [G]o...wherever religion is still conserved, the honour of our family is preserved...
>
> [I]f you...cancel verses in the Quran, because you are British that has no respect in Islam. Every Muslim who voted in this country has the blood of the Iraqi people on their hands, because they recommended the government who has killed the Muslims.[168]

SOS wants a restored Caliphate based on the *Shari'ah,* as is clear from its call to *mujahidin* to rid the Muslim world of apostate rulers 'to re-establish the Islamic State – al-Khilafah'.[169] Its attitude to democracy is also forthright. In his book *Allah's Governance on Earth,* Abu Hamza derides democracy as *shirk* and *kufr*:

> [F]rom the Islamic point of view, democracy is a great kufr. This is due to the fact that it is a system of insult to Allah Himself with regards to legislation...Democracy is the call of self-divinity loud and clear, in which the rights of one group of people, who have put their idea to vote, have put their ideas and their decisions over the decisions of Allah...[D]emocratic machinery exists in countries such as the United States, who from their very founding arrogantly claimed that, 'There is no god but liberty and justice is her only prophet,' as was mouthed by Thomas Jefferson...[170]

The reference to 'self-divinity' probably reflects the influence of Qutb, who is listed, along with al-Banna, as one of the 'trustworthy scholars' who have influenced SOS.[171] This demonstrates the diversity of Islamic radicalism in the UK; groups such as the ISB and MAB also declare a debt to the *Ikhwan,* but their approach to British society is vastly different. As with the Saved Sect, SOS has refined its attack on democracy by contextualising its translation of *ayat* relating to divine rule. For example, while Pickthall renders Surah Al-An'am 6:57 as 'The decision is for Allah only', Abu Hamza translates it as '*The Judgment/Legislation is only for Allah*'.[172] He comments:

> In this ayah, Allah is ordering all of creation not to associate in His Haakimiyyah [legislative right and power], but Democracy is just that, association in His legislation. These verses make it very clear that Allah doesn't share with any human being in His legislative right...
>
> [I]n Muslim societies, we had the pure light of our workable Shari'a. We did not need to replace it with the garbage of people's thoughts and ideologies.[173]

He dismisses as infidels people who believe in democracy and who enter parliament.[174] However, in regard to those Muslims who see parliamentary elections as a way to effect the implementation of *Shari'ah*, though he recognises their sincerity, he regards their optimism as misplaced, and quotes the case of Algeria, where the Islamists were cheated of their victory.[175] One of the major themes of the book is caution in declaring *takfir* (pronouncing people to be *kaffir*, i.e. excommunication). Rather, the way to bring about a *Shari'ah* State is through *jihad*: 'Allah has told us that the only way He...wants us to change the fitnah is by fighting, not compromising.'[176] He repeats this point, stating that those

> ...aligning themselves with the kuffar the legislators, the rulers caught in the execution and the judges in the courts of these modern days Pharaohs are all to be physically removed. They are to be fought and there is to be no truce made or no agreement signed upon. They are to step down from power or be removed. If they are killed, so be it. Those that are in the target area are not targets, but if they are in the way or used as a shield of kufr, they must know that they are in danger. Their only alternatives are to join the fight, emigrate from that area or at least keep far from the fighting so as not to be used as obstacles by the tyrants who are at war with Allah.[177]

Abu Hamza is restrained when it comes to people who vote: those committed to democracy are apostates, but others may simply be misled or pressured.[178] However, even if their motives are good, they are still being deceived by Satan.[179] This brings us back to *takfir*. Although popularly denounced as an 'extremist' by the media, Abu Hamza has actually written against extreme *takfiri* groups such as *at-Takfir wal Hijrah* ('Excommunication and Emigration') in Egypt

> ...formed by...Shukri Ahmad Mustafa Abdul 'Al...He was arrested and jailed in one of the militant cells of Ikhwan alMuslimin in 1965. When he was in prison, he was inspired by one of Shaikh Sayyid Qutb's books, entitled Ma'arif at-Tariq (Milestones). However, he went overboard with his ideas and he exaggerated some of the meanings of what was in that good book. At the end he was separated from the movement of Sayyid Qutb as well as the followers of Sayyid Qutb...
>
> ...[T]hey also made another rule, which was to stop judging a person as a Muslim initially...He classed those who are not willing to emigrate or step aside from the society as Mushrikun (pagans)...[180]

Abu Hamza rejects this group as *Khawaariji*, referring to an early group of Muslims who were disgruntled that the Fourth Caliph Ali agreed to arbitration in his dispute with Mu'awiya's rebel forces in 658, and who later assassinated Ali. Abu Hamza contrasts his stance with such people: '...Ahl us-Sunna wal Jama'ah does the opposite of the *Khawaariji*, who consider everyone kaafir (even a Muslim) until they (the people being called kuffar) prove otherwise. We consider everyone who says they are Muslim as such until we have reason to believe otherwise.'[181] He has also condemned *Khawaariji* tendencies in the Algerian *Groupe Islamique Armé* (GIA), and notably their statement that:

> ...the Algerian people were kuffar, apostates and hypocrites because they did not support the GIA against the government. Furthermore, they accepted and claimed responsibility for killing, slaughtering, massacring, burning and even kidnapping and raping women of their opponents and doing sabi to the women of their opponents.[182]

It is important to recognise these qualifications to Abu Hamza's militancy, because all too often commentators lump together all radicals, including rejectionist elements. His opposition is directed rather to 'apostate' governments, engaged in the 'deception' of mixing *Shari'ah* with *kufr* governance. He cites the great Mediaeval scholar Ibn Kathir's denunciation of the 'mixed' constitutionalism of the Tatars, who conquered the Muslim world, converted to Islam, but kept some of their own legal traditions, which rendered them *kaffirs* and objects of *jihad*:

> [T]he Tatars also judged from...a collected book from the judgments which were put together from several shari'as, from Judaism, Christianity, Islam and others. And in it (the book of Genghis Khan) are a lot of judgments taken merely from his sheer thinking and desire...[T]hey preferred it to the legislation of the Book of Allah and the Sunna of the Messenger...So whoever does that, then he has become a kaafir, and it is compulsory to fight him, until he returns to the legislation of Allah and His Messenger. So no one other than He...should judge or legislate in any matter, be it small or large.[183]

The *jihad* considered in this respect concerns insurgency against *internal* foes – the 'apostate' Muslim rulers who do not rule by pure *Shari'ah*. However, it is clear that SOS approves of *jihad* against infidel occupiers as well. Among the sheikhs praised in *Allah's Governance* are Abdullah Azzam and 'Usaamah ibn Laadin'.[184] (The SOS website features Azzam's two most famous works, *Defence of Muslim Lands* and *Join the Caravan*, as well as *The Islamic Ruling with Regards to Killing Women and Children in Jihaad*, which justifies such action in certain circumstances, demonstrating their identification with the theology of Azzam and Al-Qaida.) SOS and Al-Muhajiroun sponsored a 9/11 conference on 11 September 2002 called 'A Towering Day in History' (see below), leaving no doubt as to the position of SOS on Al-Qaida. Its attitude to Western forces in Iraq is equally forthright:

> We call upon the Muslims in the Middle East to rise up and repel this invasion by the kufr forces. This can be done by attacking the kufr forces and their national interests throughout the Middle East, and indeed throughout the Muslim World...[T]his crusader war does not even conform to the kuffars own

criterion, thus making the crusader rabble, war criminals. Therefore, any kafir mercenary captured should either be executed for war crimes or preferably be exchanged for the blessed Muslims being held in the Guantanamo Bay concentration camp.[185]

As for UK Muslims being involved in *jihad*, Abu Hamza denies despatching people, but openly inspires them to engage in such actions: 'I don't send particular people...I give a message. I say to Muslims get out of these societies, they are toxic for you, they will damage your religion. Go and support the cause of Muslims with regards to Jihad.'[186] We have seen that there are allegations, denied by Abu Hamza, that, prior to the 2001 Burnley riots, he incited Muslims to attack local 'infidels', though his website and books never recommend this.

The rejectionist attitude to *kufr* society is matched by antipathy towards participationist Muslims. When MAB supporters succeeded in wresting Finsbury Park Mosque from SOS, the latter condemned them as 'sell-out Muslims', and commented that al-Banna 'would have condemned them today for their collaboration with "*Kafir*" authorities'.[187] Comparing the MCB to the heterodox Qadiani (Ahmadiyya) sect (which, it alleges, supported the British Raj in the subcontinent), it denounced the organisation for its 'loyalty to the...British government' and for having Shia members, whom SOS also regards as heretics.[188] It thus equated the MCB both with collaboration with the enemy, and with heresy. It went on to denounce the MCB for supporting democracy and voting in UK elections:

> With the upcoming elections the MCB will be out as usual trying to get Muslims to disobey Allah (SWT) by participating in the '*Democratic (shirk) Process*' through voting. Even though this is a principle of the Muslims of [*Ahl us-Sunnah wal-Jamaah*], that Allah (SWT) is the **ONLY** Legislator and the laws in the Qur'an and Sunnah form the **FINAL SHAREEAH**.[189]

Hence, the MCB was derided as *munafiqeen* (hypocrites), *murtadeen* (apostates) and *collaborators*.[190]

THE SAVED SECT

Since much of the concern with Islamist elements dates from 9/11, it is well worth examining in detail this section of radicals, who openly support Al-Qaida – even though their numbers and influence are limited.[191] Their attitude to democracy and *jihad* is unambiguous. The 'Saved Sect' (until Omar Bakri's exit from Britain, known as the 'Saviour Sect') actually denies that it is a group, but however it defines itself, it is associated with the teaching of Sheikh Omar Bakri Muhammad, the Syrian asylum-seeker who started his political life in Britain as leader of the UK wing of Hizb ut-Tahrir. He then founded Al-Muhajiroun, which he disbanded in 2004. He explained his departure from HT as being

> ...in response to a violation of Islamic rules by the worldwide Amir of Hizb-ut-Tahrir...The real dispute was over the methodology to establish the Khilafah, they did not like me attacking man-made laws here in the UK, and they did not like the fact that I was condemning the policy of John Major and the British government.[192]

However, on 9 August 2005 HT issued a release stating that: 'Omar Bakri Mohammed was not the founder of Hizb ut-Tahrir in Britain. He was expelled from the party in 1996 and has had no relationship whatsoever with the party for over 9 years.'[193]

Since his departure, he has moved towards Salafi ideology, which he defines as following 'the pious predecessors':

> The followers of ASWJ [*Ahl us-Sunnah wal-Jamaah*], in summary, follow only the Quran and the Sunnah in accordance to the understandings of the Companions and the Family of the Prophet Muhammad. We follow the Nahj-ul-Salaf (the path of the pious predecessors). The central theme is Al-Talazum (Correlation), which forbids divorcing Shari'ah from Aqeedah. In the Salafi worldview there can be no separation between Aqeedah and Shariah; they have to be moulded together. Moreover Iman (faith) is no longer an issue of the heart, Iman must automatically entail action. It goes further than this, insofar as there must be a union between Koran and the Sunna as core constituents of Wahy (revelation).[194]

The Sect's website reflects this approach, basing its stance on a *hadith* that emphasises the purity of the first three generations:

'Verily the best among you (to follow) is my generation (the messenger Muhammad (saw) and his Companions (ra)), then those who follow them, and then those who follow them…' (Saheeh Muslim, Book: the Virtues of the Sahaabah, chapter 52 hadeeth #2535)

From this hadeeth we can understand the following – undoubtedly, the best people to understand Islaam, the Qur'aan, Sunnah, and Sharee'ah terminology etc. is the first generation in Islaam – the Messenger Muhammad (saw) and His Companions (ra). The Messenger Muhammad (saw) also praised those who follow this first generation, and then those who follow the followers of the first generation. In other words, the best generations in Islam are:

a) The first generation – the Messenger Muhammad (saw) and His Companions

b) The second generation – those who followed the first generation (known as the *Taabi'een*)

c) The third generation (ended 240–260 AH) – those who followed the Taabi'een (known as *Taabi' ut-Taabi'een*).[195]

However, it must be emphasised that they emphatically dissociate themselves from those traditionally seen as Salafis – the Wahhabi scholars collaborating with what the Sect sees as the '*kaafir*' Saudi regime, which should caution commentators against too easily associating Salafis and Wahhabism with political militancy. 'So-called' Salafis are denounced as those who:

…do not enter any struggle against kufr, shirk or the Tawaagheet. If their own practicing of the deen leads them to any such struggle, they will leave it completely and follow a different deviant Tareeqah (path). However, they are happy and content with just speaking about Allaah's names and attributes all day (without understanding them) and always dig on the mistakes of Muslims. They are hardcore Khawaarij when it comes to the Mujaahideen (they call them kaafir, a'oodhu-billaah), Murji' when it comes to the apostate rulers, and Zindeeq in other areas.

The Jaamiyyah and Madkhaliyyah within the fake
Salafees follow the governmental 'scholars' of Saudi Arabia and
work as freelance informers and government spies.[196]

Sheikh Omar's moves reflect partly a spiritual odyssey towards a
clear-cut Salafi position, but also his determination to display an open
and activist interaction with British society. It is not in his character to
be a shrinking violet; 'jesuitical' is not a description that could ever be
applied to him, and his comments are always a manifestation of his
refusal to compromise. However, his granite opinions are matched by a
genial disposition that makes him a good public figure, especially on
television. He is even generous to opponents in debate who manifest
uncompromising courage, such as the UK-based American Evangelical
Jay Smith: 'I feel very comfortable with Jay – with him, what you see is
what you get. He is no hypocrite, and neither are Salafis. His words and
actions match his heart. He does not pretend by saying soft words
about Islam...Most U.S. evangelicals refuse to debate Muslims, unlike
the courage of Jay who boldly cries "Jesus is Lord!" I am always willing
to meet him.'[197]

As part of its response to the London bombings, the Government
declared its intention of excluding certain imams from Britain. The first
object of the new policy was Omar Bakri. Bakri left Britain for Lebanon
on August 6, apparently to visit his mother, but on 12 August Home
Secretary Charles Clarke took the opportunity to exercise his 'personal
power' to exclude him from returning.[198] The ban was welcomed by
some Muslims. Inayat Bunglawala, media spokesman for the Muslim
Council of Britain, said most Muslims would not miss him: 'Bakri has
been the source of an immense amount of frustration and dismay to
Muslims ever since he came to these shores 20 years ago,' said Mr
Bunglawala. 'With his very provocative language, he has contributed
enormously to the demonisation of British Muslim community.'[199] The
Muslim Weekly exclaimed 'Good riddance, hatemonger.'[200]

On the other hand, Bakri's supporters mourned his departure.
Anjem Choudary 'described the move as "a kangaroo system" of
justice...They say that there's freedom of expression here but he's been
banned because he was a voice of dissent... He has committed no
offence here, he has children and grandchildren here and he has never
encouraged anyone to commit acts of violence. I will miss him

enormously."'[201] The Al-Ghurabaa website issued a release saluting Bakri:

> Remember how you found yourself in a land where you were surrounded and imprisoned by the diseases of democracy, freedom and perversity. By the grace of Allah, the source of all power, might, majesty and glory you struck the neck of the evil with the sharp words of truth, those words, which still stand out clearly today like the sun in the middle of the day, even though the kuffar hate it.
>
> Your da'wah was able to reach throughout the UK and the world. By the permission of Allah you were able to raise two generations of steadfast and uncompromising people of Tawheed and Sunnah. In the time when the people were chanting for 'Halal meat', you gave us the vision of superiority and supremacy for the Deen of Allah, you called for the message of Tawheed, the message that the worship, obedience and sovereignty is for none but Allah, you rose with the message of the truth and you spoke when others were afraid to speak.
>
> Though the disbelievers and hypocrites were many in number and wealth and claimed you were dreaming, to their nightmare and the promise of Allah your call, the call of the prophets and scholars before you for the rule to be for none but Allah is ever closer to reality.
>
> Verily, while his flags are at half mast, Mr Tony Blair cannot spend his days in power without fear from your promise of the black flag of Islam flying high over 10 Downing Street.
>
> Now that Allah has freed you from this prison of Britain, do not feel that those behind you have forgotten the call of Tawheed and piety, rest assured that we will continue to call on the same path as those pious predecessors before us.[202]

The related 'Saved Sect' website issued a message referring to him as 'our beloved teacher and scholar', and spoke of the divine favour that allowed them 'to learn Islam with a scholar of Ahl us-Sunnah wal-Jamaa'ah such as yourself. We thank Him (swt) for guiding us to the Deen of Islam and allowing us to have such a great teacher who sacrificed his life for the sake of Allah and for the Deen of Islam to be supreme and dominant above all other ways of life and ideologies.' It continued:

We were once upon a time on the road to apostasy and Hellfire, following the British way of life and ideology, and looking to make this world our permanent place of residence. Like all other British Muslims, we never used to know the true meaning of the Kalimah [Islamic creed – no God but Allah and Muhammad is His Messenger], and hence we used to urge our parents to become apostates by voting for man-made law and to integrate with this corrupted and non-Islamic society.

In a time when we used to be clean shaven, listen to music, smoke, free-mix in colleges and universities, disrespect our parents, wear designer clothes, swear, betray our covenants, not pray, and knowingly disobey our Lord; you were the only one who was out there challenging the Western (non-Islamic) way of life openly and publicly, not fearing from the blame of the blamers and the propaganda of the media.

You were one of those very few scholars of ḥaq who took time out to learn the language of the people (i.e. English) in order to convey the message of Islam here and to teach the Muslims in this country the correct understanding of the Deen and political analysis based upon the Qur'aan, Sunnah and guidance of the Salaf.

The more we used to see the disbelievers and hypocrites attacking you, the more it increased our faith and belief that you were speaking the ḥaq (truth), as this is something which the Messenger of Allah used to face on a daily basis from the enemies of Islam.

You will be pleased to know that we will continue with our work here in order to distinguish ourselves from the disbelievers and fulfil our duties and obligations wherever we are. However, our activities here should not be linked to you in any way as we follow Islam in accordance with the understanding of the Messenger Muhammad (saw) and his Companions, and not your understanding.

Our dear Sheikh, remember that you have a great obligation on your neck and you will be severely tested by Almighty Allah (swt).

You will be greatly missed here by thousands of Muslims, and we pray that Allah (swt) unites us again, if not in this world, inshaa-Allah in the Hereafter.[203]

It is doubtful that Bakri's exclusion will prevent his influencing British Muslims in the future. His followers here will continue to proclaim his message, and nothing will prevent Bakri from establishing websites abroad that Britons can access. It should be remembered that Bakri's followers are generally British-born UK citizens; these cannot be deported. We may have seen the last of Bakri in Britain, but it is unlikely that we have *heard* the last of him – or from him.

LeBor notes that, while he was leader of HT, Sheikh Omar emerged as a 'hate figure in the British media' ever since the Gulf war, 'when he was reported to have called for the assassination of John Major, which he strongly denies'.[204] The *Guardian* quoted him as explaining his activity in *jihad* recruitment:

> ... Sheikh Omar Bakri-Muhammad...personally arranged the recruitment of the three students through his contacts in Britain and abroad...He said: 'I believe in the divine cause for Muslims to struggle.'
>
> Al-Muhajiroun, which has a network of centres around the world, is divided into two wings, said Sheik [*sic*] Bakri. 'There is the Da'wah (propagation) network, and there is the Jihad Network,' he added. It is the Jihad Network of the party that recruits people for military campaigns, while the Da'wah wing 'spreads the word of Islam' through lectures, conferences, stalls and leaflets.[205]

After 9/11 and America's preparation for war against Afghanistan, some Al-Muhajiroun members purportedly volunteered to fight the Taliban, though their numbers were small.[206] There were claims that the Tel Aviv bombers were somehow linked to the group.[207] Sheikh Omar denied that they were members of Al-Muhajiroun, although he praised their self-sacrifice: '"These two brothers have drawn a divine road map, one which is drawn in blood"...Bakri...was quick to add that neither Hanif nor Sharif were members of his group nor were they recruited by him to go abroad and fight the jihad.'[208] Probably as a result of changes in anti-terrorist legislation, Sheikh Omar became more circumspect in his *public* comments about alleged involvement in recruitment for *mujahidin*. The 2000 Terrorism Act allows for groups to be banned, assets confiscated and members jailed if it can be proved that they conspired to commit a terrorist offence abroad. On 30 July 2003, on the basis of this Act, 'British police and Specialist officers, upon the orders of the Blair regime, raided the houses of Sheikh Omar Bakri Muhammad (Amir of Al-Muhajiroun) and Mr Anjem Choudary (The UK leader) and the movements [*sic*] offices in North London.'[209] The statement denied that Al-Muhajiroun involved 'themselves in military activities or recruiting people for operations'.

However, Sheikh Omar has never been reticent about his public support for *mujahidin* such as Al-Qaida. For example, on 11 September 2002 – that is, the first anniversary of 9/11 – Al-Muhajiroun, in conjunction with SOS and Abu Qatada, organised a closed conference at Finsbury Park Mosque entitled 'A Towering Day in History'; it was advertised by a poster depicting the second aeroplane heading for the World Trade Center. The following year a similar conference – entitled 'The Magnificent 19' – was advertised by posters and stickers with the faces of the 9/11 *mujahidin*. The press release for the event explained its motivation:

> ...the event entitled the 'Magnificent 19', to be held on the 11th September 2003, is not a celebration, this has not been suggested and this is not our intention. Rather the purpose of the commemoration of the 11th September 2001, is to examine its root causes and the driving force and motivation of the 19 men who partook in the operation, in order to have a clearer understanding and in order to discuss whether the continuation of the causes might result in a recurrence of such events, albeit by utilising different ways and means.[210]

In an interview with this author, Sheikh Omar explained his position on 9/11, and the motivation and justification for this action and other manifestations of modern *jihad*, such as the Beslan incident:

> 9/11 was undoubtedly an unpleasant moment for its targets or their relatives (Muslims and non-Muslim), but those committing it acted as a result of the predestined divine decree...
>
> The 'Magnificent 19' or 'terrorists' are personally accountable for their actions. If these were based on God's

commands, they will be rewarded; if against his commands, they will be punished.

The 19 referred to a divine text, Surah Al-Baqara 2:190: 'Fight in the way of Allah against those who fight against you...'

...The USA is a *kaffir* state – and *kaffir* includes those U.S. Muslims who ally with non-Muslims, e.g. in the U.S. Army, as in Iraq, and are therefore legitimate targets of jihad.

...U.S. terrorism in Iraq is anti-God. U.S. voters have joint liability with the government they choose, as do Russian voters in regard to the actions of their government in Chechnya – yet they voted for Putin. Complicity in the acts of one's rulers makes one a legitimate target...

Again, speaking objectively as a Muslim scholar, and not inciting such acts, 9/11 was justifiable because America had no Covenant of Security with the Muslims, although Muslims in the U.S. are under a Covenant of Security whereby they may not act militarily against America...

9/11 was not an attempt to conquer America, but rather an act of retaliation. Its aim was to force America out of the Muslim world by inflicting the same pain on them as they inflict on Muslims.[211]

Sheikh Omar is also explicit about democracy, which he rejects as enshrining popular, rather than divine, sovereignty. He therefore envisages Britain becoming an Islamic State, by means of both *da'wah* and *jihad*, which he regards as a *fard* obligation:

To him 'sovereignty is for God, not for people'. He said Al-Muhajiroun's sole purpose is to 'establish the Islamic state,' through both propagation and jihad. 'I want Britain to become an Islamic state. I want to see the flag of Islam raised in 10 Downing Street.'...Islamising Britain is a 'divine duty'.[212]

Al-Muhajiroun was always very public in its *da'wah* activities – not only in the usual way of having literature tables in public places, debates in colleges, etc., but also by making controversial statements about *jihad* that regularly hit the headlines, and by holding an annual summer 'Rally for Islam' in Trafalgar Square. The purpose of the rallies was to invite non-Muslims to convert to Islam, and they included a specific invitation to Her Majesty the Queen, the Prime Minister and the general British public to embrace Islam on pain of hell-fire. In an interview with the author at the 1999 rally, Anjem Choudary, Sheikh Omar's right-hand man, predicted that Britain would become predominantly Muslim within a century. Sometimes people from other faiths are invited to address the rally, and converts declare their *shahadah* ('*La Ilaha illala Muhammadur Rasullah*' – 'There is no God but Allah and Muhammad is his Messenger'). These actions are based on the *Sunnah*: Muhammad himself sent invitations to contemporary rulers inviting them to Islam.[213]

The 2002 rally was particularly tense, with counter-demonstrations from the National Front and the Iranian and Iraqi Communist parties. Only the massive police presence prevented a riot. One speaker started chanting in support of bin Laden, whilst another (a white convert) accused Blair and Bush of being the real war criminals. When Abu Hamza appeared as the last speaker, the opposition crowd surged forward with clear violent intent. Undeterred, the group staged a repeat rally the following year, but the 2004 rally was moved to Essex, because of possible confrontation with a large group of Sikh counter-demonstrators, as well as with pickets from the National Front and the United British Alliance. Choudary stated: 'We could not guarantee the safety and security of the attendees. There were a number of people coming from all over the country...it would be very difficult for us to control.'[214]

It can be seen how Islamic missionary activity (at least as envisaged by some groups) is distinct from its Christian equivalent, in that it has a *political*, indeed *constitutional*, element. It is not simply about converting people to a certain faith; it also involves the restructuring of the political order. Sheikh Omar wants to see a restored Caliphate that would ultimately include Britain and other Western countries, and would involve a radical re-orientation of the nature of British society:

> Under the *Khilafah*, authority is centralized, but not administration. The Caliph appoints ministers, judges, governors, army commanders, etc. Constitutionally, although all analogies are imperfect, the *Khilafah* is closer to the U.S. presidential system than to the U.K. parliamentary system with a Prime Minister, although the major difference is that the Caliph operates under a divine mandate.

There could be no non-Muslim judges. Effectively, the Qur'an and Sunnah...are the Constitution, Shari'ah is the law. The Caliph is chosen by Muslims, whether by popular election, or selection by Majlis as-Shura...Non-Muslims can enter the Majlis to represent their own community...

As citizens, in terms of welfare and security, education, etc., they will be equal. They will be exempt from national service, although they can volunteer. They will pay the *Jizya* poll-tax for security and signifying that they submit to Islamic law, except if they join the army. This need not be levied with humiliation. Nor is it levied on women, children, clergy, elderly, etc., only on mature, working males.

No private schools will be allowed, and there will be an Islamically influenced national curriculum. No new churches will be permitted, but existing ones will be allowed. Private consumption of alcohol will be permitted, but not its public sale. All state officials must be Muslims, save for the Caliph's assistants to advise him about relations with non-Muslim citizens. Muslims could not convert to Christianity on pain of execution. Evangelistic campaigns would be forbidden, but people would be free to present Christianity on TV, in debates, etc.[215]

In a surprise announcement on 8 October 2004, Sheikh Omar dissolved Al-Muhajiroun.[216] After explaining his move towards explicit Salafism, he said he was taking this decision in order to consolidate the pro-*jihadi* forces:

In light of the new reality after the blessed 9/11, the evil forces having united against the Ummah and Islam...there is nothing left except that the sincere Muslims who fight with their lives, flesh and wealth unite for the sake of Allah...[V]erily the strategic threat which is posed by the Jihadi movement from the followers of Ahl ul-Sunnah Wa al-Jamma' and those who support them – poses a real threat to USA...However, this requires a brave decision and the moulding together of all the Islamic movements and groups and the propagation of the Jihadi notion of the Ummah...I truthfully and sincerely declare...the dissolving of the entity of Al-Muhajiroun...We are keen for the safety of the path to the way of the salaf and in support of the Mujahideen and Jihad...[217]

It is hardly cynical to view this dissolution as a tactical move, not least in the light of the group's commitment to *jihad*. In an article about the dissolution, 'The leader of the group's Luton branch, using the pseudonym Saif al-Islam, suggested the dissolution would lead to members going "freelance".'[218] Obviously, if there is no organised 'group' as such, but merely a 'sect' of believers without any hierarchy, then it is difficult to proscribe the 'grouping', or to confiscate its assets. When demonstrations are held, it is simply a collection of individuals gathering together. Sheikh Omar's influence becomes *ideological*, rather than administrative; the prosecution of 'leading' Sect followers would be more difficult, and would have fewer consequences.

By the advent of the 2005 general election, the Saviour Sect had made its appearance. Its name reflects a *hadith* predicting sectarian divisions in Islam.[219] Its website explained matters thus:

Website established on the 4th of February 2005

This website aims to represent the views of the Saviour Sect in Islam...[T]he reason why we have named our website 'the Saviour Sect' is in order to remind the Muslims of returning back to the best people who walked the face of this earth – the messenger Muhammad (saw) and his companions (may Allah be pleased with them), who are the Saviour Sect.

We are followers of Ahl us-Sunnah wal-Jamaa'ah and we aim to only produce material which is based upon the teachings of as-Salaf us-Saalih (the Pious Predecessors) and never to deviate from their path by referring to the Khalaf (those who came after) over the best first three generations in Islam.

We are not a group, as groups (who do not follow the Saviour Sect) in our present day reality are the cause of disunity and trials amongst the Ummah, and neither are we an organisation. We are a number of individuals who follow Nahj us-Salaf (the path of the Pious Predecessors), working to spread the correct 'Aqeedah (Islamic belief) and Manhaj (method) for revival.[220]

Nonetheless, this sect does engage in political activity. The self-designation and description of the sect is that of *Salafis*, adhering to the *Ahl us-Sunnah* ('People of the *Sunnah*'):

> … Ahl us-Sunnah wal-Jamaa'ah are the only saved sect out of 73, and it is a duty upon every Muslim to learn about their attributes and characteristics in order to make one of their aims in life to be from among them in this dunyaa and in the Aakhirah (Hereafter).[221]

The restoration of the Caliphate abolished by Ataturk in 1924 remains their principal objective, but they reject the Ottoman Empire as the ideal model for the State, looking instead to Muhammad himself and the reign of the *Khulafa Rashidun* ('Righteous Caliphs'), in keeping with their position as Salafis:

> …we should always remember that the Ottoman Empire was not our role model or perfect example. Rather, our best example to follow are as-Salaf us-Saaliḥ, the Pious Predecessors, and we should look to how they used to run the affairs of mankind – by the Book of Allaah (swt) and the Sunnah of the messenger Muhammad (saw) and his Companions (ra).[222]

The *Khilafah* they envisage will be a Jihad State, leading to the conquest of the West: 'Only with the implementation of the Sharee'ah will we see the Hypocrite system of the Saudi government and the so-called super power – USA destroyed and the black flag of Islaam elevated over 10 Downing Street and the White House, inshaa-Allaah.'[223] As with Hizb ut-Tahrir and Al-Muhajiroun, they are adamant that democracy is not only incompatible with Islam, but is actually *kufr*, and indeed *shirk*:

> Another meaning for the term Democracy…is that it is *'the rule for the people, by the people'*, in other words, it is a system where the people legislate laws that suits their own desires. Therefore, whether we like it or not, Democracy is not only a form of consultation (Shooraa) as the secular 'Muslims' like to claim in order to justify their kufr, but it is primarily a mechanism and system that allows people to leave the commands of Allah (swt) and to legislate their own

laws...Muslims are **not allowed** to have any opinion on the Divine Rules (al-Ahkaam ash-Shar'iyyah) of Allah, and commenting on any of Allah's law is considered to be Kufr Akbar which takes you outside the fold of Islam...[T]hose who call for Democracy are calling for shirk, kufr and a Deen other than Islam, which are all major forms of apostasy...'Freedom' is a form of Taaghout (false God or deity), and Muslims are obliged to reject anything that is worshipped, obeyed or followed other than Allah...[224]

Similarly, the Sect presented a detailed statement concerning its position on the 2005 election, called *A Guide for the Muslims Regarding the Upcoming Elections: Exploring the Issues Affecting the Muslims*. Right from the start there was no question as to its policy on the subject: participation is apostasy, a capital offence resulting in eternal damnation. This was backed up by the following *hadith*:

It is reported on the authority of Abu Hurayrah that when the verse, **'When comes the Help of Allaah and the Victory, And you will see the people enter into Allaah's Religion in crowds.'** [Nasr 1-2] was revealed the Prophet (saw) said, 'They (the Muslims) will leave Islaam in crowds the way they entered into it as crowds.' [Sunan ad-Daarimi][225]

The authors straightaway declared not only a tactical opposition to voting in the particular election under consideration, but even to democracy in general, and, furthermore, implied that those participating in the election would be in eschatological danger:

[W]e hope that it can be used as a testimony on the Day of Judgement against those who participate in the Kufr Electoral process...

It is an undisputable fact that the Muslims living in the West are living in countries which are known as Daar ul-Kufr, the lands of Kufr. This is because the law and order that prevails in these countries are not based upon the Shari'ah (the law of Allaah) but are based upon the whims and desires of those Kuffar (disbelievers) in the parliament...

212

The people who *initially* elected these ministers into parliament are the ones who are ultimately accountable for the final decisions made.

Now, if these ministers deem by their majority opinion that alcohol should be permitted (as it is in this Kufr society) then this would be accepted as law (*qanoon*). In addition if people deem that prostitution, gambling, paedophilia, killing Muslims (as in the wars on Afghanistan, Iraq and the ongoing war on Islam), homosexuality, permissibility of same-sex marriages etc. is beneficial for the people, then through the process of majority voting, these and other motions would be accepted and implemented as law, such that the people will live and judge by them.[226]

The reference to the 'War on Terror' as 'the ongoing war on Islam' which involves 'killing Muslims' is important. The *Qur'an* forbids intra-Muslim slaughter, except under certain conditions (i.e. capital crime, rebellion, etc.), under pain of damnation: Surah Al-Furqan 25:68: 'nor slay such life as God has made sacred except for just cause'; Surah An-Nisa 4:93: 'If a man kills a believer intentionally, his recompense is Hell, to abide therein (For ever): And the wrath and the curse of God are upon him, and a dreadful penalty is prepared for him.' The implication of the authors is that by participating in the British electoral process, UK Muslims will become complicit in the slaughter of fellow-Muslims, and will thus be damned. It can be appreciated how this is a powerful deterrent to such participation.

Not content with rejecting the British electoral system, the publication also demonstrates its adherence to the principle of *takfir* by slating major Muslim groups as 'extreme secularists' and thus effectively apostates:

The extreme secularists such as the Muslim Parliament, the MCB, MPAC, the Islamic Party of Britain (ISB), YM, YMO and their ilk may argue that Allaah (swt) has created the Muslims for worship and this worship is in prayer, zakaat and hajj, and has no bearing on affairs outside the mosque. Such statements are simply at best due to their grave ignorance about Islam and the Arabic language or at worst their disbelief in the true tenets of Islam.[227]

213

The significance of this is, of course, that these groups all accept the principle of electoral participation. The problem, as seen by the Sect, is that given the *kufr* nature of British constitutionalism, electoral participation by Muslims effectively causes everyone involved in the process at any level to become *mushrikun* – polytheists, because they 'associate' something with one of Allah's attributes, which is a forbidden act of apostasy: 'they associate with Allaah (swt) others in the Actions which Allaah (swt) has made specific to Himself. Now turning to the issue of passing laws and orders, we know that Allaah (swt) has said, "*Verily the absolute right of legislating is for none but Allaah (swt)*" [*Yusuf* 12:40]'.[228]

It should be noted that the Pickthall translation renders this *ayah* thus: 'Those whom ye worship beside Him are but names which ye have named, ye and your fathers. Allah hath revealed no sanction for them. The decision rests with Allah only, Who hath commanded you that ye worship none save Him.' The word translated as 'decision' or 'command' is rendered by the authors of the Saviour Sect publication as 'legislate' – a common theme in their literature. Arguably, this ironically represents a contextualisation of their message for the British situation. They elaborate on how voting in a *kufr* state involves *shirk* by referring to texts in the *Qur'an* and *hadith* which equate the obedience given by Jews and Christians to their religious leaders who deviated from God's law with 'worship' of such leaders; for, by obeying them rather than God, they 'worshipped' those leaders. Hence, obeying the *kufr* British political system by participating in it is also *shirk*:

> 'They took their Rabbis and their Monks to be their Lords and Legislators besides Allaah...[N]one has the right to be worshipped or followed and to legislate but he, praise and glory be to him from having the partners they associate with him.' [at-Tauba 9:30–31]...The above ayah was revealed in the following circumstances. It has been reported by Hudhayfah in Ahmad, Tirmidhi and Ibn Jareer that the Messenger Muhammad (saw) was reciting the above verse and Udayy (ra) said to him (saw),
>
> 'O Prophet of Allaah! They do not worship the Rabbis and the Monks!' To which he (saw) replied: 'The Rabbis and Monks make that which is lawful unlawful and that which is unlawful lawful and they i.e. the people, follow them, and by doing so they worship them.' Allaah (swt) and the Prophet (saw)

therefore considered that as making them lords and gods besides Allaah (swt), because the obedience (*taa'ah*) in legislation is worship, and must not be for any one except Allaah (swt).[229]

Although the original context only refers to following religious leaders in theological matters, the text is employed to argue that such legislation that is the result of human initiative is essentially *idolatry*, because it usurps a divine prerogative, and is thus *haram* for Muslims. The usual argument of Islamist democrats – that democracy is analogous to *shura* – is forcefully rejected:

> Unfortunately Muslims today have sought to equate the Islaamic principle of Shooraa i.e. consultation, with democracy. Shooraa means engaging in mutual consultation or discussion regarding a particular matter…Whilst the Muslims are a source of authority, sovereignty belongs to the Sharee'ah. So in the case of shooraa although the Muslims have a right to be consulted in everything, their opinion will not necessarily be transferred into law. This is unlike in a democracy where in theory the people are sovereign and their will is transferred into law. In Islaam the Divine Law is sovereign and consultation cannot overrule it…
>
> …Shooraa in legislative matters is restricted to outweighing and favouring one opinion according to the strength of the evidence in the case of plurality of opinions and understandings…[T]he head of state is the sole body with the mandatory power to make the opinion binding and law on all Muslims. Evidence for this is extracted from what took place during the peace treaty of Hudaybiyah when the Muslims objected to what Allaah's Messenger (saw) signed with Quraysh, he (saw) followed the revelation and ignored the Muslim's [*sic*] opinion and objection…
>
> If the Majlis ash-Shooraa disagrees with the ruler over an action from the viewpoint of Sharee'ah, the matter is to be decided by the court for the unjust acts. This consists of a small band of jurists, who are qualified with the ability to make Ijtihaad (juristic exertion), thus able to determine whether the ruler has acted in accordance with the divine law…
>
> Every Muslim of the Islaamic state has the right to become a member of the Majlis ash-Shooraa, provided that is, that he or she is mature and sane. Non-muslims can be members

215

of the Majlis ar-Ri'ayyah but their presence is confined to representing their community in respect of their grievances against the ruler and issues which affect them specifically.[230]

The consequence of this is that British democracy – which has no written constitution, which proceeds on the basis of parliamentary supremacy, with the Legislature able to pass any law it chooses, and which is open to the full and equal membership of all people, irrespective of creed – is necessarily rejected, as is Muslim participation therein. Saviour Sect followers demonstrated their opposition in very practical ways during the 2005 general election. Firstly, according to a statement posted on their other website – 'Al Ghurabaa – Followers of Ahl Al Sunnah Wal Jama'ah' – on 18 April 2005, their followers took pre-emptive action against an MCB pre-election meeting:

> A MCB press conference organised at the London Central Mosque in central London calling upon Muslims to apostate from Islam was left in shatters this morning. As the MCB were preparing to further cement themselves as lackeys of the British Government, Muslims from the Followers of Ahl Us Sunnah Wal Jama'ah interrupted the meeting, disrupting its proceedings and eventually bringing it to an abrupt and premature end.
>
> The MCB had organised the event to launch it's [sic] campaign for greater participation of the Muslim Vote on May 5th 2005, promoting a vote card outlining issues that Muslims should take into consideration when casting their vote.
>
> Incensed by the MCB encouraging Muslims to vote in the forthcoming elections, General Secretary for the MCB, Iqbal Sacranie and his cohorts were confronted about there [sic] alliance with the Labour government, there [sic] Kufr (non-Islamic) call, for Muslims to vote in the elections and their support for a government that is engaged in a war against Islam and Muslims, arresting, murdering and raping Muslims.[231]

The Sect also distributed a leaflet with the warning 'Caution! Stay Muslim – Don't Vote!' This claimed that voting is *shirk*, and that Parliament is a place of *kufr*. Indeed, the leaflet went further and claimed that Parliament was a '*taaghout*' ('tyrant'). The Sect was especially active in Tower Hamlets, where George Galloway stood for RESPECT, and where he was courting the Muslim vote. It denounced

RESPECT as '...a Kaafir (non-Muslim) organisation which, like every other political party, believes that sovereignty belongs to man and not Allah'.[232] It also claimed, wrongly, that Galloway 'was also one of the MPs who supported the war and occupation of Afghanistan'. It can be seen that the position of the Sect is at variance with leading UK Muslim organisations, *and specifically elements that represent the contextualised opinions of the* Jama'at *and* Ikhwan.

As for *jihad*, we have seen that Sheikh Omar stated in an interview that a 'covenant of security' precludes resident Muslims from attacking the non-Muslim country in which they reside:

> ... 9/11 was justifiable because America had no Covenant of Security with the Muslims, although Muslims in the U.S. are under a Covenant of Security whereby they may not act militarily against America.[233]

However, he has since reportedly stated that, in view of recent UK anti-terror legislation, which he interprets as an assault on Muslims, this covenant has been removed, and that resident Muslims may indeed attack Britain:

> Muslims in Britain must either leave the country or take up jihad...Sheikh Omar Bakir Muhammed [*sic*]...told UPI the actions of the British government against Muslims – anti-terror legislation and indefinite detention of terror suspects – has [*sic*] broken the covenant of security under which Muslims in Britain previously lived. Muslims are therefore now at war with the government...[234]

The Times reported him elaborating on this:

> 'I believe the whole of Britain has become Dar ul Harb. That Dar ul Harb has not started yet, but still really they start it. They arrest ulema (religious men), they arrest scholars...they declare your job is to divide the Muslims, promote secularism and the kuffar has said use of IDs, integration, etc, and you should report to the police. This is what makes it Dar ul Harb.'[235]

This ties in with a previous statement, made in an interview with this author, explaining how America could become a legitimate target for those Muslims resident there:

The USA ceases to be Dar al-Amen for Muslims in America if: (1) America declares Islam to be the enemy; (2) it starts arresting or killing Muslims; (3) it bans Islamic preaching. Muslims are not allowed to fight America from within its borders when they normally live there – they must leave and then fight.[236]

There has also been an apparent shift from the position of Al-Muhajiroun in regard to *offensive jihad*. We have already seen that it is only possible when there is a Caliph, and therefore a corresponding Islamic Caliphate. However, a small change to the Sect's presentation on *jihad* suggests that, in their view, this may not be completely essential: 'This type of Jihaad is usually only carried out by the Islaamic state.'[237] The insertion of the word 'usually' is significant. Another article seems to advocate a *coup d'etat* to establish Islamic dominance in Britain:

> So how will Islam dominate the world? Most likely by force! If the people do not embrace Islam and implement the Sharee'ah on their own accord, it becomes an obligation upon the Muslims to fight and implement Islam. In countries such as Britain and America, their people have clearly rejected to embrace Islam and will never choose to live by the Sharee'ah. Therefore, the only two ways in which these countries can become under the domain of Islam is by the last two options, a group of Muslims rise and overthrow the government, or an Islamic state is established elsewhere and comes to conquer these countries.[238]

On another Sect website, a report on an anti-voting procession in London in May 2005 is entitled 'Operation West London Takeover', and depicts a confrontation with the police that came dangerously close to violence.[239] It was alleged that police had physically abused the Muslim demonstrators, so this would be seen as defensive *jihad*. It must be understood that at the root of this confrontation lay not only testosterone, but also theology. The police are seen as agents of a Satanic infidel Government, and not as 'their' security forces, because they are the police of *Khilafah*. The Sect rejects the concept of '*British Muslim*' (as it rejects all nationalism), so no loyalty is due to the British Government or its agencies (hence in a confrontation between Afghan or Iraqi *mujahidin* and British forces, they would support the former).[240] Similarly, the Sect's demonstration against the US embassy over the *Qur'an* desecration scandal involved not only the ritual burning of the

US flag, but also the burning of a Cross (apparently as the icon of the 'Christian Crusaders' as Choudary termed them), as well as chants glorifying 9/11 and demanding more such actions; Choudary referred to Muslims as having 'desecrated' the World Trade Center, and expressed his hope, to the cheers of the crowd, that similar 'desecration' would befall the White House. Sectarian antagonism is not restricted to 'Christian Crusaders'; the Sect lauded Abu Musab al-Zarqawi's actions against the Iraqi Shia:

> The Shia are a sect that have come throughout history to distort and warp the teachings of Islam and their famous habit is always to ally with the Kuffaar to cause harm to the Muslims. This is exactly what they did during the early stages of Islam, at the time of Sheikh-ul-Islam, to the destruction of the Khilaafah and today in Afghanistan and Iraq...Today the Mujaahideen (likes of Abu Mus'ab Al-Zarqawi) do not indulge in any form of dialogue with this Taa-ifah Shirk (group of Mushrikeen) rather the only way to deal with these Shia is to make them meet their Lord. They have allied with their brothers in faith the Christian crusaders to kill the Muslims.[241]

It might be wondered why the Sect and its predecessors are so unconcerned with the inevitable bad publicity they receive as a result of some of their activities. On the one hand, it is clearly a case of Oscar Wilde's famous dictum: the only thing worse than being talked about is *not* being talked about! No one is sure of the Sect's numbers, but they probably do not exceed a few hundred, if the annual 'Rally for Islam' is anything to go by. Spectacular events and the mass publicity generated by extravagant comments thus allow the Sect to punch above its weight, and to publicise its existence across Britain. Furthermore, the bad publicity it receives from the *kufr* media does it no harm among many disgruntled Muslims, who believe the media are anyway inherently Islamophobic. Since the media are *kufr*, the Sect expects nothing but hostility from them. In fact, believing as they do that the *Kuffar* are dominated by Satan, they would be worried if they were *not* being denounced by the Devil's minions! Ironically, the attacks they endure from infidel and 'apostate' commentators in the community, media and politics only reassure them that what they are doing is right.

[1] For example, her excellent article on Muslim women and Islamophobia, 'They hate women, don't they?', *Guardian*, 21 June 2002;
http://www.guardian.co.uk/comment/story/0,,741238,00.html.

[2] Siddiqui, Kalim, *Islam and the West after Bosnia* (London: Muslim Parliament of Great Britain, 1993), p. 2.

[3] Dhalla, Musadiq, 'Creating a stately home in Slough', *Muslim News,* No. 25, March 1991, p. 7.

[4] Kepel, Gilles, *Allah in the West* (Cambridge: Polity Press, 1997),
p. 144.

[5] Masood, Ehsan, 'Preparing for Jihad', *Q-News,* 19–26 November 1993, p. 6.

[6] *Ibid.*

[7] For example, Philips dismisses Shi'ism as 'deviation', and thus rejects the Iranian Revolution as Islamic; Philips, Abu Ameenah Bilal, 'Foreword' to Ibn al-Jawzee, *The Devil's Deception* (Birmingham: Al-Hidaayah, 1996, Second Edition), p. 8.

[8] Islamic Human Rights Commission, 'Towards a new liberation theology: Reflections on Palestine'; http://www.ihrc.org.uk/show.php?id=1377.

[9] IHRC press release, 'Muslim unity march', 30 April 2005;
http://www.ihrc.org.uk/show.php?id=1364.

[10] IHRC, *The Annual Islamophobia Awards 2004* (London: IHRC, 2004), p. 3.

[11] IHRC, Introductory leaflet, April 15, 1996.

[12] *Ibid.*

[13] See Bodi, Faisal, 'Religious discrimination: A tale of two reports', *Q-News,* No. 317, March 2000, pp. 12–13, and McRoy, Anthony, 'Never again?', *Third Way,* March 2000, Vol. 23:2, pp. 8–9.

[14] IHRC broadsheet, Vol. 5, October 2004, pp. 4, 6.

[15] *Ibid.*, p. 2.

[16] *Ibid.*, p. 8.

[17] *Ibid.*, pp. 4, 6.

[18] IHRC, 'Human rights, justice & Muslims in the modern world', 7 May 2000; http://www.ihrc.org.uk/show.php?id=10.

[19] Shomali, Mohammad A., *Shi'i Islam: Origins, Faith & Practices* (London: ICAS, 2003), p. 93.

[20] Ameli, Saied Reza, *Democracy in Question – The Persecution of the Believers Or The Reverse Processing of Power and Powerlessness* (London: IHRC, 2002), p. 5.

[21] Ameli, Saied R. and Merali, Arzu, *British Muslims' Expectations of the*

Government (London: IHRC, 2004), p. 77.

[22] IHRC, 'It is not anybody who can implement Sharia – Sheikh Ibraheem Zakzaky', 8 October 1999; http://www.ihrc.org.uk/show.php?id=156.

[23] *Ibid.*

[24] IHRC, 'Civil and political rights', 15 January 2004; http://www.ihrc.org.uk/show.php?id=1010.

[25] IHRC press release, 'IHRC condemns attacks in New York & Washington; Period of calm urged; IHRC asks media to stop talking up blind retribution', 12 September 2001; http://www.ihrc.org.uk/show.php?id=33.

[26] IHRC press release, 'Urgent alert: Demonstration against Zionist "Celebration of Israel"', 10 May 2005; http://www.ihrc.org.uk/show.php?id=1376.

[27] Hansard, 18 December 2003; http://www.publications.parliament.uk/pa/cm200304/cmhansrd/vo031218/debtext/31218-18.htm.

[28] MCB press release, 'Ellman's smear against MCB-affiliated Muslim organisation rejected', 29 December 2003.

[29] Letters, *Guardian,* 22 December 2003; http://www.guardian.co.uk/letters/story/0,,1111541,00.html.

[30] RESPECT, 'Muslim Association backs Jewish "Respect" candidate', 21 April 2005; http://www.respectcoalition.org/index.php?ite=709&rlid=8.

[31] MAB press release, 'Muslim community gives Sheikh Qaradawi rapturous welcome', 11 July 2004.

[32] Muslim Association of Britain, 'MAB responds to vile attack'; http://www.mabonline.info/english/modules.php?name=News&file=article&sid=105.

[33] *Ibid.*

[34] *Ibid.*

[35] MAB, 'Personalities within Islam'; http://www.mabonline.info/islam/modules.php?name=News&file=article&sid=14.

[36] http://www.mabonline.info/english/modules.php?name=About.

[37] Carlin, Brendan, 'Backlash as Muslims are urged: Don't vote Labour', *Yorkshire Post,* 19 May 2004; http://www.yorkshiretoday.co.uk/viewarticle2.aspx?ArticleID=793020&SectionID=5.

[38] MAB, 'Who to vote for on May 5th', 5 May 2005; http://www.mabonline.info/english/modules.php?name=News&file=article&sid

=371.

[39] MAB, 'Salma Yaqoob: Respect due';
http://www.mabonline.info/english/modules.php?name=News&file=article&sid
=400.

[40] Tamimi, Azzam, 'Fundamentalism & violence: An Islamic viewpoint';
http://www.ii-pt.com/web/papers/view.htm.

[41] Smallman, Lawrence, 'When hostages become captives';
http://english.aljazeera.net/NR/exeres/BA590075-7765-4122-B54B-
EEAA8A7A1926.htm.

[42] MAB, 'Salma Yaqoob: Respect due'.

[43] *Ibid.*

[44] Vasagar, Jeevan, 'Palestinian radical was guest of US ambassador', *Guardian*,
21 December 2002;
http://www.guardian.co.uk/international/story/0,,863922,00.html.

[45] Tamimi, Azzam, 'The legitimacy of Palestinian resistance: An Islamist
perspective'; http://www.ii-pt.com/web/papers/legitimacy.htm.

[46] Tamimi, Azzam, 'Hizbollah's gift to Palestine'; http://www.ii-
pt.com/web/articles/hizbollah.htm.

[47] Tamimi, Azzam, 'America's Crusade'; http://www.ii-
pt.com/web/articles/oct01.htm.

[48] MAB press release, 'MAB denounces killing of Kenneth Bigley', 8 October
2004.

[49] Saved Sect, 'Exposing the Munaafiqeen of Britain;
http://www.thesavedsect.com/articles/CurrentAffairs/HypocritesBritain.htm.

[50] MAB press release, 'New management for Finsbury Park Mosque',
7 February 2005.

[51] Nasr, Seyyeid Vali Reza, *Mawdudi and the Making of Islamic Revivalism*
(New York & Oxford: Oxford University Press, 1996), pp. 126f.

[52] *Ibid.*, p. 110.

[53] *Ibid.*, p. 55.

[54] *Ibid.*, p. 75.

[55] *Ibid.*, p. 37.

[56] *Ibid.*, p. 77.

[57] *Ibid.*, p. 76.

[58] *Ibid.*, p. 84.

[59] UK Islamic Mission;
http://ukim.org/DesktopDefault.aspx?tabindex=3&tabid=10.

[60] Dawatul Islam, 'Interview'; http://www.dawatul-islam.org.uk/pastpresent.htm.

[61] YMUK, '*Shumuliyyah* (Comprehensiveness)'; http://www.ymuk.net/articles-02/?action=disparticle&id=16.

[62] IFE, 'Hizb Allah, Israeli army exchange fire'; http://www.islamicforumeurope.com/live/ife.php?doc=newsitem&itemId=1284.

[63] IFE press release, 'British Muslims heed IFE's election guidance', 6 May 2005; http://www.islamicforumeurope.com/live/ife.php?doc=articleitem&itemId=231.

[64] Islamic Society of Britain, *Islam – a Vision for Britain* convention brochure (Leicester: Islamic Society of Britain, 1995), pp. 10–12.

[65] Muslim Council of Britain, *Invitation* (Bradford: MCB, 1996), p. 12.

[66] *Ibid.*

[67] Muslim Council of Britain, *Seeking the Common Good* (London: MCB, 1997), p. 13.

[68] *Ibid.*

[69] Adil, Abdul, 'A new Muslim body inaugurated', *Muslim News*, No. 104, December 1997; http://www.muslimnews.co.uk/mcb104.html.

[70] MCB, *Seeking the Common Good*, p. 8.

[71] MCB, *Invitation*, p. 9.

[72] *Ibid.*, p. 11.

[73] Sacranie was knighted in 2005.

[74] UKACIA, *Elections 1997 and British Muslims: For a Fair and Caring Society* (London: UKACIA, 1997), pp. 5, 11n.

[75] For example, '...Muslims are not and do not seek to be a ghetto community.' *Ibid.*, p. 4. Cf. MCB, *Invitation*, p. 8: 'The Muslim community in Britain is not and cannot be a ghetto community.'

[76] UKACIA, *Elections 1997*, p. 4.

[77] UKACIA, 'Announcements', 10 June 1997; www.ukacia.com.

[78] Muslim Council of Britain (briefing paper), *Question on Religious Affiliation in the 2001 Census* (London: July 1998).

[79] UKACIA, *Elections 1997*, p. 9.

[80] MCB, *Invitation*, p. 12.

[81] Taylor, Jenny, 'An Islamic vision for Britain?'in Newbigin, Lesslie, Sanneh, Lamin, and Taylor, Jenny, *Faith and Power: Christianity and Islam in 'Secular' Britain* (London: SPCK, 1998), p. 124.

[82] Faraz, Mohammad, 'MCB: Dad's Muslim Army', *Q-News*, No. 287–288, April 1998, p. 21.

[83] Adil, 'A new Muslim body inaugurated'.

[84] MCB press release, 'Don't do business with Putin', 13 April 2000.

[85] Muslim Council of Britain, *The Common Good*, Vol. 1:2, December 1999, p. 6.

[86] Muslim Council of Britain, *The Common Good*, Vol. 1:1, March 1999, pp. 1, 3.

[87] 'Muslim Council of Tricks', *Q-News*, No. 317, March 2000, p. 17.

[88] MCB, *The Common Good*, 1:1, p. 1.

[89] *Ibid.*, p. 1.

[90] *Ibid.*, p. 4.

[91] MCB, *The Common Good*, 1:2, p. 2.

[92] Casciani, Dominic, 'UK Muslim loses top peace award', 1 June 2004; http://news.bbc.co.uk/1/hi/uk/3766567.stm.

[93] Sacranie, Iqbal, 'Why you should exercise your vote', *Q-News*, No. 255–259, March 1997, p. 26.

[94] With the qualification, of course, that, like Christianity, Islam began in the Middle East.

[95] Muslim Public Affairs Committee, 'What is MPACUK?'; http://www.mpacuk.org/content/view/307/34/.

[96] *Ibid.*

[97] MPAC press release, 'Lobbying works and MPAC proves it', 25 November 2002.

[98] MPAC press release, 'Another MPAC success', 19 December 2002.

[99] MPAC, 'What is MPACUK?'.

[100] MPAC, 'MPACUK meets U.S. Christian Evangelicals'; http://www.mpacuk.org/content/view/90/.

[101] Saleem, Sara, 'Labour in trouble in its northern heartlands', *Muslim News*, 28 April 2005, http://www.muslimnews.co.uk/news/news.php?article=9096.

[102] MPAC, 'What is MPACUK?'.

[103] See http://www.mpacuk.org/content/view/662/34/.

[104] MPAC press release, 'Is Islam and democracy the same?', 14 November 2003.

[105] MPAC press release, 'Neutralising Khilafah', 25 July 2002.

[106] MPAC press release, 'Al Mahaja-loon idiots do all they can to get media spotlight 4 Palestine crises', 1 May 2003.

[107] MPAC press release, 'Does this man represent 'YOU'??', 18 February 2003.

[108] MPAC, 'MPACUK's commitment to democracy';
http://www.mpacuk.org/content/view/627/.

[109] MPAC, 'Islam and democracy – Part 1';
http://www.mpacuk.org/content/view/491/.

[110] MPAC, 'True meaning of Jihad';
http://www.mpacuk.org/content/view/4/623/103.

[111] MPAC press release, 'Sept 11th media alert', 10 September 2002.

[112] Channel Four, *Operation Muslim Vote*, 16 May 2005.

[113] MPAC press release, 'MPACUK condemns anti-Semitism', 16 April 2005.

[114] MPAC, 'Success: MPACUK strikes back – Rochdale falls';
http://www.mpacuk.org/content/view/637/.

[115] MPAC, 'Float like a butterfly'; http://www.mpacuk.org/content/view/676/.

[116] An-Nabhani, Taqiuddin, *The Islamic State* (London: Al-Khilafah
Publications, 1998 edition), p. 168.

[117] *Ibid*., pp. 169–174.

[118] *Ibid*., pp. 174–175.

[119] *Ibid*., p. 221.

[120] *Ibid*. p. 222.

[121] *Ibid*.

[122] *Ibid*., p. 223.

[123] *Ibid*., p. 225.

[124] *Ibid*., p. 221.

[125] *Ibid*., pp. 236, 238.

[126] *Ibid*., pp. 148f.

[127] Rashid, Ahmed, *Jihad: The Rise of Militant Islam in Central Asia* (New
Haven & London: Yale University Press, 2002), p.115.

[128] Taji-Faruki, Suha, *A Fundamental Quest: Hizb al-Tahrir and the Search for
the Islamic Caliphate* (London: Grey Seal, 1996), p. 178.

[129] LeBor, *A Heart Turned East: Among the Muslims of Europe and America*
(London: Little, Brown and Company, 1997), p. 140.

[130] Taji-Faruki, *Quest*, p. 181.

[131] *Ibid*., p. 177.

[132] LeBor, Adam, *A Heart Turned East*, p. 140.

[133] Taji-Faruki, *Fundamental Quest*, pp. 181–182. I was present at this
conference, and think this numerical estimate too low. Significantly, most of
those attending did *not* seem to be members, but rather interested newcomers.

[134] *Ibid.*, p. 182.

[135] *Ibid.*, p. 184. The quote of Badawi comes from the *Sunday Telegraph*, 7 August 1994.

[136] 'Islam-bashing at NUS conference', *Muslim News*, No. 73, April 1995, p. 3.

[137] 'A historic handshake at NUS', *Muslim News*, No. 84, April 1996, p. 3.

[138] 'HT activists defy Birmingham ban', *Q-News*, No. 189, 10 November 1995, p. 2.

[139] Schogger, Damian, 'Radical Muslims defy ban to spread campus propaganda', *Jewish Chronicle*, 30 October 1998; http://www.jchron.co.uk/jc/jcdat/98/Oct30/story_4.htm.

[140] Taji-Faruki, *Fundamental Quest*, p. 175.

[141] Aslam, Dilpazier, 'I could scream with happiness. I've given hope and strength to Muslim women', *Guardian*, 3 March, 2005; http://www.guardian.co.uk/uk_news/story/0,,1429072,00.html.

[142] Mendick, Robert and Randhawa, Kiran, 'Muslim girl's brother linked to Islam radicals', *Evening Standard*, 4 March 2005; http://www.thisislondon.co.uk/news/articles/17038092?source=Evening%20Standard.

[143] Saviour Sect, 'School girl gives a bad name to Islaam and Muslims'; http://www.thesavioursect.com/articles/currentAffairs/shabinaBegum.htm.

[144] Aldred, Jessica, 'Muslims are being asked to abandon part of their identity', *Guardian*, 30 November 2004; http://www.guardian.co.uk/islam/story/0,,1360589,00.html.

[145] Abedin, Mahan, 'Inside Hizb ut-Tahrir: An interview with Jalaluddin Patel, Leader of Hizb ut-Tahrir in the UK'; http://jamestown.org/terrorism/news/article.php?articleid=2368393.

[146] Kassem, Farid, 'Voting in non-Islamic elections: a sinful diversion', *Muslim News*, No. 94, February 1997, p. 5.

[147] HT; http://www.standforislam.org/.

[148] *Ibid.*

[149] HT, 'Religious Hatred Bill'; http://www.1924.org/opinion/index.php?id=1978_0_34_0_M.

[150] HT, *Hizb ut-Tahrir* (London: Al-Khilafah Publications, 2000), pp. 39–40.

[151] *Ibid.*, p. 52.

[152] *Ibid.*, pp. 67–68.

[153] HT, 'What can Muslims in Britain and other non-Muslim countries do to re-establish the Khilafah?'; http://www.islamic-state.org/west/.

[154] *Ibid.*

[155] HT, *The Methodology of Hizb ut-Tahrir for Change* (London: Al-Khilafah Publications, 1999), p. 32.

[156] *Ibid.*, pp. 38–39.

[157] Abedin, 'Inside Hizb ut-Tahrir'.

[158] *Ibid.*

[159] HT release, 'Hizb ut-Tahrir Britain condemns Tony Blair's announcement to ban the Party', 5 August 2005; http://www.hizb.org.uk/press/index.php?id=2127_0_45_20_M98.

[160] MCB release, 'Banning non-violent groups is not the solution', 5 August 2005; http://www.mcb.org.uk/.

[161] MAB release, 'Freedom and civil liberties must not be forsaken', 5 August 2005; http://www.mabonline.info/english/modules.php?name=News&file=article&sid=474.

[162] 'The Law: Conspiring to terrorise', *Q-News*, No. 295, September 1998, p. 6.

[163] Yaqub, Shagufta, 'Conversation with Sheikh Abu Hamza', *Q-News*, No. 301, February 1999, p. 25.

[164] SOS, 'How can I be a "member" of Supporters of Shareeah?'; http://www.shareeah.org/news/joinsos.html.

[165] SOS press release, 'Finsbury Park raided', (undated); http://www.shareeah.org/news/release1.html.

[166] SOS press release, 'Torture & attempted murder at Belmarsh', (undated); http://www.shareeah.org/news/tortureatbelmarsh.pdf.

[167] SOS, 'Questions and answers'; http://www.shareeah.org/ba/articles/004.html 2005; SOS press release, 'The U.K. Governments [*sic*] Re-Arrest Of Shaykh Abu Hamza Al-Masri', (undated).

[168] Yaqub, Shagufta, 'Conversation with Sheikh Abu Hamza', *Q-News*, No. 301, February 1999, pp. 25–27.

[169] SOS press release, 'The stance against the war on Iraq', (undated); http://www.shareeah.org/ba/articles/006.html.

[170] Al-Masri, Sheikh Abu Hamza, *Allah's Governance on Earth* (London: SOS, 2001), pp. 410, 414.

[171] SOS, 'About Supporters of Sharee'ah'; http://www.shareeah.org/about/index.html.

[172] Al-Masri, *Allah's Governance*, p. 416.

[173] *Ibid.*, pp. 416, 417.

[174] *Ibid.*, p. 423.

[175] *Ibid.*, p. 429.

[176] *Ibid.*

[177] *Ibid.*, pp. 451–452.

[178] *Ibid.*, pp. 435f.

[179] *Ibid.*, p. 454.

[180] Al-Masri, Sheikh Abu Hamza, *Khawaarij and Jihaad* (London: SOS, 1999); http://www.shareeah.org/ba/books.html - PDF file, pp. 103, 106.

[181] *Ibid.*, p. 70.

[182] *Ibid.*, pp. 158f. *Sabi* is defined by the author as taking women as booty – 'what the right hand possesses', allowing them to be enslaved and raped, even if married. He holds that this does not apply to Muslim women.

[183] Al-Masri, *Allah's Governance*, pp. 249f. (emphasis in original).

[184] *Ibid.*, p. 16.

[185] SOS, 'The stance against the war on Iraq'.

[186] Yaqub, 'Conversation with Sheikh Abu Hamza', pp. 26–27.

[187] SOS release, 'Statement regarding the occupation of Finsbury Park Masjid', (undated).

[188] SOS release, 'MCB: The Qadiani & Shia link', (undated).

[189] *Ibid.* (emphasis in original).

[190] *Ibid.*

[191] This is effectively admitted by their article 'Should we follow majority or the minority?'; http://www.thesavedsect.com/articles/Ruling/MajorityMinority.htm.

[192] Abedin, Mahan, 'Al-Muhajiroun in the UK: An interview with Sheikh Omar Bakri Mohammed', 23 March 2004; http://www.jamestown.org/news_details.php?news_id=38.

[193] HT release, 'Omar Bakri was not the founder of Hizb ut-Tahrir', 9 August 2005; http://www.hizb.org.uk/press/index.php?id=2201_0_45_10_M98.

[194] Abedin, 'Al-Muhajiroun in the UK'.

[195] Saved Sect, '*Al-Quroon ath-Thalaathah al-Faadilah* (the Best Three Generations)'; http://www.thesavedsect.com/articles/Aqeedah/BestThreeGenerations.htm.

[196] Saved Sect, 'The ten main divisions in the Ummah today'; http://www.thesavedsect.com/articles/Aqeedah/TenMainDivisions.htm.

[197] McRoy, Anthony, 'There can be no end to Jihad', interview with Omar Bakri Muhammad, *Christianity Today*; http://www.christianitytoday.com/ct/2005/105/22.0.html.

[198] Travis, Alan and Gillan, Audrey, 'Clarke uses "personal power" to ban Bakri from UK', *Guardian*, 13 August 2005;
http://www.guardian.co.uk/guardianpolitics/story/0,,1548375,00.html.

[199] *Ibid*.

[200] 'Situation vacant: Islamic bogeyman needed urgently', *Muslim Weekly*,
12 August 2005;
http://www.themuslimweekly.com/fullstoryview.aspx?NewsID=5F0240F57EE6D
DB6ED66FF67&MENUID=EDITORIAL&DESCRIPTION=Editorial.

[201] Travis and Gillan, 'Clarke uses "personal power" to ban Bakri from UK'.

[202] Al-Ghurabaa release 20 August 2005, 'Salutations to Sheikh Omar Bakri
Muhammad'; http://www.al-ghurabaa.co.uk/pr/salaamsheikh.htm.

[203] Saved Sect; http://www.islamasitis.info/maqaalaat/MessageOBM.htm.

[204] LeBor, *A Heart Turned East*, p. 141.

[205] Taher, Abul, 'Call to arms', *Guardian*, 16 May 2000;
http://www.guardian.co.uk/guardianeducation/story/0,,221145,00.html.

[206] Harris, Paul, Wazir, Burhan and Burke, Jason, 'We will replace the Bible with
the Koran in Britain', *Observer*, 4 November 2001;
http://observer.guardian.co.uk/islam/story/0,1442,587375,00.html.

[207] Norton-Taylor, Richard and Wilson, Jamie, 'Suicide bombers were known to
MI5', *Guardian*, 5 May 2003;
http://www.guardian.co.uk/terrorism/story/0,12780,949701,00.html.

[208] Britten, Nick, Waterhouse, Rosie, and O'Neil, Sean, 'Al Muhajiroun under
scrutiny', *Daily Telegraph*, 2 May 2003;
http://www.telegraph.co.uk/news/main.jhtml;jsessionid=VJWHMGFYPOC3NQF
IQMFCNAGAVCBQYJVC?xml=/news/2003/05/02/wbomb202.xml.

[209] Al-Muhajiroun press release, 'Al-Muhajiroun raided by Blair regime',
30 July 2003.

[210] Al-Muhajiroun press release, 'Magnificent 19 conference';
www.almuhajiroun.com.

[211] McRoy, 'There can be no end to Jihad'.

[212] Taher, 'Call to arms'.

[213] Narrated by Anas ibn Malik
Sahih Muslim 4382
The Prophet of Allah (peace be upon him) wrote to Chosroes (King of Persia),
Caesar (Emperor of Rome), Negus (King of Abyssinia) and every (other) despot
inviting them to Allah, the Exalted...

[214] Iyer, Vik, 'Al-Muhajiroun moves rally', *Muslim News*, 25 July 2004;
http://www.muslimnews.co.uk/news/news.php?article=7802.

215 McRoy, 'There can be no end to Jihad'.

216 Sheikh Omar Bakri Muhammad, 'An official Declaration dissolving Al-Muhajiroun'; http://www.almuhajiroun.net.

217 *Ibid.*

218 Al-Yafai, Faisal, 'Monitored Islamist group shuts down', *Guardian*, 13 October 2004; http://www.guardian.co.uk/uk_news/story/0,,1325840,00.html.

219 Narrated by Abdullah ibn Amr

Mishkat Al-Masabih 0171

Allah's Messenger (peace be upon him) said: There will befall my Ummah exactly (all those) evils which befell the people of Isra'il…if the people of Isra'il were fragmented into seventy-two sects my Ummah will be fragmented into seventy-three sects. All of them will be in Hell Fire except one sect.

They (the Companions) said: Allah's Messenger, which is that? Whereupon he said: It is one to which I and my companions belong.

Transmitted by Tirmidhi.

220 Saviour Sect, http://www.thesavioursect.org.uk/about.htm.

221 Saved Sect, 'Where does the name *Ahl us-Sunnah wal-Jamaa'ah* come from?'; http://www.thesavedsect.com/articles/Aqeedah/NamesTitlesASWJ.htm.

222 Saved Sect, 'The 3rd of March 1924'; http://www.thesavedsect.com/articles/Ruling/3rdMarch1924.htm.

223 *Ibid.*

224 Saved Sect, 'The Islamic ruling on democracy, freedom and participating in elections'; http://www.thesavedsect.com/articles/Ruling/Democracy.htm.

225 Osama, Abu and Ziyaad, Abu, *A Guide for the Muslims Regarding the Upcoming Elections: Exploring the Issues Affecting the Muslims* (Ad-Dawah Publications, undated), p. 4.

226 *Ibid.*, pp. 5–6.

227 *Ibid.*, p. 7.

228 *Ibid.*, pp. 7–8.

229 *Ibid.*, pp. 8–9.

230 Saved Sect, 'The difference between *Shooraa* in Islaam and the concept of Democracy'; http://www.thesavedsect.com/articles/Ruling/ShooraaDemocracy.htm.

231 Al-Ghurabaa press release, 'Mushrik Council Of Britain (MCB) shamed', 19 April 2005; http://www.al-ghurabaa.clara.co.uk/oldvotingarticles/PR_mcb.htm.

[232] Ul-Mutakabbir, 'Abd, 'Exposing the truth behind the Respect Party and those Munaafiqeen who vote for them'; http://www.thesavioursect.com/articles/currentAffairs/respectParty.htm. See also Saved Sect, 'Exposing the Respect Party and those Munaafiqeen who vote for them'; http://www.thesavedsect.com/articles/CurrentAffairs/RespectParty.htm.

[233] McRoy, 'There can be no end to Jihad'.

[234] 'British Muslims urged to take up jihad', *Washington Times*, 10 January 2005; http://washingtontimes.com/upi-breaking/20050110-102516-5703r.htm.

[235] O'Neill, Sean and Lappin, Yaacov, 'I don't want you to join me, I want you to join bin Laden', *Times*, 17 January 2005; http://www.timesonline.co.uk/article/0,,2-1443909,00.html.

[236] McRoy, 'There can be no end to Jihad'.

[237] Saved Sect, 'An introduction to Jihaad'; http://www.thesavedsect.com/articles/Jihaad/IntroJihaad.htm.

[238] Saved Sect, 'How Islam will dominate the world'; http://www.thesavedsect.com/articles/Jihaad/IslamDominate.htm.

[239] ASWJ Videos, 'Operation West London takeover'; http://www.aswjvideos.com/aswjvideos/home/htm_home.htm.

[240] Saved Sect, 'The difference between a Muslim and a British Muslim'; http://www.thesavedsect.com/articles/CurrentAffairs/DifferenceBritishMuslim.htm.

[241] Saviour Sect, 'Abdillaah, Abu, 'Ibn Taymiyyah vs Ibn Mutahhir: A debate between a Muwahhid and a Shiite'; http://www.thesavioursect.com/articles/notes/ibnTaymiyyah_ibnMutahhir.htm.

CONCLUSION

In order to understand the radicalisation of the British Muslim community as a whole, as well as the emergence of specific radical groups within it, we have to understand the impact of several crises upon the community, how they affected the self-identity, assertiveness and organisation of British Muslims, and indeed, the *psychological* impact of the crises. In temporal terms, everything seemed to hit the community at once. The Rushdie affair began in 1988 and continued into 1990. In 1990–91, the Gulf crisis occurred. Soon after began the disintegration of Yugoslavia, and the resultant Bosnian conflict. The Rushdie affair saw Muslims accused of possessing values hostile to the cultural norms of modern Britain. During the Gulf crisis, there were accusations that they were disloyal to Britain in a war situation. The Bosnian crisis shocked the community, leading to concern that they could be the next victims of European Islamophobia. The events of 11 September 2001 have been even more traumatic, but it should be noted that the mainstream leadership of British Muslims generally negotiated these challenges with a great deal of skill and sensitivity.

As we saw when we examined the 2001 Northern riots, traditional sociological explanations for such disturbances are invalid. It is not social deprivation that causes Islamic radicalism; it is cultural and religious factors. Essentially, these are *izzat* and *ghairat*. When young Muslims first led the sometimes violent anti-Rushdie protests, they defended the honour of the Prophet and of themselves – *izzat*. Hence, for younger Muslims in particular, the issue was an important one of honour. Ruthven writes:

> In Britain, where Muslims are encouraged to see themselves as a small, embattled minority seeking to preserve their identities against the assimilationist pressures of the wider society, the Qur'an and the figure of the Prophet are deeply implicated in the communal *izzat*. An attack on the sacred text and the person of its revelator, which is what *The Satanic Verses* was seen to be, was experienced as an attack on the honour of the whole community.[1]

Akhtar makes this very point, that Khomeini's *fatwa* defended the 'honour' of the Prophet.[2] In Eastern societies threats to *izzat* frequently lead to violence, even murder, such as when a daughter is suspected of sexual transgression, or when a family member apostatises.[3] Modood adds another dimension to this issue of 'honour' – that of *ghairat*:

> *Izzat* is a form of honour important to Muslims, usually associated with the social standing or respectability a family may enjoy. The issue here, however, is *ghairat*: while izzat is about the respect others accord to one, *ghairat* is about the quality of one's pride or love – pride in one's religion or the Prophet. While izzat is something to be maintained, ghairat is something to be tested. *The Satanic Verses*, then, is for many Muslims an unavoidable challenge to demonstrate their attachment to and love for their faith: their *imani ghairat*. And naturally the more the book is lauded as a literary masterpiece and so on, the greater the challenge, and greater the response required.[4]

This is helpful in seeking to understand the British Muslim reaction to Rushdie. Here was a Briton of Muslim background who both shamed the community in the face of the Muslim world, a question of *izzat*, and who did so by insulting the Prophet, provoking *ghairat*. British Muslims felt literally honour-bound to respond passionately, even aggressively, to what they saw as a violation of their religion. The famous book-burning and the filming of young men angrily stamping on it should be understood in terms of *izzat* and *ghairat*, rather than Nazi book-burning, to which comparison was made in several quarters.[5] The Nazi action was an expression of *censorship* against dissident opinions; in contrast, it was defence of *honour* that motivated the Muslims.[6]

The same motivation lay behind the 2001 riots. It must be remembered that until the 1980s, Paki-bashing would have been a frequent phenomenon in Muslim areas. In those days the victims usually did not fight back. That is a source of shame for the younger generation, a response they will not repeat, and their violent actions retrieved the honour of the community. When media and Government ignore their concerns, Muslims are often prone to view this as an insult. This also explains 9/11. Most hijackers were well-educated, had not been to *madrassas*, and were not poor. The basis of their action was the defence of the honour of Islam, 'defiled' by the 'desecrating' presence of US troops in their Holy Land. This, together with the *Ummah* concept,

234

also explains why British-born Muslims are willing to fight and die abroad – for the honour of the *Ummah* and Islam – and why some are even ready to bomb their own country, as on 7/7. It follows that if British Muslims can defend this honour *politically* as they are now doing, especially since the 2003 local council elections, then they are less likely to seek the redress of honour through violence.

We have seen that Islamic radicalism in the UK is not a monolith, and we must be careful when referring to 'Muslim radicals' because they are a very diverse body. Most are participationist, but some are rejectionist, and even among the latter there are very different nuances. In fact, some expressions of Muslim radicalism are now the dominant and guiding forces in British Islam. At the start of the twenty-first century many British Muslims remain quite alienated from government policies in many ways, notably on foreign policy matters. As was demonstrated by 7/7, some are violently inclined, but most are much more confident and able than they were when Rushdie's book first led to public awareness of their distinctive identity. Like everyone, they have learned from their mistakes. But something else has occurred, too: the old traditional, subcontinental Islam, with its cultural accretions, has lost out to challenges from the contextualised radicalism of Mawdudism, Qutbism and Khomeinism, and even from home-grown strategies, as with MPAC. In particular, Muslims are more confident in their British identity, partly as a result of their own social engineering policies, partly through natural integration, but also because of more positive public attitudes – such as the mass turnout at anti-war rallies over Iraq. Again, as a consequence of this war, Muslims have managed to implement strategies for tactical voting, and have seen the fruit of it. This holds out the prospect for a more peaceful and cohesive future – *Insh'allah*.

[1] Ruthven, Malise, *A Satanic Affair: Salman Rushdie and the Rage of Islam* (London: Chatto & Windus, 1990), p. 8.

[2] Akhtar, Shabbir, *Be Careful with Muhammad!: The Salman Rushdie Affair* (London: Bellew Publishing, 1989), p. 64.

[3] *Ibid.*, p. 74. He notes a contemporary case in Birmingham where a Bengali father murdered his daughter for becoming a Jehovah's Witness.

[4] Modood, Tariq, 'Muslims, incitement to hatred and the law' in Horton, John (ed.), *Liberalism, Multiculturalism and Toleration* (London: Macmillan, 1993), repr. in UKACIA, *Muslims and the Law in Multi-Faith Britain: The Need for Reform* (London: UKACIA, 1993), p. 72.

[5] Lewis, Philip, *Islamic Britain* (London: I.B. Tauris, 1994), p. 158; Webster, Richard, *A Brief History of Blasphemy* (Southwold: Orwell Press, 1990), p. 126.

[6] Kepel, Gilles, *Allah in the West* (Cambridge: Polity Press, 1997), p. 136.